THE MODERN LAW OF ANIMALS

The Modern Law of Animals

By

P. M. NORTH, B.C.L., M.A.

Fellow of Keble College, Oxford

LONDON

BUTTERWORTHS

1972

ENGLAND: BUTTERWORTH & CO. (PUBLISHERS) LTD.
                LONDON: 88 KINGSWAY, WC2B 6AB
AUSTRALIA: BUTTERWORTH & CO. (AUSTRALIA) LTD.
                SYDNEY: 586 PACIFIC HIGHWAY, CHATSWOOD, NSW 2067
                MELBOURNE: 343 LITTLE COLLINS STREET, 3000
                BRISBANE: 240 QUEEN STREET, 4000
CANADA: BUTTERWORTH & CO. (CANADA) LTD.
                TORONTO: 14 CURITY AVENUE, 374
NEW ZEALAND: BUTTERWORTH & CO. (NEW ZEALAND) LTD.
                WELLINGTON: 26–28 WARING TAYLOR STREET, 1
                AUCKLAND: 35 HIGH STREET, 1
SOUTH AFRICA: BUTTERWORTH & CO. (SOUTH AFRICA) (PTY.) LTD.
                DURBAN: 152–154 GALE STREET

66274

ISBN 0 406 63070 4 ✓

PRINTED AND BOUND IN GREAT BRITAIN
BY CHAPEL RIVER PRESS, ANDOVER, HANTS

PREFACE

It is now over thirty years since Professor Glanville Williams' scholarly and authoritative monograph on *Liability for Animals* was published. Not only have there been a number of judicial developments of the law relating to liability for harm done by animals since then, but a movement for the reform of this area of the law which started at least twenty years ago has culminated in the Animals Act 1971. Were it not for this legislation it might have been thought presumptuous for anyone to attempt what Professor Glanville Williams had already accomplished. The law has, however, been altered in a number of significant respects by the 1971 Act and the purpose of this book is to provide an account of the modern law of civil liability for harm done by animals in the light of this legislation. Nevertheless, the assistance which I have derived from Williams on *Animals* has been considerable. I have endeavoured to build upon his historical account in order to present a view of the modern law.

The modern law of animals is to be found both in common law decisions and in the new legislation. The Animals Act 1971 depends in many areas on established general common law principles. Some rules of the common law relating to harm done by animals are untouched by the Act. Furthermore, despite the specific abolition of some specialised common law heads of liability for harm done by animals, a number of the elements of such liability appear in the statutory provisions of the 1971 Act. Where that is so, I have relied on some of the old common law decisions as being still illustrative of the law. Indeed, where relevant in indicating what may be the law of England and Wales, I have drawn on decisions from further afield, notably from Australia, Canada and New Zealand, and also from Scotland.

v

A number of my friends and colleagues have helped me with their patient answers to my perplexed questions. I am especially grateful to Mr. J. D. Heydon, Fellow of Keble College, Oxford, who has been kind enough to read the whole typescript and to assist me with his varied comments and to Dr. Bernard Rudden, Fellow of Oriel College, Oxford, who read the book in proof. Finally, my wife has made time both to type part of the book and to read most of the proofs and, again, I am indebted to her.

I have endeavoured to state the law as it was on October 1st, 1971, the date on which the Animals Act 1971 came into force.

Keble College, Oxford.   P.M.N.
February, 1972

CONTENTS

TABLE OF STATUTES

References in this Table to "*Statutes*" are to Halsbury's Statutes of England (Third Edition) showing the volume and page at which the annotated text of the Act will be found.

* Indicates where the Act is set out.

TABLE OF CASES

In the following Table references are given where applicable to the
English and Empire Digest where a digest of the case will be found.

PAGE

1

INTRODUCTION

(a) The General Position

"The law of torts has grown up historically in separate
compartments and . . . beasts have travelled in a compartment
of their own."[1]

Whilst you may find a few animals in the other compartments of the torts train, it is undoubtedly true that since
mediaeval times specialised rules of liability have been developed
to deal with the question of harm done by animals.[2] Not only
is liability imposed for such harm under the general application
of the torts of nuisance, negligence, trespass and the like, but
two common law actions, the *scienter* action and cattle trespass,
and one statutory head of liability, under the Dogs Acts
1906–1928, existed to provide redress for a person who, or
whose property, was injured by assorted animals. It is with
these specialised rules of liability and the effect upon them of
the Animals Act 1971 that this book is primarily concerned,
although consideration is given also to liability for harm done
by animals under the more general heads of tortious liability.

The general common law position has been described as:

"a pot-pourri of specialised rules of mediaeval origin. These
special rules, for the most part, are such as to give rights of action
which are additional to the rights of action which, in modern
times, lie in respect of damage generally (that is, whether or not

[1] *Read* v. *J. Lyons & Co., Ltd.*, [1947] A.C. 156, 182.
[2] For a discussion of these rules, see Williams, *Liability for Animals, passim*
(hereafter referred to as Williams); Delany (1953) 10 N.I.L.Q. 135; Davis
(1964) 1 N.Z.U.L.R. 206.

the damage was caused by an animal). A person who has suffered damage caused by an animal can frame his action for redress on modern principles—for example, in negligence; or he can frame it under the special rules which are peculiar to liability for damage done by animals; or he can, by including separate causes of action in the one proceeding, get the better of both worlds—modern and mediaeval."[3]

Dissatisfaction with these mediaeval rules, or aspects of them, as well as with the application of the law of negligence to liability for harm done by animals straying onto the highway has been evident for some considerable time. A special committee was established in 1951, under the chairmanship of Lord GODDARD, C.J., which reported in 1953 on the Law of Civil Liability for Damage done by Animals;[4] the Law Reform Committee for Scotland reported on the same topic in 1963;[5] and the Law Commission reported in 1967 on Civil Liability for Animals,[6] their Report[7] containing draft legislation which has been substantially implemented in the Animals Act 1971.[8] There had also been varied attempts to introduce Private Member's Bills to amend the law of negligence relating to animals straying onto the highway.[9]

One might ask what was so wrong with the common law that it provoked so much reforming activity in the course of twenty years. It is proposed to examine briefly the different areas of liability for harm done by animals and to consider the various recommendations for their improvement which have been made.

---

[3] Report of the New South Wales Law Reform Commission on Civil Liability for Animals, (1970) L.R.C. 8, §. 5.
[4] Cmnd. 8746 (1953). Lord GODDARD had, in fact, recommended the establishment of such a committee a decade earlier: *Hughes* v. *Williams*, [1943] K.B. 574, 580.
[5] Twelfth Report of the Law Reform Committee for Scotland, Cmnd. 2185 (1963).
[6] Law Com. No. 13; see Roberts (1968) 31 M.L.R. 683.
[7] See also the Report of the New South Wales Law Reform Commission on Civil Liability for Animals (1970) L.R.C. 8.
[8] The Act came into force on October 1st 1971; see Animals Act 1971, s. 13 (3). The Act applies to England and Wales, but not to Scotland or Northern Ireland: s. 13 (4). Brief commentaries on the Act are to be found by Samuels (1971) 34 M.L.R. 550; Powell-Smith (1971) 121 N.L.J. 584; and see Winfield and Jolowicz, *Tort*, 9th ed., chapter 17.
[9] North (1966) 30 Conv. (N.S.) 44.

There were, however, two general complaints made of the law; they were that it was uncertain and obscure and that the development of fine distinctions had led to "excessive complexity and sometimes quite unreasonable results."[10]   This is harsh condemnation of an area of law:

> "which touches so closely the lives of ordinary people [that it] should be simple and certain.   Unhappily, at present that is not so.   It is one of the most intricate, complex and uncertain branches of our common law, much of it going back to conditions which prevailed centuries ago, before the Industrial Revolution."[11]

(b)   Liability for dangerous animals: the scienter action

The keeper of an animal was liable without proof of fault if the animal caused any injury to person or property provided the animal either belonged to the class of wild animals, animals *ferae naturae*, or, if it was a tame animal, *mansuetae naturae*, provided it had a vicious propensity known to the keeper. Another way of expressing this would be to say that the keeper was only liable where he knew of his animal's vicious propensity, but that such knowledge was irrebuttably presumed in the case of wild animals.   The reason for such a basis of liability was probably that:

> "there had to be some culpability in the owner . . . and of this culpability knowledge of the animal's past mischief was a rough practical test."[12]

Some of the defects and complexity in this area of law, as with others concerned with liability for harm done by animals, stemmed from the fact that a "tendency . . . has existed towards treating cases which were . . . decided as matters of fact as if they laid down principles of law."[13]   Amongst the problems with the developed *scienter* action were the difficulty and inflexibility of deciding whether an animal belonged to a species *ferae naturae*, the fact that that decision was made with regard to the species and not to the particular animal and that danger

---

[10] 795 H.C. Deb. c. 510.
[11] *Ibid.*, c. 508.
[12] Williams, 282.
[13] Report of the Goddard Committee (1953), §. 1.

to mankind was the sole criterion of "wildness", without any
reference to danger to property. The complaint has been
made that to:

> "focus attention . . . upon animals such as fully grown lions is but
> to ignore the difficulties of defining a test for the assigning of all
> animals to one or the other of two groups.   Such a division is not
> to be found in nature.   The different species of animals in fact
> present different degrees of danger to mankind and within each
> species the danger presented is not constant but varies according
> to age, sex, time of the year and many other matters; and
> individual animals within the one species differ."[14]

When one turns to liability for harm done by animals
mansuetae naturae the common law suffered from a further
variety of complexities and uncertainties.   The defendant had
to have knowledge of his animal's vicious propensity; it was
not enough that he had the means of knowing this or that he
ought to have known this.   It was debatable whether there
was liability for damage inflicted other than by an "attack", or
for injuries caused by a natural propensity of the animal.   It
was unclear whether the animal had to have escaped from his
keeper's control, whether there was strict liability as between
master and servant or what was the scope of the defences to the
action, particularly whether act of a third party was a defence.

Given all these varied defects, reform appeared inevitable,
but it posed a fundamental choice.

> "Reform may take one of two general courses.   It may modify or
> replace these special rules which are collateral to the general body
> of the law; or it may take the bolder course of sweeping aside
> these special rules, thereby leading to the result that liability for
> damage done by animals will be determined exclusively by the
> same principles which pertain in respect of damage otherwise
> caused."[15]

The majority of those bodies which reported on liability under
the *scienter* action preferred the bolder, more fundamental,
course.   The Goddard Committee recommended that the
scienter action should be abolished and:

---

[14] Report of the New South Wales Law Reform Commission (1970) §. 9.
[15] *Ibid.*, § 6.

"that (subject to the law of cattle trespass . . .) liability for the acts of every class of animal should be based upon negligence. This need not result in any practical diminution of an owner's responsibility for a dangerous animal because the degree of care which must be exercised in the keeping of an animal will depend upon its nature and will obviously be far higher in the case of a tiger than of a dog."[16]

The one qualification of this general liability was the further recommendation relating to burden of proof that:

"it should be for the defendant to show that he acted without negligence and not for the plaintiff to adduce affirmative proof that negligence existed."[17]

The basic recommendation of the Law Reform Committee for Scotland was similar, though with no suggestion for the reversal of the burden of proof.

"We recommend that liability for injury caused by animals should . . . depend on whether there has been a failure to exercise reasonable care to prevent the animal causing the injury. We believe that this simple principle could be effectively applied in all cases and that it is flexible enough to allow the court to have regard to all the circumstances of a particular case."[18]

The New South Wales Law Reform Commission agreed with this general recommendation that *scienter* liability should be abolished and harm done by dangerous animals should be dealt with under the general law of negligence.[19]

The one law reform agency which has taken a different view is the Law Commission whose recommendation for the formal abolition of the *scienter* action and its replacement by a similar statutory liability for dangerous animals has been implemented in the Animals Act 1971.[20] They agreed that the common law as to *scienter* was antiquated and complex but considered that that was an argument "for its simplification rather than for the abandonment of its underlying principle."[1] This presupposes

---

[16] Report of the Goddard Committee (1953), § 2.
[17] *Ibid.*, §. 6.
[18] Twelfth Report of the Law Reform Committee for Scotland, §. 11.
[19] Report of the New South Wales Law Reform Commission (1970) §. 13.
[20] See Chapter 2.
[1] Law Commission Report, §. 14.

that there is some fundamental principle contained therein which would be abandoned with the abandonment of strict liability. The one such principle given is that

"With regard to animals we see a great deal of common sense in the broad distinction which the law makes between dangerous and non-dangerous animals. It does not seem unreasonable that the keeper of a dangerous animal should bear the special risk which is created by keeping it; moreover, it is a risk against which he can more conveniently insure than can the potential victim."[2]

Whilst many would accept the force of the latter part of this reasoning, it does not necessarily indicate that liability should be strict, given the present structure of the law of torts. The whole point of the recommendations of the Goddard Committee[3] was that the standard of care expected of the keeper varied according to the type of animal. If it is wild and dangerous a far higher degree of care will be expected than if it is tame and docile. In a plea for reform of the law of *scienter*, DEVLIN, J., supported the use of the flexible principles of the law of negligence. He argued that the *scienter* doctrine:

"with all its rigidity—its conclusive presumptions and categorisations—is outmoded and the law favours a flexible and circumstantial approach to problems of this sort. Four years ago a committee appointed by the Lord Chancellor and presided over by Lord GODDARD, C.J. recommended that the scienter action should be abolished and that liability for harm done by an animal should be the same as in the case of any other chattel; it should depend on the failure to exercise the appropriate degree of care; which might in the case of very dangerous animals be 'so stringent as to amount practically to a guarantee of safety': *per* Lord MACMILLAN in *Donoghue* v. *Stevenson*.[4] . . . This branch of the law is badly in need of simplification."[5]

A flexible test based on negligence would enable liability to depend on less rigid and illogical factors than the legal distinctions between different classes of animal. No doubt the

---

[2] Law Commission Report, § 14.
[3] Report of the Goddard Committee (1953), §. 6.
[4] [1932] A.C. 562, 612.
[5] *Behrens* v. *Bertram Mills Circus, Ltd.*, [1957] 2 Q.B. 1, 14.

keeper of a wild animal is the person to insure against the risk of its causing injury, but he will be wise to insure whether liability is based upon strict liability or negligence for he is likely to be liable on either basis. Furthermore, the main incidence of claims under the *scienter* action concerned animals which fell into the non-dangerous category. Instead of basing liability in such cases on the flexible fault concept, detailed specialised rules are to be retained to decide the circumstances where the keeper shall be liable, even though the underlying basis of those rules in mediaeval law, long before the development of the tort of negligence, was, as we have seen,[6] that knowledge was a rough practical test of culpability. Why retain the rough test when a more sophisticated one is available?

Having accepted that the common law of *scienter* should be simplified rather than abandoned, the Law Commission made recommendations for such simplification. These took the form of the abolition of the common law action and its replacement with a new, but very similar, statutory action of strict liability based upon a classification of animals into dangerous and non-dangerous categories, with liability in the latter depending upon the keeper's knowledge of the animal's abnormal characteristics. Their specific recommendations were that:

"(i) Strict liability at common law for animals *ferae naturae* and for animals with known fierce propensities should be abolished.

(ii) Strict liability should be imposed in respect of any injury or damage done by animals belonging to a species which presents a special danger to persons or property. A species presents a special danger when animals belonging to it are likely to cause damage or any damage which they may cause is likely to be severe.

(iii) The question whether an animal belongs to such a species should depend as at present on a test prescribed by law; in determining this question a court should regard as the decisive consideration the risk to persons or property in the circumstances of this country. A species of animals which is generally domesticated in the British Isles should not be regarded in law as dangerous, but with regard to other species their domesticated or

---

[6] *Supra,* p. 3.

non-domesticated character abroad should be taken into account only to the extent that this factor may be relevant to the degree of risk which such species present in the circumstances of this country.

(iv) Strict liability should also be imposed in respect of injury or damage of any kind done by an animal which does not belong to a dangerous species, if the particular animal had dangerous characteristics known[7] to its keeper[8] which made it likely that injury or damage of that kind would occur or that any injury or damage of that kind which might occur would be severe. Such characteristics should be capable of giving rise to strict liability even if they are shared by other animals within the species, whether at a particular age, at certain times of the year or in certain conditions.

(v) Strict liability in respect of either of the two above categories should not depend on escape from control.

(vi) The fact that the plaintiff by reason of his negligence was solely responsible for the injury or damage, his voluntary assumption of the risk, and, to the extent that it contributed to the injury or damage, contributory negligence should be defences. But liability should not be restricted between employer and employee on the ground of voluntary assumption of risk. It should also be a defence that the plaintiff was at the time of the injury or damage a trespasser on the property where the animal was kept and, where the animal does not belong to a dangerous species, it was not kept there to cause damage to trespassers and, where the animal

---

[7] As to the requirement of knowledge, the Law Commission recommended, Report §. 97, that "Knowledge of dangerous characteristics of an animal should be imputed to a person in the following cases: (i) Where a servant of his who has charge of the animal knows of its dangerous characteristics. (ii) Where a member of his household under the age of sixteen who is a keeper of the animal knows of its dangerous characteristics." See now Animals Act 1971, s. 2 (2) (c).

[8] The Law Commission Report, §. 96 recommends that strict liability for injury or damage caused by an animal should be imposed on "in the case of an action brought to enforce strict liability for animals of a dangerous species or with known dangerous characteristics, as well as for injury by dogs to livestock, the 'keeper'—i.e. the owner or possessor of the animal—and a person a member of whose household under the age of sixteen is a keeper. If at any time the animal ceases to have a keeper a person who immediately before that time was a keeper should continue to bear responsibility for the animal until some other person becomes the keeper. But a person who takes in an animal to prevent it causing damage or to restore it to its owner should not be regarded as a keeper for this purpose." See now Animals Act 1971, s. 6 (3).

belongs to a dangerous species, it was not kept there to deter or cause damage to trespassers."[9]

In substance, all these recommendations have been implemented by the Animals Act 1971.[10] Whether this implementation may be said to remedy all the defects of the old law depends on whether one accepts that they can be remedied within the framework of specialised rules of strict liability. Undoubtedly many anomalies have gone, but fine distinctions remain. Animals are still classed by species, as a matter of judicial notice, into dangerous and non-dangerous categories. Although the line is drawn in a different place, it is still drawn and, as has been said earlier, "such a division is not to be found in nature."[11] To take just one other example, liability for injuries to a trespassing plaintiff depends in part on whether the animal which injured him was kept on the premises "for the protection of persons or property."[12] Consequently, difficult distinctions may have to be drawn in relation to the purposes for which the animal was kept. Dogs are often kept both for companionship and for protection.

(c) Straying animals: cattle trespass

The owner of animals which fell within the legal definition of "cattle", which encompassed most domestic animals but excluded cats and dogs, was strictly liable if his animals trespassed on another's land. He was liable whether they injured the land, the occupier's chattels or the occupier himself.

There were two basic areas of discontent with this tort of cattle trespass. Its detailed rules produced anomalies and, secondly, the incidence of strict liability for trespassing cattle required justification at a time when other forms of trespass were coming to be based upon proof of fault,[13] especially in the light of the modern extension of cattle trespass to include

---

[9] Law Commission Report, §. 91.
[10] Animals Act 1971, ss. 1, 2, 5, 6, 10.
[11] Report of the New South Wales Law Reform Commission (1970), §. 9.
[12] Animals Act 1971, s. 5 (3), *infra*, pp. 77–83.
[13] *Fowler* v. *Lanning*, [1959] 1 Q.B. 426.

liability for personal injuries inflicted on the occupier of the land trespassed upon.[14] It was anomalous that if cattle trespassed onto a man's land and injured both him and his employee, the former but not the latter could claim in cattle trespass, for only the former had sufficient interest in the land to maintain trespass to land, of which cattle trespass was a specialised derivative. An allied anomaly was that there was a right to detain trespassing cattle under the law of distress damage feasant but the detainer had no real power of sale or disposal of the cattle. There was also uncertainty as to the meaning of "cattle" and as to the scope of the defences to cattle trespass.

The most fundamental issue was, as mentioned above, whether strict liability for cattle trespass in any form could be justified. The New South Wales Law Reform Commission felt that the anomalies of cattle trespass destroyed any case for its survival, stating:

> "Anomalies such as these lead us to the conclusion that the tort of cattle-trespass is no longer worthy of a place in the law. It developed, long before the advent of the modern tort of negligence, as an expedient to enable recovery of damages for harm done by trespassing cattle in cases other than those where the cattle were deliberately driven onto the land. The tort of negligence, however, also achieves this result; but it does so more flexibly and more justly."[15]

The Goddard Committee, although seeing the logic of such an approach, took the view that "this class of liability is of interest only to farmers and landowners and the general public are not affected thereby. The evidence satisfied us that the general incidence of liability is well understood by the former class who are in favour of the law as it stands."[16] No substantial change was recommended, and the Law Commission took a similar view on the basis that "those bodies in touch with the farming community wish to retain strict liability for cattle trespass."[17] Nevertheless, the anomalies and uncertainties had to be dealt

---

[14] *Wormald* v. *Cole*, [1954] 1 Q.B. 614.
[15] New South Wales Law Reform Commission Report (1970), §. 25.
[16] Report of the Goddard Committee (1953), §. 3.
[17] Law Commission Report, §. 62.

with, and so, once again, the Law Commission recommended that cattle trespass, as such, should be abolished, to be replaced by a new form of statutory strict liability to provide a clear rule of liability which would enable disputes to be settled between neighbours without recourse to litigation. Their recommendations were that:

"(i) The present rules of strict liability for cattle trespass should be abolished, and a new form of strict liability for straying livestock should be provided.

(ii) The straying of livestock should only be actionable upon proof of actual damage; this should cover reasonable expenses incurred in detaining the livestock where there is a right to do so or in finding the person to whom it belongs, but should otherwise be limited to damage to land and chattels.

(iii) Normally the occupier of the land strayed upon should be the only person to rely upon this strict rule of liability.[18] However, an owner of land out of possession whose interest in the land or in chattels thereon is damaged should also be able to do so.

(iv) The following should be defences to a claim under this rule of strict liability:

(a) The fact that the plaintiff by reason of his negligence was wholly responsible for the damage and, to the extent that it contributed to the damage, the partial defence of his contributory negligence. But neither of these defences should be available by reason only that the plaintiff could have prevented the straying by fencing, unless the straying would not have occurred but for the breach of a duty to fence by a person other than the defendant having an interest in the land upon which the livestock strayed.

(b) The fact that the livestock had strayed from a highway where it lawfully was."[19]

Recommendations to replace the law of distress damage feasant were also made, as follows:

"(i) The right of distress damage feasant in respect of animals should be abolished. In its place there should be provided a new remedy whereby a person finding livestock which has strayed on to

---

[18] The person to be held liable is the possessor of the livestock: Law Commission Report, §. 96 (ii).
[19] Law Commission Report, §. 93.

land in his occupation may detain it as security against payment of compensation for the damage which he has suffered and certain reasonable expenses.

(ii) The new remedy should be on the lines suggested by the Goddard Committee[20] but should be elaborated, modified and extended in certain respects, in particular to give a power of sale to the detainer to cover not only the cost of detaining the animal but also the damage which it has caused."[1]

These various recommendations are carried into effect by the Animals Act 1971, both as to cattle trespass[2] and as to distress damage feasant.[3]   Undoubtedly the new law is better than the old, though areas, particularly in relation to the defences, are of a complexity such that they can hardly provide for the settlement of disputes between farmers without the intervention of legal advisors.   One general critical comment is that the reforms appear to have been designed on the advice of the farming community and with them in contemplation, even though a farmer's domestic animals may stray into gardens as well as into adjoining fields.   This is seen especially in the context of the right to detain such animals.   It is quite unrealistic to expect an ordinary householder to detain an errant sheep or cow for fourteen days before selling it,[4] though a farmer well might and could.

(d)   Special rules relating to dogs

Legislation was introduced in the nineteenth century to make special provision for liability for injuries done by dogs. This culminated in the Dogs Acts 1906–1928.   Under these Acts, the owner of a dog was held strictly liable for any injury done by his dog to cattle or poultry, these being defined to include most domesticated animals.   By and large, this legislation appeared to work quite well, but the Goddard Committee recommended[5] that liability should be extended to

---

[20] Report of the Goddard Committee (1953), §. 9.
[1] Law Commission Report, §. 94.
[2] Animals Act 1971, ss. 1, 4, 5, 10.
[3] *Ibid.*, s. 7.
[4] *Ibid.*, s. 7 (4), *infra*, pp. 122–123.
[5] Report of the Goddard Committee (1953), §. 6.

the keeper of the dog as well as the owner and that new provision should be made for the imposition of liability on a person in whose household a dog is kept. The Dogs Acts 1906–1928 had unduly complex provisions on this matter. These recommendations were accepted by the Law Reform Committee for Scotland[6] and were adopted by the Law Commission who also chose to resolve a number of doubts as to the scope and existence of the various defences to liability under the Dogs Acts 1906–1928. Again, their recommendations took the form of the abolition of the old remedy to be replaced by a new, but similar, statutory remedy. They recommended that:

"The strict liability at present imposed by the Dogs Acts 1906 to 1928 for injury by dogs to cattle or poultry should be retained but the principles of the liability should be restated in new legislative provisions. The fact that the plaintiff was by reason of his negligence the sole cause of the injury and, to the extent that it contributed to the injury, his contributory negligence, should be defences to an action brought under this form of strict liability. It should also be a defence that the livestock were straying on the land where they were attacked by the dog and the dog belonged to the occupier of the land or its presence there was authorised by him."[7]

Whilst these wholly desirable recommendations find legislative effect in the Animals Act 1971,[8] the form in which they have been drafted contains the seeds of difficulties other than those they are intended to cure. For example, instead of discussing the liability of the keeper of a dog which kills or injures livestock, liability is imposed for causing "damage by killing or injuring livestock",[9] which raises the question whether there is strict liability for damage other than the death of or injury to the livestock.[10]

It might be asked why special legislation is justified in the case of injuries by dogs. Although dogs have such physical

---

[6] Twelfth Report (1963), §. 15.
[7] Law Commission Report, §. 95. Liability should be imposed on a newly-defined "keeper" of the dog: see Law Commission Report, §. 96, quoted *supra*, p. 8.
[8] Animals Act 1971, ss. 1, 3, 5, 6, 10, 13.
[9] Animals Act 1971, s. 3.
[10] Discussed *infra*, pp. 185–189.

attributes as enable them to inflict serious injuries on persons and property and have a natural tendency to chase and worry other animals, there are other animals which have a potentiality for causing even greater damage. Why should dogs be singled out for the imposition of strict liability on their keepers? The answer would appear to be that:

> "what places dogs in a special position is that despite their canine characteristics and the rapidly increasing urbanisation of our society it is still popularly accepted that, broadly speaking, dogs are privileged to roam and that, in ordinary circumstances, the owner of a dog does not act unreasonably towards others in permitting it to do so. No like privilege is conceded to any other animal which is as likely as is a dog to inflict serious injury.[11] The position of dogs is special; and this warrants the imposition of special liability in respect of them."[12]

Cogent though this argument is, it either proves too much or points to a defect in the English law as to strict liability for dogs. The two characteristics of dogs which, combined with their special place in society, justify the imposition of special rules of liability are their characteristic of attacking, worrying and chasing other animals and their characteristic of occasionally attacking people, with the ability to inflict severe injury. This latter would support the imposition of strict liability for personal injuries which was lacking in the Dogs Acts 1906–1928 and is similarly lacking in the Animals Act 1971, for liability there is based upon the killing or injuring of livestock. It is as true of the Animals Act as it was of the Dogs Acts that: "Parliament thought that sheep require more protection than human beings."[13]

Allied to the question of liability for harm done by dogs is that of the measures which an occupier of land may take against dogs roaming on his land where his animals are put in jeopardy by their presence, and, especially, the circumstances in

---

[11] A similar, if not wider, privilege is afforded to cats; but they have far less potentiality for causing substantial injury or damage.
[12] Report of the New South Wales Reform Commission (1970) §. 35. There has long been strict liability in N.S.W. for injuries to the person inflicted by dogs; see Report, §. 38.
[13] *Hughes* v. *Williams*, [1943] K.B. 574, 580.

which such dogs may be shot. There is no doubt that a serious social problem is involved here. For example, in 1966 over four thousand sheep and over seven thousand head of poultry were killed by dogs in England and Wales.[14] The common law position[15] was that a dog could be shot if it was actually attacking farm animals or was likely to renew an attack so that the animals were in real and imminent danger. Shooting had to be only the practicable means open to the farmer to protect his animals or it must have been reasonable to regard it as such. It was generally considered that the right to shoot trespassing dogs was unduly restricted by these rules, for they were inapplicable to the case of the dog making off after an attack nor did they apply to the dog which was about to attack for the first time.

Whilst the Law Commission accepted that three factors had to be balanced, namely the interests of owners of livestock, the interests of dog owners and the inherent dangers in the use of firearms, they did conclude that some extension of the law was called for.[16] Accordingly they recommended that:

"(i) With regard to measures taken in protection of livestock against dogs, the defence to a civil action arising out of injury to a dog which was recognised in *Cresswell* v. *Sirl* should be extended to cover reasonable belief in the existence or imminence of an attack on livestock by a dog.

(ii) It should also be a defence to such an action, subject to certain specific safeguards, that the defendant injured the dog after it had, or he reasonably thought that it had, worried livestock. Among the safeguards in particular should be the requirements that the dog was not in the control of any person, and that there were no practicable means, or the defendant reasonably believed that there were no practicable means, of ascertaining to whom the dog belonged."[17]

Detailed implementation of these recommendations is provided by s. 9 of the Animals Act 1971.[18]

---

[14] Law Commission Report, §. 81.
[15] *Cresswell* v. *Sirl*, [1948] 1 K.B. 241.
[16] Similar views had been adopted in the Report of the Goddard Committee, §. 7 and in the Twelfth Report of the Law Reform Committee for Scotland (1963), §. 16.
[17] Law Commission Report, §. 98.
[18] Discussed *infra*, pp. 195–208.

(e) Negligence

A line of cases culminating in the decision of the House of Lords in *Searle* v. *Wallbank*[19] decided that an occupier of land adjoining a highway owed no duty of care to prevent his animals escaping onto the highway. He could be as negligent as he liked, for he would incur no liability to users of the highway for injuries caused to them by such straying animals. This rule has been subjected to continual and stringent criticism, primarily on the basis that it "appears to be ill-adapted to modern conditions."[20] Hardly a single commentator has reached a conclusion different from that of the Law Commission that:

> "the case for changing the principle behind *Searle* v. *Wallbank* is overwhelming. The expanding needs of society as a whole must from time to time require some adjustment of the rights and duties of particular interests within that society; in the present context this means that the balance between the interests of the keepers of animals and users of the highway which was struck in the remote past under very different conditions cannot be wholly maintained in the twentieth century. We recognise however that any such readjustment must take account of the economic and social importance of the keeping of animals and of the burden and practical difficulties which may be involved in ensuring that they do not cause damage on the highway; but against these considerations must be weighed the danger to life, limb and property of those who use the highway."[1]

This need for readjustment of interests caused the Goddard Committee to recommend that the rule in *Searle* v. *Wallbank* be abrogated and that the general principles of negligence liability should apply to the obligation to prevent animals straying onto the highway.[2] The Scottish Law Reform Committee took a similar view[3] but judicial activity in Scotland has since rendered

[19] [1947] A.C. 341.
[20] *Hughes* v. *Williams*, [1943] K.B. 574, 576.
[1] Law Commission Report, §. 40.
[2] Report of the Goddard Committee (1953), §. 5.
[3] Twelfth Report (1963), §. 8. Similar condemnation of the rule is found in the Report of the New South Wales Law Reform Commission (1970), §§. 17–22.

legislative action unnecessary.[4] Despite a variety of attempts to promote Private Members' Bills to alter the law,[5] the antiquated rule remained in force in England, though strongly condemned by the judiciary. PEARCE, L.J. described the rule as "difficult, archaic and ill-adapted to urban communities."[6] DAVIES, L.J. was critical both of the law and of those responsible for the implementation of law reform recommendations, saying of the Report of the Goddard Committee: "Nothing has been done to implement any of those proposals, and the law remains as uncertain and unsatisfactory as ever."[7]

When they came to consider liability in negligence for harm done by animals, the Law Commission reached the same conclusion as all who had looked at the matter over the past few years and recommended that the rule in *Searle* v. *Wallbank* should be abolished. Their general recommendations on liability in negligence were:

"(i) The general principles of the present law of negligence whereby the keeper of an animal is under a duty to prevent that animal causing injury or damage should not be disturbed.

(ii) The exception to this principle recognised by the House of Lords in *Searle* v. *Wallbank* should be abolished, but in deciding whether the keeper of an animal has exercised reasonable care to prevent the animal causing damage by escaping on to the highway, regard should be had to a number of special considerations.

(iii) Notwithstanding (ii) above a person should not be regarded as committing a breach of the duty to take care by reason only of placing animals on any common land (within the meaning of the Commons Registration Act 1965) in any case where it is lawful for him to do so."[8]

Despite the history of criticism of the rule in *Searle* v. *Wallbank*, these recommendations for its abolition proved to be the most controversial aspect of the Law Commission's Report, and of the Animals Act 1971 subsequent upon it, when the relevant section of the Act, s. 8, was debated in Parliament. Two interests were ranged in opposition to each other—the

[4] *Gardiner* v. *Miller*, 1967 S.L.T. 29.
[5] See North, (1966) 30 Conv. (N.S.) 44.
[6] *Gomberg* v. *Smith*, [1963] 1 Q.B. 25, 31.
[7] *Ibid.*, at p. 40; and see *Ellis* v. *Johnstone*, [1963] 2 Q.B. 8, 27.
[8] Law Commission Report, §. 92.

farming interest and that of the general public as users of the highway. The farming lobby was powerful and succeeded in having removed from the legislation the various special considerations referred to in the Law Commission's Report[9], which had also been included in s. 8 as originally drafted. These considerations[10] were intended merely as guide-lines for a court faced with the issue of deciding whether a farmer has been negligent.[11] Their removal from the Act will, it is suggested, have no direct effect on liability, for they are factors which will be relevant to a determination of liability whether specifically mentioned or not. Nevertheless, their exclusion may mean that they are not necessarily in the forefront of judicial consideration, nor of counsel's consideration, which might, marginally, benefit defendants. There is no doubt, however, that s. 8 of the Animals Act marks the successful culmination of a long struggle to remove the outdated and illogical *Searle* v, *Wallbank* rule from the common law.

(f) Conclusions

It might be apposite to ask at this juncture to what extent the Report of the Law Commission and the Animals Act 1971, spawned by that Report, have provided satisfactory solutions to the problems posed by the common law relating to civil liability for harm done by animals. One immediate difficulty is that this is a branch of the law on the reform of which all regard themselves as expert. As Lord HAILSHAM, L.C. has said:

> "I would say that of all types of law reform which are difficult to get through Parliament that relating to animals is one of the most intractable, because almost everybody likes talking about animals, either on their behalf or against them."[12]

---

[9] Law Commission Report, §. 92 (ii).
[10] They were: "(a) the nature of the land and its situation in relation to the highway; (b) the use likely to be made of the highway at the time the damage was caused; (c) the obstacles, if any, to be overcome by animals in straying from the land on to the highway; (d) the extent to which users of the highway might be expected to be aware of and guard against the risks involved in the presence of animals on the highway; (e) the seriousness of any such risk and the steps that would have been necessary to avoid or reduce it." Law Commission Draft Animals Bill, Cl. 8 (2).
[11] As in the Occupiers' Liability Act 1957, s. 2 (3).
[12] 312 H.L. Deb. c. 229.

The Law Commission Report and the Animals Act 1971 have not had a wholly favourable reception. Of the Report it was asked: "Why is it that the Commission has concentrated its attention upon the details and preserved a general framework which has so little to commend it?"[13] The Animals Act 1971 has been described as "a kind of mongrel Bill"[14]; as an Act parts of which "bristle with practical difficulties"[15]; and as one some of whose basic concepts are "divorced from reality."[16]

Undoubtedly there is much that is good in the Report and in the Animals Act 1971. The demise, at last, of *Searle* v. *Wallbank*[17] is a wholly beneficial measure, as are many of the details of the recast liability for dangerous animals and for straying livestock. The main and, it is suggested, all-pervading criticism is that the Act is fundamentally misconceived. Nor does it do what it is intended to do. These criticisms are interrelated for it could not achieve all its objectives in its present form. The purpose of the Act is to provide "a new and clearer statement in statutory form of the law"[18] relating to animals, with the objective of removing anomalies and uncertainties and providing rules more suited to modern than mediaeval conditions. Many of the uncertainties and anomalies stemmed from the basic distinctions of the old law. Once the crucial decision is taken not to adopt the radical solution[19] of abandoning the old categorisation in favour of the flexible concept of negligence, but to retain different specialised categories of liability, the problems created by such categorisation remain. Although the specialised categories of dangerous and non-dangerous animals are different from those under the

---

[13] Roberts, (1968) 31 M.L.R. 683, 684.
[14] 815 H.C. Deb. c. 612.
[15] Powell-Smith, (1971) 121 N.L.J. 584.
[16] Samuels, (1971) 34 M.L.R. 550.
[17] [1947] A.C. 341.
[18] 795 H.C. Deb. c. 512.
[19] The fact that the Act is not radical may be seen from the comments upon it by Lord HAILSHAM, L.C.: "If Clause 8 were not in the Bill it would hardly be worth Parliamentary time at all. There are marginal advantages to be gained in the other clauses, but Clause 8 is the only one which it is really worth passing at all. Personally, I do not know whether I should have troubled to take the Bill to Parliament if it had not contained Clause 8. The rest of the Bill is polishing up fairly well known areas of the law, with minor improvements." 312 H.L. Deb. cc. 887–888.

scienter action, rigid distinctions still have to be drawn.   Such
distinctions create new anomalies and new uncertainties and, to
echo the Law Commission's own assessment of the old law of
animals, the drawing of such distinctions makes little sense in
modern conditions.[20]   One can but agree with the commentator
on the Animals Act 1971 who said:

> "It is hardly a logical pattern to find liability as follows in these
> situations: (1) a cow escapes from farm A to farm B—strict
> liability; (2) a cow escapes from farm A onto the highway—
> negligence; (3) a cow escapes from common land onto the
> highway—no liability; (4) a cow escapes from the highway
> onto farm B—negligence."[1]

One of the features of the Animals Act 1971 which has
provoked comment is that it is written in English which
ordinary educated people may understand.   Indeed, the
Parliamentary draftsmen were complimented for having got the
Act "into such an unfamiliar shape".[2]   Nevertheless, there are
a number of difficulties of interpretation with this Act, primarily
because it is overlaid upon a basis of common law liability.
Even though the specific heads of common law liability are
abolished, much of the learning from them will be apposite in
applying the new statutory heads of liability.   To take just
three examples, the meaning of "knowledge of abnormal
characteristics,"[3] the definition of a "highway"[4] or of
"trespassers"[5] must all be referred to the common law.   Indeed,
common law concepts are specifically included by reference on
matters such as assumption of risk[6] and the obligation to fence.[7]

The new law of animals will be a statutory framework laid
upon a common law basis.   Much of it is good.   One can only
hope that the gloomy prognostications as to other parts will be
confounded by the judicial experience in administering the
Animals Act 1971.

---

[20] Law Commission Report, §. 1.
[1] Samuels, (1971) 34 M.L.R. 550.
[2] 305 H.L. Deb. c. 547.
[3] Animals Act 1971, s. 2 (2).
[4] *Ibid.*, s. 5 (5), s. 8.
[5] *Ibid.*, s. 5 (3).
[6] *Ibid.*, s. 5 (2).
[7] *Ibid.*, s. 5 (6).

2

STRICT LIABILITY FOR DANGEROUS ANIMALS

(A) INTRODUCTION

At common law, under the *scienter* action,[1] the keeper of an animal with a propensity to do harm was held strictly liable for any such injury caused. Such mischievous animals fell into two legal categories: animals *ferae naturae* and animals *mansuetae naturae*. It had long been established that the liability of the keeper varied according to such categorisation and according to his knowledge of the animal's viciousness.[2]

When the Law Commission came to examine this head of liability they approved the broad general distinction between liability for dangerous and non-dangerous animals, especially as the keeper of a dangerous animal can more conveniently insure against the risk of its causing injury than can the plaintiff.[3] They concluded that such rules of strict liability should be amended and simplified, rather than abandoned.[4] This could best be done by abolishing the common law rules of the *scienter* action and replacing them by reformulated rules relating to strict liability for dangerous animals.

---

[1] On the development of this common law action, see Williams, Chapters 15–21; Delany, (1953) 10 N.I.L.Q. 135, 135–137; Davis, (1964) 1 N.Z.U.L.R. 206, 222–223.

[2] 1 Hale P.C. 430–431; *R. v. Huggins* (1730), 2 Ld. Raym. 1574, 1583.

[3] Law Commission Report, §. 14.

[4] *Ibid.*, §. 18. *Cf.* the Report of the Goddard Committee (1953), §. 6, which recommended the abolition of the *scienter* action and the absorption of liability for dangerous animals into the law of negligence.

This has now been done by the Animals Act 1971. Section 1 abolishes the *scienter* action. It is provided by s. 1 (1) (a) that the provisions of the 1971 Act replace "the rules of the common law imposing a strict liability in tort for damage done by an animal on the ground that the animal is regarded as ferae naturae or that its vicious or mischievous propensities are known or presumed to be known".

The replacement for the *scienter* action is to be found in s. 2, as follows:

"(1) Where any damage is caused by an animal which belongs to a dangerous species, any person who is a keeper of the animal is liable for the damage, except as otherwise provided by this Act.

(2) Where damage is caused by an animal which does not belong to a dangerous species, a keeper of the animal is liable for the damage, except as otherwise provided by this Act, if—

(a) the damage is of a kind which the animal, unless restrained, was likely to cause or which, if caused by the animal, was likely to be severe; and

(b) the likelihood of the damage or of its being severe was due to characteristics of the animal which are not normally found in animals of the same species or are not normally so found except at particular times or in particular circumstances; and

(c) those characteristics were known to that keeper or were at any time known to a person who at that time had charge of the animal as that keeper's servant or, where that keeper is the head of a household, were known to another keeper of the animal who is a member of that household and under the age of sixteen."

It will be obvious that the effect of s. 2 is to define the liability of the keeper of a dangerous animal differently according to whether the animal belongs to a dangerous species or not.[5] This means that any discussion of liability under s. 2 must be divided into a consideration, first, of liability for

---

[5] There is no definition of "animal" provided by the Animals Act 1971, but it is suggested that the term would include birds, reptiles and insects, but not bacteria.

animals belonging to a dangerous species and then of the liability for other animals known to be dangerous. There are,
however, various issues relating to liability under s. 2 which
are common to both types of case. In discussing those issues,
such as the question of who is the proper defendant to an action
under s. 2, it will not be necessary to distinguish between the
two types of case.

(B) WHO IS LIABLE?[6]

Liability under s. 2 of the Animals Act 1971 is placed on the
keeper of the dangerous animal in question and the issue of who
is its keeper is dealt with by s. 6 as follows:

"(3) Subject to subsection (4) of this section, a person is a
keeper of an animal if—

  (a) he owns the animal or has it in his possession; or
  (b) he is the head of a household of which a member under the
      age of sixteen owns the animal or has it in his possession;

and if at any time an animal ceases to be owned by or to be in
the possession of a person, any person who immediately before that
time was a keeper thereof by virtue of the preceding provisions of
this subsection continues to be a keeper of the animal until
another person becomes a keeper thereof by virtue of those
provisions.

(4) Where an animal is taken into and kept in possession for
the purpose of preventing it from causing damage or of restoring
it to its owner, a person is not a keeper of it by virtue only of that
possession."

The basic liability, under s. 6 (3) (a), is that of the owner or
the possessor of the animal. The normal defendant, as at
common law, will be the person who has control of and "keeps"[7]
the animal, i.e. the possessor of the animal[8]. The statutory
liability in this context is the same as that at common law and

---

[6] This discussion is applicable also to the liability of the keeper of a dog for
injury done to livestock by that dog, under s. 3 of the Animals Act 1971,
infra, pp. 189–190.
[7] E.g. *Jackson* v. *Smithson* (1846), 15 M. & W. 563, 565; *May* v. *Burdett* (1846),
9 Q.B. 101, 110; *Knott* v. *L.C.C.*, [1934] 1 K.B. 126, 143–144.
[8] *Cf. Breen* v. *Slotin*, [1948] 4 D.L.R. 46.

the decisions thereunder will be relevant to an examination of who is a keeper within the meaning of s. 6 (3).

The possessor is liable whether or not he is the owner of the animal. Thus, in *M'Kone* v. *Wood*[9] the defendant was held liable for injuries caused by a dog, known by him to be vicious, which had been left on his premises by a former servant of his. Lord TENTERDEN, C.J. said:

> "It is not material whether the defendant was the owner of the dog or not; if he kept it, that is sufficient; and the harbouring a dog about one's premises, or allowing him to be there or resort there, is a sufficient keeping of the dog to support this form of action."[10]

Undoubtedly the man who harbours a dog will be held to have it in his possession for the purposes of s. 6 (3) (a). It is more doubtful whether merely allowing a dog to resort to one's premises will result necessarily in the conclusion that the dog is, thereby, in one's possession.

Liability has been imposed at common law and would be imposed under s. 2 by reason of s. 6 (3) (a) on the trainer of a horse kept in his stables by a third party for a weekly sum,[11] and where the defendant paid his foreman 1*s.* per week for the use of the latter's dog to watch his premises.[12] Indeed, it has even been suggested, at common law, that "if one out of charity harboured a dog and gave it food and it did mischief, then one was liable where there was evidence of *scienter*".[13] In such a case, it might well be that the defendant had acquired possession of the dog and would be liable under s. 2 of the 1971 Act.

On the other hand, the mere fact that the plaintiff has been injured by an animal on the defendant's premises does not necessarily impose liability on the defendant. So, where a stray dog ran on to the defendants' station and, in the course of two hours, attacked a passenger, a cat and then the plaintiff, there was no liability in the *scienter* action as there was no

---

[9] (1831), 5 C. &. P. 1.
[10] *Ibid.*, at p. 2.
[11] *Walker* v. *Hall* (1876), 40 J.P. 456.
[12] *Bolton* v. *Webster* (1895), 59 J.P. 571.
[13] *Ibid.*; and see *Judge* v. *Cox* (1816), 1 Stark. 285.

evidence that the defendants had any possession of the dog.[14]
Again, where a school caretaker kept a dog on the premises, the
school authority was not liable when the dog bit a cleaner for
they neither knew of the dog's existence nor of its vicious
propensity and "had neither property in nor possession of it
and made no use of it."[15]   These common law decisions remain
unaffected by the Animals Act 1971.   There is no possession
and so no liability under s. 2.   If, therefore, an occupier of
premises employs a security firm to guard his premises with
dangerous dogs which are brought to the premises each night
by their handler, the occupier of the premises will not be a
keeper of the dogs as he is neither their owner nor their possessor.   He will not, therefore, be strictly liable under s. 2 for
any injuries they cause, though he would be liable at common
law if his conduct was in any way negligent towards an injured
plaintiff. The responsibility under s. 2 rests in such a case solely
on the security firm whose dogs they are.[16]

The second type of defendant to consider is the owner who
has neither possession nor control of his dangerous animals.
Varied dicta at common law suggested that such an owner
would be liable for his dangerous animals, and ATKIN, L.J.
has asked:

"Can the person who has acquired a tiger, so long as he remains
its owner, relieve himself of responsibility by contracting with a
third person for its custody?"[17]

Nevertheless an owner out of possession had never been held
liable, at least where the animal was in the control of another
person.   Section 6 (3) is quite unequivocal.   The owner of a
dangerous animal is a keeper of it and is, therefore, subject to
liability under s. 2.   It does not matter that he has neither
possession nor control of it so long as the conditions of liability

---

[14] *Smith* v. *Great Eastern Rail. Co.* (1866), L.R. 2 C.P. 4.
[15] *Knott* v. *L.C.C.*, [1934] 1 K.B. 126, 142.
[16] Unless the occupier is held vicariously liable for his independent contractors
on the basis of the much criticised "Dangerous operations doctrine": see
Atiyah, *Vicarious Liability*, Chapter 32.
[17] *Belvedere Fish Guano Co., Ltd.* v. *Rainham Chemical Works, Ltd.*, [1920]
2 K.B. 487, 504; and see *Brackenborough* v. *Spalding U.D.C.*, [1942] A.C.
310, 324; *Knott* v. *L.C.C.*, [1934] 1 K.B. 126, 141; though *cf. Ibid*, at p. 140.

laid down in s. 2 are satisfied. When the owner sells the animal to another person, the latter is liable in the case of a dangerous species immediately title has passed. Where the animal does not belong to a dangerous species then even if the first owner knew of its dangerous characteristics he will not be liable under s. 2 once he has parted with title in and possession of the animal. It has been suggested[18] that the old owner should continue to be liable until the new owner becomes aware of the viciousness, thereby giving an incentive for the transferor to inform the transferee of the dangerous characteristics. There is no such provision in s. 6 (3) and the old owner's liability ceases immediately on there becoming a new keeper, i.e. a new owner. Of course, the new owner will not be liable under s. 2 until he acquires knowledge of the dangerous characteristics,[19] and a seller will not be inclined to stress the dangerous nature of the animal he is selling.

In the case of the hire purchase of domestic farm animals[20] the hire purchase company will, as owner, be a keeper of the animal within the meaning of s. 6 (3). It will, normally,[1] avoid liability under s. 2, however, by reason of lack of knowledge of the dangerous characteristics of the animal: a state of ignorance which, no doubt, it will be anxious to perpetuate.

If the animal is under the care and control of the owner's employee, neither at common law[2] nor under the Animals Act 1971 will this, in any way, relieve the owner from liability. Furthermore, the obligation of the owner would not appear to be delegable to an independent contractor.[3] On the other hand, merely to employ the keeper of a vicious monkey where the injury is done by the monkey neither on the defendant's premises nor in circumstances such as to give the defendant

---

[18] Williams, 326.
[19] Section 2 (2) (c).
[20] Hire purchase agreements relating to livestock are quite common: Goode, *Hire Purchase Law and Practice,* 2nd ed., 41; and see, e.g. *Tucker* v. *Farm and General Investment Trust, Ltd.,* [1966] 2 Q.B. 421.
[1] Hire purchase of dangerous animals for a wild life park will involve liability without any knowledge, under s. 2 (1).
[2] *Baldwin* v. *Casella* (1872), L.R. 7 Exch. 325, *infra,* p. 61.
[3] *Pinn* v. *Rew* (1916), 32 T.L.R. 451, unless that case be restricted to liability for dangerous activities on or near a highway.

any control over the keeper or the monkey would not be sufficient to impose liability, under s. 2 and s. 6 (3), on the defendant
as a keeper.[4]

The third type of defendant to be considered is that best
illustrated by the problem of the "family pet". It may well
be that a child is the owner of a dangerous dog; the problem of
liability for such an animal is dealt with in s. 6 (3) (b). A
person is a keeper of an animal if "he is the head of a household
of which a member under the age of sixteen owns the animal
or has it in his possession." The liability of the head of the
household under this subsection is dependent on the fact that
he is not himself the owner or possessor of the animal, for
otherwise he would be liable under s. 6 (3) (a). Furthermore, he
is only liable if the member of his household who owns or
possesses the animal is under the age of 16. These factors
might be illustrated by the common law decision in *North* v.
Wood.[5] The defendant's seventeen year old daughter kept a
bull terrier, known by the defendant to be dangerous, on the
defendant's premises. The dog attacked and killed the
plaintiff's dog. The defendant was held not liable at common
law and he would not be liable under the Animals Act 1971,
s. 2. He was not in control or possession of the animal. It
was in the possession of his daughter who both owned it and
paid for its keep and so s. 6 (3) (a) is not satisfied so far as the
defendant was concerned. Furthermore, the case does not fall
within s. 6 (3) (b) because the daughter was over 15. On the
other hand, there may well be cases[6] where the fact that a
spouse or child over 15 owns the animal does not relieve from
liability the other spouse or parent in whose house it is kept,
especially in the case of a family pet. Such a pet may well not
be in the exclusive possession of any one member of the family
and so the parent who occupies the house where it is kept may
be liable as a possessor of it.[7] Such a conclusion in favour of

---

[4] *Cf. Connor* v. *The Princess Theatre* (1912) 27 O.L.R. 466.
[5] [1914] 1 K.B. 629; approved in *Knott* v. *L.C.C.*, [1934] 1 K.B. 126.
[6] *Cf. Dawson* v. *Warren* (1884), 2 N.Z.L.R. 255; *Wood* v. *Vaughan* (1889),
28 N.B.R. 472, affirmed (1890) 18 S.C.R. 703; *Stanford* v. *Robertson*, [1946]
3 D.L.R. 313; affirmed, [1947] 1 D.L.R. 493.
[7] *Stanford* v. *Robertson*, [1946] 3 D.L.R. 313, 316.

possession may be the more likely if he exercises some control over it.[8]   However, the mere fact that someone is the head of a household does not mean that he necessarily possesses all the animals therein, hence the need for s. 6 (3) (b).

Quite what constitutes a "head of a household" within the meaning of s. 6 (3) (b) is none too clear,[9] particularly as many wives claim rights equal to those of their husbands in running the household;[10] though it may be improbable that we shall have many instances of a husband sheltering in his wife's petticoats from liability for a child's pet by claiming that his wife is the head of the household.[11]   Equally it is unclear who are the members of a "household".   It is assumed that parents and children living together are included; but it is debatable whether the head of a household is liable for injuries caused by the dangerous dog belonging to a fourteen year old friend of one of his children who is staying, with his dog, in the household for a week.

The fourth class of possible "keeper" to be considered is that of the owner or possessor of an animal that has escaped.   Does his liability continue after the animal has escaped and, if so, for how long?   This problem is dealt with in that part of s. 6 (3) of the Animals Act 1971 which provides that "if at any time an animal ceases to be owned or to be in the possession of a person, any person who immediately before that time was a keeper thereof by virtue of the preceding provisions of this subsection continues to be a keeper of the animal until another person becomes a keeper thereof by virtue of those provisions".   This provision needs to be examined in the context of the escape of three different types of animal.

The first is the indigenous wild animal, such as a fox.   It is

---

[8] *Dawson* v. *Warren, supra,* at pp. 260, 262.
[9] Who is the head of a household belonging to and run by two widowed sisters, with children under the age of 16?   See 305 H.L. Deb. cc. 1436–1437.
[10] Perhaps the answer is joint and several heads of the same household.
[11] In *Richardson* v. *Dorn,* [1937] 1 W.W.R. 143 a husband kept a dangerous bull on his wife's farm and the wife was held not liable for injuries it caused, for it remained in the husband's control.   *Cf. Shaw* v. *M'Creary* (1890), 19 O.R. 39 where a wife who allowed her husband to keep a bear on premises owned and occupied by him was held liable for harbouring the animal, though it is not clear how far the bear was not in the exclusive control and possession of the husband: Williams, 325.

not usual for foxes to be kept as pets. It might also be said that foxes are a dangerous species because they are not "commonly domesticated in the British Islands" and they are likely to cause severe damage to chickens[11a]. The problem of the escaped fox was considered at common law as long ago as 1676 in *Mitchil* v. *Alestree*,[12] where it was said by TWISDEN, J.:

> "If one hath kept a tame fox, which gets loose and grows wild, he that kept him before shall not answer for the damage the fox doth after he hath lost him, and he hath resumed his wild nature."[13]

Liability seemed, therefore, at common law, to continue after an escape until the animal had resumed its wild natural state, but not thereafter.[14] However, the effect of s. 6 (3) is that liability is to continue until someone else becomes owner or possessor. This seems unduly wide in the case of the indigenous wild animal which, once it has returned to its wild state, is unlikely to be caught again. If a person owns a tamed fox with a known taste for chickens,[15] should he be liable for all the proven depredations of his fox, even after it has escaped back to its wild state, for the rest of the fox's life, except in the unlikely event of its becoming owned by someone else?[16]

The second type of animal is the non-indigenous wild animal such as a lion, tiger, puma or cheetah. The risk of the escape of such animals is greatly increased by the present proliferation of wild life parks. In such a case the original keeper, whether he be owner or possessor, remains liable until someone else becomes the keeper of the animal. Even if the escape of such an animal does terminate ownership or possession of it,[17] it is obviously desirable that liability under s. 2 should be unaffected by the escape. By reason of s. 6 (3) liability continues

---

[11a] See the discussion of the definition of a "dangerous species", *infra*, pp. 38–43.

[12] (1676), 1 Vent. 295; and see *Brady* v. *Warren*, [1900] 2 I.R. 632, 640. [13] *Ibid.*

[14] The distinction drawn in *Andrew* v. *Kilgour* (1910), 13 W.L.R. 608, 613, between escape in town and in the country could be justified on the grounds that in the latter case the fox has regained its wild state merely by escaping.

[15] Thereby avoiding any doubts as to whether the fox is dangerous species.

[16] Perhaps some consolation may be derived from the Law Commission's view. Report §. 76, that this question "arises in theory, although seldom in practice".

[17] *Cf.* Law Commission Report, § 76, note 123.

until the animal acquires a new keeper.

The third class of case is that of the escape of an animal not belonging to a dangerous species but which has known dangerous characteristics. If the original keeper is the owner he is most unlikely to cease to be owner because of the escape; but even if he is merely the possessor and he loses possession because of the escape, the effect of s. 6 (3) is that he continues to be liable until the animal acquires a new "keeper". Therefore, liability will continue even after the escape[18] and it cannot be avoided by abandoning the animal, and certainly not by abandoning it *after* it has caused injury.[19] However, liability for any future conduct ceases once the animal has passed into the possession of a third party, even though that third party has not yet become aware of the animal's dangerous characteristics.[20]

A final problem relating to escapes is that of the liability of the former keeper of an animal not belonging to a dangerous species which has escaped and become wild, as perhaps with cattle in some jurisdictions[1] and which might occur in this country with, e.g. cats or tame deer[2]. Here again, s. 6 (3) seems unbending. Liability will continue until the unlikely eventuality of the animal acquiring a new keeper.

There are two general points to be made as to the interpretation of s. 6 (3). The first is this. The keeper of an animal is, under s. 6 (3) (a), the owner or the person in possession of the animal and he, or they,[3] remain keepers until another person becomes a keeper. Let us assume that a lion is owned by A and is in the possession of B. The lion escapes. Both A and B continue to be keepers until the lion comes into the possession of C. B then ceases to be keeper because he is no longer a possessor under s. 6 (3) (a) and his continued obligation for an escaped animal, under s. 6 (3), has now ceased. What about A? He is the owner throughout and the fact that the animal

---

[18] *Cf.* the deer in *Brady* v. *Warren*, [1900] 2 I.R. 632.
[19] *Dee Conservancy Board* v. *McConnell*, [1928] 2 K.B. 159, 163.
[20] *Cf.* Williams, 325–326.
[1] *Falkland Islands Co.* v. *R.* (1863), 2 Moo. P.C. N.S. 266, as discussed in *Reeve* v. *Wardle, Ex parte Reeve*, [1960] Qd. R. 143, 147–150; Williams, 148–149; though *cf. Scott* v. *Edington* (1888), 14 V.L.R. 41.
[2] *Cf. Brady* v. *Warren, supra.*
[3] The problems of their being joint tortfeasors are discussed, *infra*, pp. 32–33.

has changed possessors should not affect his status as a keeper under s. 6 (3) (a). It is not, in fact, affected by the general provisions of s. 6 (3) relating to escaping animals for they merely state the circumstances in which the status of keeper continues notwithstanding apparent loss within the terms of s. 6 (3) (a). If A is still owner, he is still a keeper no matter what happens to the lion.

The second point relates to the liability of the head of a household, under s. 6 (3) (b), if the animal escapes. Let us assume that A is the head of a household and that his 15 year old son, B, has a dog known to be dangerous. Let us assume also that this dog is possessed, but not owned, by B. If that dog escapes so that B ceases to possess it, then A continues to be liable, until the dog acquires a new keeper. It does not matter that during that period B becomes 16. Although A would not now be responsible as head of the household for B's dog because of B's age, he was responsible for it when it left B's possession and s. 6 (3) states that "any person who immediately before [it ceased to be owned or possessed] was a keeper thereof by virtue of the preceding provisions of [s. 6 (3)] continues to be a keeper until another person becomes a keeper". The justification for holding A liable for an escaped dog, though not for one still in B's possession, must be that A is taken to bear some responsibility for the escape. Of course, in this type of case there is no doubt that B is liable throughout as former possessor of the dog.

Let us now assume the similar but more normal case of the facts being the same, except that B is the owner of the dog. If the dog escapes it does not cease to be owned by B though it may cease to be possessed by B. A's liability as head of the household for B's dog would appear at first sight to end when B becomes 16 for, although the dog has escaped, B still remains its owner. However, s. 6 (3) appears to continue A's liability notwithstanding that there is no loss of ownership by B. A's obligation as keeper, stemming from his headship of the household, continues, under s. 6 (3), "if at any time an animal ceases to be owned by or to be in the possession of a person". Although B has not ceased to own the dog, he has, in the above example, ceased to possess it and, because of that, A's liability will continue until the dog acquires a new keeper. But what if, in either of these cases, i.e. whether B owned or merely possessed the dog, no one else is known to have acquired the dog and eventually it is restored to B's possession? Can A now ever lose responsibility for it, even though B is well over the age of 16 and no longer a member of the household? Indeed B has, by virtue of s. 6 (3), remained a keeper of it throughout, even though he lost possession, for no new person has become a keeper of it; and if B remained a keeper, so did and, apparently, does A.

The liability of the captor of an escaped animal is dealt with in s. 6 (4):

> "Where an animal is taken into and kept in possession for the purpose of preventing it from causing damage or of restoring it to its owner, a person is not a keeper of it by virtue only of that possession."

Quite properly, such a captor of an escaped animal should not be held strictly liable for all injuries done by the animal. If, however, the captor is the owner he will be liable under s. 6 (3) notwithstanding the fact that he merely has possession for the purposes of restoring it to its original possessor.

One point of detail in s. 6 (4) is that it refers to capture of the animal for the purpose "of restoring it to its owner". It does not include the case of restoration to its possessor. Assume that the captor takes the animal into his possession and whilst in his possession the animal causes injury, if the captor then restores it to a possessor other than the owner he will have to rely on the argument that he captured it "for the purpose of preventing it from causing damage". Such minor difficulties might have been avoided if "keeper" had been substituted for "owner" in s. 6 (4).

Problems of joint liability will arise, under s. 2, from the fact that more than one person may be a keeper of the same dangerous animal at the same time.[4] It is suggested that where both the owner and the possessor of a dangerous animal are its keepers, they will be joint tortfeasors if the animal causes damage. That being so they will be jointly and severally

---

[4] Joint liability for harm done by dogs, under s. 3, is considered *infra*, pp. 194–**195**.

liable.   The plaintiff may recover in full from either, but the keeper who is thus held responsible may seek apportionment from his fellow keeper under the Law Reform (Married Women and Tortfeasors) Act 1935, s. 6.   The apportionment will be on the basis of that which is "just and equitable having regard to that person's responsibility for the damage".[5]   Although the court should look both to the relative blameworthiness of the defendants and to the extent to which each contributed to the cause of the damage, it may well be that in many cases of liability under s. 2 apportionment will be equal.   Of course, if there are two keepers and the animal does not belong to a dangerous species and thus falls under s. 2 (2), there will only be joint liability if the various conditions of liability laid down in s. 2 (2) are satisfied with regard to both keepers.   If only one of them knows of the animal's abnormal characteristics,[6] and the other does not, then the keepers will not be joint tortfeasors.   The one who has no knowledge will not be liable at all, and the other keeper will bear the full burden of damages.

This might be an appropriate point at which to examine the liability of the Crown under the Animals Act 1971, even though the provisions of the Act in that respect are general and are not confined to the case of liability under s. 2.   Section 12 states:

"(1) This Act binds the Crown, but nothing in this section shall authorise proceedings to be brought against Her Majesty in her private capacity.

(2) Section 38 (3) of the Crown Proceedings Act 1947 (interpretation of references to Her Majesty in her private capacity) shall apply as if this section were contained in that Act."

The effect of s. 12 (1) is to make the Crown liable for injuries caused by animals to the extent provided by the Crown Proceedings Act 1947, s. 2 (2) of which states that:

"Where the Crown is bound by a statutory duty which is binding also upon persons other than the Crown and its officers, then, subject to the provisions of this Act, the Crown shall, in respect of a failure to comply with that duty, be subject to all those liabilities in tort (if any) to which it would be so subject if it were a private person of full age and capacity."

---

[5] Law Reform (Married Women and Tortfeasors) Act 1935, s. 6 (2).
[6] Animals Act 1971, s. 2 (2) (c).

In other words, the Crown will be fully liable for injuries caused by animals.[7]

The effect of s. 12 (2) of the Animals Act 1971 is that the phrase "Her Majesty in her private capacity" has the extended meaning of including a reference to "Her Majesty in right of her Duchy of Lancaster and to the Duke of Cornwall".

(C) LIABILITY FOR ANIMALS OF A DANGEROUS SPECIES

The special issues relating to liability, under s. 2 (1), for animals of a dangerous species must now be considered. The first problem is one, however, which has necessary implications for s. 2 (2), for it is that of defining an animal of a "dangerous species". This is the crucial factor which decides whether s. 2 (1) or s. 2 (2) is the relevant subsection applicable to the animal in question and the most important difference between them is that there will only be liability under s. 2 (2) if the keeper has knowledge of the animal's dangerous characteristics, whereas such knowledge is not necessary under s. 2 (1).

(i)   The meaning of "dangerous species"

The general distinction under discussion here is that between domesticated animals which are not normally dangerous and those wild animals which are generally dangerous to mankind. The elements of the distinction were stated by the Law Commission thus:

> "The question whether an animal belongs to a dangerous species should depend, as is at present the position with the category of animals *ferae naturae,* upon a test prescribed by law; and in determining this question a court should regard as the decisive consideration the risks to persons or property in the circumstances of this country.   A species of animals which is generally domesticated in the British Isles should not be regarded in law as dangerous, but with regard to other species their domesticated or non-domesticated character abroad should be taken into account only to the extent that this factor may be relevant to the degree of risk which such species present in the circumstances of this country."[3]

---

[7] See Williams, *Crown Proceedings,* Chapter 2.
[8] Law Commission Report, §. 25 (ii).

The test for the determination of a "dangerous species" is provided by s. 6 (2) of the Animals Act 1971, as follows:

"A dangerous species is a species—

(a) which is not commonly domesticated in the British Islands; and

(b) whose fully grown animals normally have such characteristics that they are likely, unless restrained, to cause severe damage or that any damage they may cause is likely to be severe."

There are several general issues relevant to this subsection to examine before considering the two specific conditions for classification as a "dangerous species".

The question whether a species of animal is dangerous or not is, as with the distinction between animals *ferae naturae* and *mansuetae naturae,* a question of law and a matter of judicial notice.[9] Subject to the operation of the doctrine of precedent, a classification once made on the basis of an interpretation and application of s. 6 (2) is binding, for "it is not competent to the Courts to reconsider the classification of former times and to include domestic animals of blameless antecedents in the class of dangerous animals even when wandering on the roadsides".[10] An animal is considered dangerous if it belongs to a species which is decided, in accordance with s. 6 (2), to be a dangerous species. It matters not what the characteristics of the individual animal of that species may be. Thus, it has been held, at common law, that all elephants are *ferae naturae*[11] and indeed they are likely to be classed as a dangerous species under s. 6 (2),[12] even though the particular elephant in question is tame and causes damage from fright rather than viciousness. The peculiarity of this situation is well revealed by DEVLIN, J. in *Behrens* v. *Bertram Mills Circus, Ltd.*[13]:

"The particular rigidity in the scienter action which is involved in this case . . . is the rule that requires the harmfulness of the

---

[9] *Behrens* v. *Bertram Mills Circus, Ltd.* [1957] 2 Q.B. 1.
[10] *Heath's Garage, Ltd.* v. *Hodges,* [1916] 2 K.B. 370, 383; and see *Behrens* v. *Bertram Mills Circus, Ltd., supra,* at p. 30.
[11] *Filburn* v. *People's Palace and Aquarium Co., Ltd.* (1890), 25 Q.B.D. 258; *Behrens* v. *Bertram Mills Circus, Ltd., supra.*
[12] *Infra,* p. 41.
[13] [1957] 2 Q.B. 1, 14–15.

M.L.A.—3

offending animal to be judged not by reference to its particular training and habits, but by reference to the general habits of the species to which it belongs. The law ignores the world of difference between the wild elephant in the jungle and the trained elephant in the circus. The elephant Bullu is in fact no more dangerous than a cow; she reacted in the same way as a cow would to the irritation of a small dog; if perhaps her bulk made her capable of doing more damage, her higher training enabled her to be more swiftly checked. But I am compelled to assess the defendants' liability in this case in just the same way as I would assess it if they had loosed a wild elephant into the funfair."

This rule and the problem just exemplified remain unaffected by the Animals Act 1971. Criticised though the rule has been, some justification for applying a fixed rule to all animals of one species, however tame, might be that:

"a wild animal may become tame and kind. Its nature may sleep for a time, but it may also wake up, and, if the animal has lost its fear of mankind, it is undoubtedly more dangerous."[14]

The second general issue relates to the meaning of "species". The only assistance in determining what constitutes a species is provided by s. 11 of the Animals Act 1971 which states that " 'species' includes sub-species and variety". This can be interpreted in two different ways. First, it can mean: "Wherever the word 'species' appears, the phrase 'sub-species' may be substituted". According to this interpretation one must examine the dangerousness of animals according to the sub-species to which they belong. Thus if one sub-species of monkey is dangerous and another is not, the categorisation of the particular monkey in question would depend on the sub-species to which it belonged. The other interpretation is quite the opposite: "All sub-species and varieties of an animal have the same characterisation as dangerous or non-dangerous as is given to the species as a whole." On this analysis, if elephants are classed, as a species, as dangerous, then no distinction can be based on the fact that a sub-species of elephant could be classed as non-dangerous.

---

[14] *Andrew* v. *Kilgour* (1910), 13 W.L.R. 608, 613; and see *Besozzi* v. *Harris* (1858), 1 F. & F. 92, 93; *Temple* v. *Elvery*, [1926] 3 W.W.R. 652, 655.

This latter approach is certainly that which was favoured at common law, in relation to both elephants and monkeys.   In *Behrens* v. *Bertram Mills Circus, Ltd.*,[15] DEVLIN, J. was not prepared to distinguish between different varieties of elephants and he refused to hold that, whilst elephants generally are wild, Burmese elephants are not.   He said that:

"Common knowledge about the ordinary course of nature will extend to a knowledge of the propensities of animals according to their different genera, but cannot be supposed to extend to the manner of behaviour of animals of the same genus in different parts of the world.   Nor can one begin a process of inquiry which might lead in many directions (for example, I am told that female elephants are more docile than male, and that is why circus elephants are usually female) and be productive of minute subdivisions which would destroy the generality of the rule."[16]

Again, monkeys have caused difficulties of classification in the *scienter* action.   In *May* v. *Burdett*[17] the keeper of a monkey was held liable when it bit the plaintiff, but here the defendant was proved to have known of this particular monkey's vicious propensity so it did not matter how a monkey was classified. It has been argued since that "ape or monkey"[18] does not include every species within the generic term "monkey" and that not all "monkeys" are wild or dangerous by nature.[19] However, it does seem to have been assumed in Canada, at least, that some if not all monkeys are wild animals.[20]

The problems of interpretation raised by s. 11 might be illustrated further by the status of a cat.   The cat is a commonly domesticated animal in the British Islands.[1]   There is, however, also the case of the wild cat found in Scotland.   It would seem very strange if the domesticated nature of the former should be held also to include the latter.   A similar difficulty can be seen with domesticated and wild rabbits.[2]

---

[15] [1957] 2 Q.B. 1.
[16] [1957] 2 Q.B. 1, 16.
[17] (1846), 9 Q.B. 101.
[18] Hale 1 P.C. 101.
[19] *Brook* v. *Cook* (1961), 105 Sol. Jo. 684; and see *ibid.*, at pp. 1094–1095.
[20] *Connor* v. *The Princess Theatre* (1912), 27 O.L.R. 466; and see *Andrew Baker's Case*, cited by Hale, 1 P.C. 430.
[1] Animals Act 1971, s. 6 (2) (a).
[2] Rabbits may fall within s. 6 (2) (b) because they could be thought likely to cause severe damage to property.

Do the former cause the latter to be classed as non-dangerous? Such problems might favour the first interpretation of the definition of "species" given above.   On the other hand it is open to DEVLIN, J.'s objection that it may lead to minute sub-divisions of species and a variation of the legal rule dependent upon the categorisation of the sub-species.

The first specific condition for classification as a dangerous species provided in s. 6 (2) is that the species "is not commonly domesticated in the British Islands".[3]   This has the effect that all such commonly domesticated animals are excluded from classification as dangerous without proof of knowledge despite the fact that they may commonly be regarded as dangerous as well as domesticated.   Thus, not only cats[4] are excluded by this provision but so also are bulls.[5]

Under s. 6 (2) (a) the species must be one that is *commonly* domesticated in the British Islands.   The original draft Bill referred to a species that was *generally* domesticated, but it was amended in the House of Lords.   It may be difficult to envisage "commonly" and "generally" as other than synonyms, but the main difference is that "commonly" is less wide in its ambit than "generally".   The practical consequence of this is that if an animal is a member of a species which is frequently domesticated in the British Islands, it will fall outside the class of dangerous animals even though the species is not normally domesticated.   As Lord WILBERFORCE has said:

> "If one takes 'commonly' and applies it to rabbits, rabbits are 'commonly domesticated', one would say, even though the majority of them are not domesticated;   and that is all right.   As regards camels, elephants, cheetahs, snakes or crocodiles, they are not 'commonly domesticated' in this country, although there may be some that are."[6]

The consequence of this approach is that the tame rabbit, mouse and pigeon, for example, may well remove their wild

---

[3] Section 6 (2) (a).
[4] E.g. *Buckle* v. *Holmes,* [1926] 2 K.B. 125.
[5] E.g. *Hudson* v. *Roberts* (1851), 6 Exch. 697;   *Dobbie* v. *Henderson,* 1970 S.L.T. (Sh. Ct. Rep.) 27.
[6] 305 H.L. Deb. c. 1433.

cousins from any possible category of dangerous animals,[7] unless one says that wild rabbits and the like belong to a different species or sub-species from tame rabbits.

The species must also be "domesticated". If "domesticated" meant merely "tame"[8] then it would be true to say, contrary to the view of Lord WILBERFORCE, that the majority of elephants, and even camels, found in the British Islands are tame. However, the meaning of "domesticated" is narrower than this and would seem to relate only to those animals which are found in or near a household or farm.[9] This would exclude those animals found in, but rarely outside, a zoo. Even then, it is not abundantly clear how to classify a pet monkey. Many are kept in private homes. These would seem to be domesticated. It is debateable whether enough are so kept to justify the conclusion that monkeys are "commonly domesticated".

The only domestication that is relevant under s. 6 (2) (a) is domestication in the British Islands.[10] If an animal is domesticated in those parts of the world where it is indigenous, as may be the case with the elephant and the camel, then this is a factor relevant, perhaps, under s. 6 (2) (b) as to whether the animals have such characteristics that they are likely to be dangerous; such foreign domestication is irrelevant to s. 6 (2) (a). Thus, if the facts of *McQuaker* v. *Goddard*,[11] where the plaintiff was bitten by a camel at Chessington Zoo, were to recur, the fact that camels are usually domesticated in those countries where they are commonly found would not be conclusive as to the camel's character, as dangerous or non-dangerous, in England.

The requirement that the species is one not commonly domesticated in the British Islands is not, quite properly, the sole test of a species' dangerous quality. The provisions of s. 6 (2) (b) must also be satisfied. It must be a species:

"whose fully grown animals normally have such characteristics

---

[7] 312 H.L. Deb. c. 869.
[8] 305 H.L. Deb. c. 1451.
[9] The definition in the Shorter Oxford English Dictionary is "living in or near the habitations of man".
[10] "British Islands" is defined by the Interpretation Act 1889, s. 18, as "the United Kingdom, the Channel Islands, and the Isle of Man".
[11] [1940] 1 K.B. 687.

that they are likely, unless restrained, to cause severe damage or that any damage they may cause is likely to be severe."

The characteristics relevant here are not those of the particular animal in question but are those of the "reasonable adult animal of the species". If the young of the species do not normally evidence the tendency to cause severe damage although full grown animals do, then if a young animal causes any damage, its keeper will be strictly liable. The relevant characteristics are those which full grown animals of the species "normally have". If the tendency to cause severe damage is abnormal, the condition is not satisfied. However, the tendency may be subject to the further condition that it is normal in such animals but only at particular times. It is well-known that some females can be very fierce in protection of their young, even though generally docile. Their ferocious behaviour is only normal in the special circumstances. There is no indication in s. 6 (2) (b) whether such circumstances are relevant to a determination of normal behaviour.[12] The question whether animals of the species under consideration have dangerous characteristics is likely to be treated by the courts as a matter of judicial notice, as is the whole question of classification.[13] Indeed, it has been said of the common law distinction:

> "The doctrine has from its formulation proceeded upon the supposition that the knowledge of what kinds of animals are tame and what are savage is common knowledge. Evidence is receivable, if at all, only on the basis that the judge may wish to inform himself. This was clearly settled by the Court of Appeal in *McQuaker* v. *Goddard*,[14] where CLAUSON, L.J.[15] said: 'The reason why the evidence was given was for the assistance of the judge in forming his view as to what the ordinary course of nature in this regard in fact is, a matter of which he is supposed to have complete knowledge.' "[16]

The species envisaged by s. 6 (2) (b) fall into two categories. There are, first of all, those obviously fierce wild animals which

---

[12] *Cf.* Animals Act 1971, s. 2 (2) (b).
[13] *Supra*, pp. 35–36.
[14] [1940] 1 K.B. 687.
[15] *Ibid.*, at p. 700.
[16] *Behrens* v. *Bertram Mills Circus, Ltd.*, [1957] 2 Q.B. 1, 16.

are likely to cause severe damage. This would include animals such as bears,[17] leopards,[18] lions,[19] tigers,[20] wolves,[1] gorillas,[2] and, possibly, zebras;[3] though it is perhaps, debatable whether zebras are likely to cause *severe* damage unless restrained.

The second category is that of more normally peaceful, but undomesticated, animals. They are included in the category of dangerous animals if they have a potential for causing severe damage. They are animals which are unlikely to cause damage in normal circumstances. If, however, they do cause any damage it is likely to be severe damage. The best illustration of this type of animal is the elephant. It is normally quite docile and unlikely to cause any damage, severe or otherwise. If however, it does cause damage because, for example, it has been frightened, then there must be little doubt that it is likely to cause severe damage to person or property because of its great size.[4] One result of its classification as dangerous from its sheer size will be that its keeper will be strictly liable even though the damage it actually causes does not result from its size,[5] as where it takes and eats property using its trunk.

Both these categories involve the requirement of likelihood of causing severe damage. Whether damage is likely to be severe is a judgement which must be left to the court. "How severe is severe?" is a question which cannot be answered in the abstract. It may well be a factor which will vary from species to species. It is, of course, crucial to the issue whether the animal falls within the strict liability of s. 2 (1) or liability

---

[17] E.g. *Besozzi* v. *Harris* (1858), 1 F. & F. 92; *'Wyatt* v.*'Rosherville Gardens Co.* (1886), 2 T.L.R. 282, 283; *Shaw* v. *McCreary* (1890), 19 O.R. 39.
[18] E.g. *Sylvester* v. *Chapman*, [1935] 1 L.J.C.C.A. 261, 264.
[19] E.g. *Pearson* v. *Coleman Bros.*, [1948] 2 K.B. 359; *Young* v. *Green*, [1958] O.W.N. 426; and see *Besozzi* v. *Harris* (1858), 1 F. & F. 92, 93; *cf. Murphy* v. *Zoological Society of London*, [1962] C.L.Y. 68.
[20] E.g. *R.* v. *Huggins* (1730), 2 Ld. Raym. 1574, 1583; *Wyatt* v. *Rosherville Gardens Co.* (1886), 2 T.L.R. 282, 283; *Buckle* v. *Holmes*, [1926] 2 K.B. 125, 128; *Behrens* v. *Bertram Mills Circus, Ltd.*, [1957] 2 Q.B. 1, 17–18.
[1] E.g. Hale, 1 P.C. 430; and see *Temple* v. *Elvery*, [1926] 3 W.W.R. 652, esp. at p. 654: a cross between a dog and a wolf, classed as *ferae naturae*.
[2] E.g. *Buckle* v. *Holmes*, [1926] 2 K.B. 125, 128.
[3] *Marlor* v. *Ball* (1900), 16 T.L.R. 239.
[4] E.g. *Behrens* v. *Bertram Mills Circus, Ltd.*, [1957] 2 Q.B.1.
[5] *Cf. Filburn* v. *People's Palace and Aquarium Co., Ltd.* (1890), 25 Q.B.D. 258; and see the report of the facts in 6 T.L.R. 402.

only on proof of knowledge of its dangerous characteristics under s. 2 (2).

If "severity" is incapable of precise definition, "damage" creates less difficutly. At common law, the test for deciding whether an animal was *ferae naturae* was whether it was dangerous to mankind[6] and the fact that an animal was naturally dangerous to property was not relevant.[7] It was, therefore, necessary to exclude from consideration, for example, the natural propensity of a cat to eat pigeons[8] or to fight dogs.[9] A corollary of this principle was that a number of species of "wild animals" fell within the category of animals *mansuetae naturae,*[10] such as camels,[11] rabbits,[12] and, probably, "hares, pheasants and partridge",[13] as well as bees.[14] On the other hand an indigenous wild animal has been classed as *ferae naturae,* as with the raccoon in Canada.[15]

Undoubtedly many "harmless wild animals", i.e. animals not commonly domesticated in the British Islands, are very destructive of property,[16] but the common law position was that there was no liability for damage to property by an animal likely only to damage property. However, as there seems little reason to doubt that the strict liability for animals *ferae naturae* extended to damage to property,[17] there was such liability for damage to property by an animal classed as "wild" because of its tendency to injure mankind.

---

[6] *Buckle* v. *Holmes,* [1926] 2 K.B. 125, 129; and see *Filburn* v. *People's Palace and Aquarium Co.* (1890) 25 Q.B.D. 258, 260; *Clinton* v. *J. Lyons & Co., Ltd.,* [1912] 3 K.B. 198, 202, 207; *McQuaker* v. *Goddard,* [1940] 1 K.B. 687, 695; *Behrens* v. *Bertram Mills Circus, Ltd.,* [1957] 2 Q.B. 1.

[7] *Filburn* v. *People's Palace and Aquarium Co., Ltd., supra,* at p. 260.

[8] *Buckle* v. *Holmes,* [1926] 2 K.B. 125, 129.

[9] *Clinton* v. *J. Lyons & Co., Ltd.,* [1912] 3 K.B. 198.

[10] Thus revealing the fallacy in equating "domesticated animals" with "animals *mansuetae naturae*"; cf. *McQuaker* v. *Goddard,* [1940] 1 K.B. 687; though see Williams (1940) 56 L.Q.R. 354.

[11] *McQuaker* v. *Goddard,* [1940] 1 K.B. 687; *Nada Shah* v. *Sleeman* (1917), 19 W.A.L.R. 119.

[12] *Behrens* v. *Bertram Mills Circus, Ltd.,* [1957] 2 Q.B. 1, 14.

[13] *Filburn* v. *People's Palace and Aquarium Co., Ltd.* as reported in (1890), 59 L.J.Q.B. 471, 472.

[14] *O'Gorman* v. *O'Gorman,* [1903] 2 I.R. 573, 581, 583, 588; and see *Robins* v. *Kennedy and Columb,* [1931] N.Z.L.R. 1134, 1142.

[15] *Andrews* v. *Kilgour* (1910), 13 W.L.R. 608.

[16] E.g. the rabbit in Australia, Fleming, *Torts,* 4th ed., 303.

[17] Williams, 297.

This anomalous situation would appear to have been altered by the Animals Act 1971. The statutory test of the dangerous nature of an animal under s. 6 (2) (b) is based upon the animal's likelihood to cause damage. There is no specific reference to the type of damage involved. The definition of "damage" in s. 11 does not resolve the matter either for it merely states that " 'damage' includes the death of, or injury to, any person (including any disease and any impairment of physical or mental condition)". This states what is included but it is neither an exhaustive definition of what is included nor is there any indication that anything is excluded. That being so, "damage" should be given its normal meaning which is broad enough to include "damage to property". Therefore, under s. 6 (2), the likelihood of animals of the species in question causing severe damage as a criterion of the dangerous nature of the species is not confined to cases of injury to mankind but will now extend to damage to property. An animal, not domesticated in the British Islands, which is likely to cause severe damage to property will be classed as dangerous. This will mean, also, that there will be strict liability where an animal, classed as dangerous because likely to cause one type of damage, in fact causes a different type.

The criterion of damage to property may raise some difficulties in that many English "wild animals" are likely to cause damage to property, though not to persons. Obvious examples would be rabbits, squirrels and pigeons. If one of these creatures was in captivity, then its keeper might be held strictly liable for any injury it caused because of the potential of such animals to cause damage to property, provided one can say that fully grown rabbits,[18] squirrels and the like[19] are likely to cause severe damage to crops.[20] If that is a correct assumption, then the keeper of a caged squirrel will be strictly liable if it bites the plaintiff.

---

[18] Unless it can be said that the rabbit is "commonly domesticated" so that there is no liability under s. 2 (1) for wild rabbits; see *supra*, pp. 38–39.

[19] Another example might be the coypu: 312 H.L. Deb. c. 869.

[20] Likelihood of causing damage was amended to likelihood of causing *severe* damage in order to exclude rabbits and the like if they were not excluded already by "commonly domesticated" in s. 6 (2) (a): 313 H.L. Deb. cc. 455–456.

(ii) The scope of liability for animals of a dangerous species

It should be noted, at the outset, that it is not unlawful to keep either an animal of a dangerous species or any other animal known to be dangerous; for "the wrong is in allowing it to escape from the keeper's control[1] with the result that it does damage.   Damage is thus the gist of the action.[2]"   It has been pointed out that to admit of a rule that it is unlawful to keep dangerous animals would mean that "the proprietors of the Zoological Gardens would live in a perpetual state of law-breaking".[3]   These comments on liability under the *scienter* action are equally true of liability under s. 2 of the Animals Act 1971.   Liability arises thereunder on the causing of damage, not because a dangerous animal is being kept by the defendant.

Liability under s. 2 (1) is strict.[4]   He who keeps an animal of a dangerous species does so at his peril.   It is no defence to an action for keeping such an animal which has injured the plaintiff that the defendant did not know of its ferocity.   For it is still the law that "it cannot be doubted that a person who keeps an animal [of a dangerous species] must prevent it from doing injury, and it is immaterial whether he knows it to be dangerous or not".[5]   The honest belief in the fact that a circus elephant[6] or a performing bear[7] is harmless is irrelevant if the animal in fact causes injury; for, as in the case of the bear,

"every one must know that such animals as lions and bears are of

---

[1] Whether it is necessary for there to be an escape, or an escape from control, for liability under s. 2 is discussed, *infra*, pp. 68–71.
[2] *Knott* v. *L.C.C.*, [1934] 1 K.B. 126, 138–139; and see *Jackson* v. *Smithson* (1846) 15 M. & W. 563; *Connor* v. *The Princess Theatre* (1912), 27 O.L.R. 466, 469–470; *cf. May* v. *Burdett* (1846), 9. Q.B. 101, 111; *Card* v. *Case* (1848), 5 C.B. 622, 632–634; *Baker* v. *Snell*, [1908] 2 K.B. 825, 833, though there are suggestions that this last dictum goes too far, see BRAY, J. in *Clinton* v. *J. Lyons & Co., Ltd.*, [1912] 3 K.B. 198, 208.
[3] Winfield, *Tort*, 8th ed. 474;   and see the list there cited of statutory prohibitions against the keeping of certain creatures.
[4] Although it is strict, it is not absolute and the various defences are discussed *infra*, pp. 71–90.
[5] *Filburn* v. *People's Palace and Aquarium Co., Ltd.* (1890), 25 Q.B.D. 258, 260; and see *Wyatt* v. *Rosherville Gardens Co.* (1886), 2 T.L.R. 282, 283.
[6] E.g. *Filburn* v. *People's Palace and Aquarium Co., Ltd. supra; Behrens* v. *Bertram Mills Circus, Ltd.*, [1957] 2 Q.B.1.
[7] *Besozzi* v. *Harris* (1858), 1 F. & F. 92.

a savage nature. For though such nature may sleep for a time, this case shows that it may wake up at any time."[8]

A special problem, at common law, arising from strict liability for dangerous animals was whether their keeper was strictly liable for *any* injury caused by them or only for such injuries as could be attributed to their assumed dangerous characteristics. The problem might be illustrated by *Behrens* v. *Bertram Mills Circus, Ltd.*[9] The plaintiffs were circus midgets occupying a booth in a funfair adjoining the defendants' circus, and under licence from the defendants. The booth was in a passage way along which the defendants' elephants had to pass to get to the circus ring. One of the elephants, when frightened by a dog kept in the booth by the plaintiffs' manager, against the defendants' rules, turned to follow the dog and, in so doing, knocked the booth down, killing the dog and seriously injuring the female plaintiff. In considering the plaintiffs' claim for damages in the *scienter* action, DEVLIN, J. decided that an elephant was an animal *ferae naturae*. He then examined the problem raised by the fact that the injuries had been caused by the elephant acting out of fright rather than acting viciously or savagely against human beings. Although the keeper of an animal *ferae naturae* was presumed to have knowledge of its vicious propensity, the strict liability for such animals applied to *all* harm done by them, even though not resulting from viciousness. DEVLIN, J. accepted that he who kept an animal *ferae naturae* kept it at his peril and was liable for all harm caused by it, whether as a result of viciousness or of fright or whether by its attacking, blundering or its mere presence. He said:

> "It does not seem to me that the logic of the matter necessarily requires that an animal that is savage by disposition should be put on exactly the same footing as one that is savage by nature. Certainly practical considerations would seem to demand that they should be treated differently. It may be unreasonable to hold the owner of a biting dog responsible thereafter for everything it does; but it may also be unreasonable to limit the lia-

---

[8] *Besozzi* v. *Harris* (1858), 1 F. & F. 92, 93.
[9] [1957] 2 Q.B.1.

bility for a tiger. If a person wakes up in the middle of the night and finds an escaping tiger on top of his bed and suffers a heart attack, it would be nothing to the point that the intentions of the tiger were quite amiable. If a tiger is let loose in a funfair, it seems to me to be irrelevant whether a person is injured as the result of a direct attack or because on seeing it he runs away and falls over."[10]

The effect of the Animals Act 1971 would appear to be to leave this position unchanged. Liability is imposed under s. 2 (1) for "any damage" caused by an animal of a dangerous species; there is no need for the damage to be related to those characteristics which caused the animal to be classed as dangerous.[11] Of course, in the case of elephants the likelihood of damage caused by their sheer size is a factor which leads to their classification as dangerous. So if a horse is caused to bolt by the mere sight of an elephant and the horse is thereby injured, the keeper of the elephant will be strictly liable.[12]

It will be apparent that the phrase "any damage" is apt to cover both personal injuries to the plaintiff and damage to his property. Therefore, s. 2 (1) will apply to cases of personal injuries as a result of, for example, being mauled[13] or bitten by a bear,[14] mauled by a lion,[15] bitten by a camel[16] or a monkey,[17] or trampled on by an elephant.[18] Equally, if a marauding elephant merely damages property, an action for such damage will lie under s. 2 (1).

Damage is further defined by s. 11 to include the death of any person and so if the victim of a dangerous animal's attack is killed, his dependents will have a right of action under the Fatal Accidents Acts 1846–1959.[19] Furthermore, injury to a

---

[10] [1957] 2 Q.B. 1, 17–18.
[11] Under s. 6 (2).
[12] These are the facts of *Scribner* v. *Kelly,* 38 Barb. 14 (N.Y. 1862), though the decision there was against liability.
[13] *Besozzi* v. *Harris* (1858), 1 F. & F. 92.
[14] *Wyatt* v. *Rosherville Gardens Co.* (1886) 2 T.L.R. 282; *Shaw* v. *McCreary* (1890), 19 O.R. 39.
[15] *Cf. Young* v. *Green,* [1958] O.W.N. 426.
[16] *McQuaker* v. *Goddard,* [1940] 1 K.B. 687.
[17] *Connor* v. *The Princess Theatre* (1912), 27 O.L.R. 466.
[18] *Behrens* v. *Bertram Mills Circus, Ltd.,* [1957] 2 Q.B. 1.
[19] Under s. 10 of the Animals Act 1971 it is provided that "For the purposes of the Fatal Accidents Acts 1846 to 1959 . . . any damage for which a person is liable under sections 2 to 4 of this Act shall be treated as due to his fault".

person extends, by reason of s. 11, to cover "any disease and any impairment of physical or mental condition". If, therefore, an animal of a dangerous species is carrying a disease and the plaintiff is infected thereby, an action will lie under s. 2 (1). If the injury to the plaintiff takes the form of nervous shock or physical injury directly attributable to shock, such damage is actionable under s. 2 (1). A heart attack as a result of seeing a tiger at the end of the bed would clearly be actionable,[20] but mere "fright" at seeing a rampaging elephant would not be actionable unless it led to physical or mental impairment.[1] If, however, the fright caused the plaintiff to fall and break his wrist,[2] such damage would be actionable.

There are two final factors to consider in relation to strict liability under s. 2 (1). First, the damage complained of must have been caused by the dangerous animal. In *Brook* v. *Cook*,[3] the plaintiff fell when the defendant's monkey appeared on her garden wall. However, the County Court judge found that her fall was not caused by fright at the appearance of the monkey. Her action and her appeal to the Court of Appeal failed, as they would under s. 2 (1).

Secondly, the damage complained of must not be too remote. There is little or no direct authority on remoteness of damage in the case of animals which are *ferae naturae* or belong to a dangerous species.[4] Some of the earlier cases contain dicta indicating very wide liability,[5] in that the keeper would be liable for "any damage" caused by his animal. Later, this was modified[6] to indicate that there would be liability for any "direct damage".[7] Most recently, it has been suggested[8] that the remoteness test in the *scienter* action was "a test of foreseeability, but one which, in the case of such dangerous crea-

[20] *Behrens* v. *Bertram Mills Circus, Ltd.*, [1957] 2 Q.B. 1, 17–18.
[1] *Ibid.*, at pp. 27–28.
[2] *Cf. Brook* v. *Cook* (1961), 105 Sol. Jo. 684.
[3] *Ibid; cf. Scribner* v. *Kelly*, 38 Barb. 14 (N.Y. 1862).
[4] Williams, 320–321.
[5] *Cox* v. *Burbidge* (1863), 13 C.B.N.S. 430, 439; *Filburn* v. *People's Palace and Aquarium Co., Ltd.* (1890) 25 Q.B.D. 258, 260.
[6] *Hambrook* v. *Stokes Bros.*, [1925] 1 K.B. 141, 156.
[7] *Re Polemis and Furness, Withy & Co., Ltd.*, [1921] 3 K.B. 560.
[8] Dias, [1962] C.L.J. 178, 196.

tures as tigers, will encompass a very wide area of damage."[9] It is a matter of conjecture which approach will be regarded as relevant to liability under s. 2 (1). There is, however, no indication in the Animals Act 1971 that liability under s. 2 (1) should be other than strict which would indicate liability for all direct consequences of the animal's conduct.

(D)   LIABILITY FOR ANIMALS OF A NON-DANGEROUS SPECIES

Strict liability for harm done by animals which do not belong to a dangerous species is goverened by s. 2 (2) of the Animals Act 1971.   All animals which do not fall into the category of dangerous animals, as defined by s. 6 (2) of the Act, fall into this category.   All animals within this class are presumed to be harmless unless the necessary statutory conditions of liability laid down by s. 2 (2) are satisfied.   Once they have been satisfied, however, the keeper of the animal is liable even though he has not been proved to have been negligent.[10]   Liability is strict, subject to the various defences provided in the Animals Act 1971.[11]

The keeper of an animal not belonging to a dangerous species will be liable for damage caused by it provided the three general conditions laid down in s. 2 (2) are satisfied.   It is provided by s. 2 (2) of the Animals Act 1971 that:

"Where damage is caused by an animal which does not belong to a dangerous species, a keeper of the animal is liable for the damage, except as otherwise provided by this Act, if—
  (a) the damage is of a kind which the animal, unless restrained, was likely to cause or which, if caused by the animal, was likely to be severe; and
  (b) the likelihood of the damage or of its being severe was due to characteristics of the animal which are not normally found in animals of the same species or are not normally so found except at particular times or in particular circumstances; and

---

[9] This would accord with *The Wagon Mound,* [1961] A.C. 388 and see *The Wagon Mound (No. 2),* [1967] 1 A.C. 617.
[10] As in the *scienter* action, e.g. *Card* v. *Case* (1848), 5 C.B. 622.
[11] Discussed *infra* pp. 71–90.

(c) those characteristics were known to that keeper or were at
any time known to a person who at that time had charge of
the animal as that keeper's servant or, where that keeper
is the head of a household, were known to another keeper
of the animal who is a member of that household and under
the age of sixteen."

These conditions relate, basically, to the kind of damage
likely to be caused, the abnormal characteristics of the animal
which caused the damage and the keeper's knowledge, actual,
imputed or inferred, of those characteristics. Whilst it is
proposed to examine all three conditions, this cannot profitably
be done by considering each requirement in isolation from the
other two, for they all inter-relate.[12]

There are really two alternative requirements. The first
is that the damage is of a kind which the animal, unless
restrained, is likely to cause and this likelihood is due to abnormal characteristics of the animal known to the keeper. The
second is that the damage is of a kind which the animal is not
likely to cause but which, if caused, is likely to be severe, and
this likelihood is due to abnormal characteristics of the animal
known to the keeper. Common to both these situations is that
the likelihood of the damage or of its severity is due to the
abnormal characteristics of the animal and that the keeper has
knowledge of these.

(i) Abnormal characteristics.

The animal must have characteristics which are of one of two

---

[12] Unless s. 2 (2) (a) and s. 2 (2) (b) are read as inter-relating, s. 2 (2) (a) is
unintelligible, in part. It is not possible to indicate circumstances in which
the nature of the damage caused by an animal is likely to be severe, because
it all depends on what happens in a particular case. This might be illustrated by liability for damage done by a horse. One may well say that
horses in general and this horse in particular are not likely to bite human
beings. That being so the first alternative condition of s. 2 (2) (a) is not
satisfied. When one turns to the second and asks, "If a horse bites a human,
is the damage likely to be severe?", it is virtually impossible to answer the
question. The answer depends on where or how the person was bitten.
This is why s. 2 (2) (a) is dependent on the condition in s. 2 (2) (b), for the
likelihood of the animal causing damage or of causing severe damage must
depend on abnormal characteristics of the species. It is a far more meaning-
ful question to ask: "Did this animal have characteristics, not normally
found in animals of the same species, which would indicate that if it caused
damage it was likely to cause severe damage?"

kinds.   The first is that they are not normally found in animals of the same species.   It is not easy to see what the essence of this requirement is.   There was, at common law, considerable debate as to whether there could be liability under the *scienter* action, in the case of animals *mansuetae naturae,* for injury caused by a vice natural to the species of animal.[13]   There were suggestions, both judicial[14] and academic,[15] that there could only be liability if the defendant was proved to know that the animal had a disposition to do acts contrary to the nature of its species, and that knowledge of the natural tendency of the animal to cause the harm in question was not sufficient.   There would, however, appear to have been no decisions where a claim failed solely on the ground that the particular animal's known vice was natural to its species.   On the contrary, there have been a number of decisions where the keepers of animals have been held liable for damage caused by their animals which would seem to have acted in accordance with the generally accepted nature of the species.[16]   Thus, there has been liability for a ram butting,[17] a bull attacking a man wearing a red kerchief,[18] and for a dog biting humans,[19] other dogs[20] and other animals.[1]   A clear example of an animal acting in accordance with what might be regarded as its natural propensities is provided by *Buckle* v. *Holmes.*[2]   The defendant's cat strayed on to the plaintiff's land and there killed some of the plaintiff's pigeons and bantams.   The plaintiff failed to prove

---

[13] Williams, 318–320.
[14] *Heath's Garage, Ltd.* v. *Hodges,* [1916] 2 K.B. 370, 377–378; *Cutler* v. *United Dairies (London), Ltd.,* [1933] 2 K.B. 297, 302–303; *Fitzgerald* v. *E.D. and A.D. Cooke Bourne (Farms), Ltd.,* [1964] 1 Q.B. 249, 269–271.
[15] Salmond, *Torts,* 15th ed. 435; Law Commission Report, §. 6.
[16] *Cf. Fletcher* v. *Rylands* (1866), L.R. 1 Exch. 265, 280.
[17] *Jackson* v. *Smithson* (1846), 15 M. & W. 563; and see the comment thereon by Erle, C.J. in *Cox* v. *Burbidge* (1863), 13 C.B.N.S. 430, 437–438.
[18] *Hudson* v. *Roberts* (1851), 6 Exch. 697; *cf. Smith* v. *Cook* (1875), 1 Q.B.D. 79; though we are told that bulls are colour blind: Fleming, *Torts,* 4th ed. 305; 313 H.L. Deb. c. 457.
[19] E.g. *M'Kone* v. *Wood* (1831), 5 C. & P. 1.
[20] *Cf. North* v. *Wood,* [1914] 1 K.B. 629.
[1] *Read* v. *Edwards* (1864), 17 C.B.N.S. 245 (dog chasing pheasants); *Card* v. *Case* (1848), 5 C.B. 622 (worrying sheep); *Boulton* v. *Bankes* (1632), Cro. Car. 254 (killing a pig); *cf. Tallents* v. *Bell and Goddard,* [1944] 2 All E.R. 474 (killing rabbits).
[2] (1925), 95 L.J.K.B. 158; affirmed, [1926] 2 K.B. 125.

that the defendant knew of the propensity of his cat to kill pigeons; but, had knowledge been proved, it appeared that the plaintiff would have succeeded.[3]

If the requirement in s. 2 (2) (b) of the Animals Act that the animal must have displayed characteristics not normal to its species is given any other than a broad interpretation, it will exclude a large number of situations which, under the common law, led to liability.   It is said to be the natural tendency of horses to shy,[4] to be playful,[5] to kick and bite other horses,[6] though not perhaps to bite human beings.[7]   That being so, there would be no liability for injuries caused when a person is knocked down by a playful filly,[8] or when one horse bites another,[9] but only if it bites a person.[10]   Again it is said to be consonant with the nature of dogs to run after sheep[11] which would exclude any liability for worrying them.[12]

Examples of this type of problem could be multiplied.   The common law required that the animal evidence some vicious or mischievous propensity and it may have been that it should have had a propensity to attack humans or other animals, rather than just have had a propensity to do damage.[13]   The Animals Act 1971 will exclude liability under s. 2 (2) for any normal behaviour of an animal.   Ultimately, the whole scope of liability under s. 2 (2) will depend upon the manner in which the courts determine what are, and are not, normal characteristics of animals of non-dangerous species.   One factor that will have to be considered is the sex of the animal in question. Fierce characteristics may be normal in the male of a species but not in the female.   Goring by a bull may be expected but

---

[3] (1925), 95 L.J.K.B. 158, and see *Tallents* v. *Bell and Goddard, supra,* at p. 475.

[4] *Cutler* v. *United Dairies (London), Ltd.,* [1933] 2 K.B. 297, 303.

[5] *Fitzgerald* v. *E.D. and A.D. Cooke Bourne (Farms), Ltd.,* [1964] 1 Q.B. 249, 257.

[6] *Manton* v. *Brocklebank,* [1923] 2 K.B. 212, 222; *cf. Fletcher* v. *Rylands* (1866), L.R. 1 Exch. 265, 280.

[7] *Cf. Glanville* v. *Sutton & Co., Ltd.,* [1928] 1 K.B. 571.

[8] See *Fitzgerald* v. *E.D. and A.D. Cooke Bourne (Farms), Ltd., supra.*

[9] *Cf. Manton* v. *Brocklebank, supra.*

[10] *Pacy* v. *Field* (1937), 81 Sol. Jo. 160.

[11] *Manton* v. *Brocklebank, supra,* at p. 222.

[12] *Cf. Card* v. *Case* (1848), 5 C.B. 622.

[13] *Fitzgerald* v. *E.D. and A.D. Cooke Bourne (Farms), Ltd., supra,* at p. 270.

not by a cow.   Which are the normal characteristics of cattle?
It may be that as species "includes sub-species and variety"[14]
different rules apply to different sexes of the same type of
animal.

The second kind of abnormal characteristics envisaged by
s. 2 (2) (b) are those which are not normally found in animals
of the species in question except at particular times or in particular circumstances.   The object of this provision would
seem to be to apply to liability under s. 2 (2) a similar requirement as to abnormal characteristics to that which existed at
common law, namely that it is not necessary for the species of
animal always to reveal its dangerous or abnormal characteristics.   If a species which is normally docile reveals vicious
characteristics in certain particular circumstances, then those
characteristics, though normal to the species in those circumstances, may be classed as abnormal.   An obvious example of
such circumstances would be that a female of a species may well,
customarily, evidence fierce characteristics in the protection of
its young, though generally it is docile.   Such a situation could
be exemplified by *Barnes* v. *Lucille, Ltd.*[15]   The plaintiff had
been bitten by the defendant's chow bitch which, at the time,
had three pups, and the defendant knew that the dog, at least in
such circumstances, had a propensity to bite people.   Such
intermittent ferocity was enough.   DARLING, J. said:

> "I do not think . . . that in order to make the owner of a dog
> liable that the dog must be always and invariably ferocious.   If
> the owner knows that at certain periods the dog is ferocious,
> then he has knowledge that at those times the dog is of such a
> character that he ought to take care of it.   If a man knows that a
> bitch which is ordinarily amiable is ferocious when she has pups,
> and people go near her, I think he has knowledge that at such
> times she is of a ferocious character."[16]

This is the underlying ratio of the provision in s. 2 (2) (b) with
the added rider that, for the purposes of the Animals Act 1971,

---

[14] Animals Act 1971, s. 11.
[15] (1906), 96 L.T. 680.
[16] *Ibid.*, at p. 681; and see *Clinton* v. *J. Lyons & Co., Ltd.*, [1912] 3 K.B.
198, 202.

it does not matter that such unusual characteristics are to be expected in those unusual circumstances.   Other characteristics which would fall into the same category would, for example, be the case of "a mare at seasons when she is subject to sexual excitement",[17] or

> "an ox, ordinarily mild, brought to slaughter, [for] it is said that the animals show an instinctive revulsion from the smell of the slaughter-house and often become wild".[18]

A horse which is quite placid when used as a plough horse may bolt when put in a cart.[19]

As the damage for which liability may be imposed under s. 2 (2) must be of a kind which the animal was likely to cause and, in the present type of case, that likelihood must be due to characteristics which are only normally found in animals of the same species in particular circumstances, the keeper of the animal will only be liable if his animal causes injury during its intermittently dangerous period.   It is only during that period that the animal will be likely to cause damage of the kind in question.

Two general points might be made about the abnormal characteristics of an animal which will lead to liability under s. 2 (2).   The first is that whilst the animal's characteristics must be abnormal, they do not have to be permanent.   The keeper will be liable if his animal portrays such characteristics even though it does not do so all the time.   The animal does not have to be a recidivist;[20] for:

> "it is not necessary that the dog should run about, and show a disposition to snap at and bite everybody; a man of bad temper is not always in a bad temper".[1]

An animal of abnormal characteristics does not always reveal them.   However, the damage of which the plaintiff complains must be of a kind which the animal, because of these abnormal characteristics, was likely to cause.

---

[17] *Manton* v. *Brocklebank*, [1923] 2 K.B. 212, 227.
[18] *Howard* v. *Bergin, O'Connor & Co.*, [1925] 2 I.R. 110, 125.
[19] *Knight* v. *Knight*, [1933] G.L.R. 237.
[20] Williams, 302.
[1] *Charlwood* v. *Greig* (1851), 3 Car. & Kir. 46, 48.

Secondly, the fact that a long or short period of time has elapsed between the animal revealing its abnormal characteristics and the harm inflicted on the plaintiff will be irrelevant. Thus, at common law, a half hour time gap has not been too short,[2] nor was four years too long[3]. Of course, it may be hard to accept that an isolated abnormal act so long ago should fix the keeper with general knowledge of the animal's abnormal characteristics or that, in such a case, the animal was likely to cause damage of the kind suffered. The two real criteria should be that sufficient time has elapsed for the keeper to take precautions to prevent the animal repeating its misdeeds,[4] and that the period should not be so long that there is now no likelihood of its causing the type of damage in fact inflicted.

(ii)   The kind of damage.

The keeper of an animal which he knows to be dangerous will only be liable for damage caused by his animal if it is either of a kind which the animal was likely to cause because of its abnormal characteristics or if the animal, though unlikely to cause damage because of such characteristics would, nevertheless, be likely, if it caused any damage, to cause severe damage.

(1)   Likely kinds of damage

Under s. 2 (2) it must be proved that the keeper had knowledge of such characteristics of his animal that it is likely to do the kind of harm actually inflicted. There will not be liability if it causes damage of a different kind from that which its abnormal characteristics would lead one to expect. This requirement might be illustrated from a number of common law decisions. If a dog has bitten a human being then it must be shown to have abnormal characteristics such that it is likely to bite human beings, though it is probably not necessary that it should be likely to bite specific human beings, e.g. small

---

[2] *Parsons* v. *King* (1891), 8 T.L.R. 114.
[3] *Gladman* v. *Johnson* (1867), 36 L.J.C.P. 153.
[4] *Parsons* v. *King, supra,* at p. 115.

boys.[5] So long as its characteristics make it liable to cause the actual damage inflicted, it need not have general dangerous characteristics. If a cat is likely to attack a person with a dog, and does so, then it does not matter that it would be unlikely to attack a person who was unaccompanied by a dog.[6] However, the fact that a dog has an abnormal tendency to worry sheep[7] or to attack goats[8] is not necessarily evidence of its likelihood to injure humans; for, under the Animals Act 1971, as under the common law,

> "in actions for injury sustained by man through the bite of a dog, the [knowledge] which it is necessary to shew is that the dog had ferocious disposition towards mankind—that he had bitten or attempted to bite mankind."[9]

It is unlikely that a tendency of a dog to worry sheep will indicate the likelihood of injury to humans. On the other hand, proof of a tendency in a dog to attack men may well constitute proof of its tendency to worry sheep, as showing evidence of its general vicious characteristics such that it is likely to cause damage to both men and sheep.[10] In the case of horses, it has been held that evidence of a tendency to bite other horses is not necessarily evidence of a tendency to bite men,[11] nor would evidence of a tendency to kick cars[12] necessarily be evidence of a tendency to kick men, or other animals. Nor, again, is evidence of a tendency to stray, proof of a tendency to leap over hedges on to passers-by.[13] However, there is some authority for the view that a tendency to attack one kind of animal is evidence of a tendency to attack other kinds of animals,[14] so that damage to the latter could be regarded as of a

---

[5] *Cf. Pacy* v. *Field* (1937), 81 Sol. Jo. 160.
[6] *Cf. Clinton* v. *J. Lyons & Co., Ltd.,* [1912] 3 K.B. 198, 208.
[7] *Cf. Hartley* v. *Harriman* (1818), 1 B. & Ald. 620.
[8] *Cf. Osborne* v. *Chocqueel,* [1896] 2 Q.B. 109.
[9] *Osborne* v. *Chocqueel,* [1896] 2 Q.B. 109, 111; and see *Whycherley* v. *Grave,* [1967] C.L.Y. 91.
[10] *Gething* v. *Morgan* (1857), 29 L.T.O.S. 106; *cf. Hartley* v. *Harriman* (1818), 1 B. & Ald. 620, 624.
[11] *Glanville* v. *Sutton,* [1928] 1 K.B. 571.
[12] *Ibid.,* at p. 577.
[13] *Brock* v. *Richards,* [1951] 1 K.B. 529, 537–538.
[14] *Quin* v. *Quin* (1905), 39 I.L.T.R. 163; and see *Jenkins* v. *Turner* (1696), 1 Ld. Raym. 109, 110.

kind which the animal is likely to cause, within the meaning of s. 2 (2) (a).

There is no requirement in s. 2 (2) that the animal's characteristics are such that it is likely to cause damage by attack. Damage caused in any way is recoverable provided both that it is likely and that this likelihood stems from the animal's abnormal characteristics. In fact this last requirement of abnormality will exclude most cases of damage caused other than by an attack. A cow is likely to cause damage to a neighbour by eating his grass, but there is nothing abnormal in a cow so acting, and so there would be no liability under s. 2 (2).

(2) *Likelihood of damage, if caused, being severe*

This second type of damage envisaged by s. 2 (2) (a) is one that must prove to be rare in practice. For there to be liability on this basis, an animal must have caused damage in circumstances where it was unlikely that an animal of that species would cause the kind of damage in question but the animal had such abnormal characteristics that it was likely that, if it did cause damage, the damage would be severe. One immediately thinks of a comparison with the classification of an elephant as a dangerous species for the purposes of s. 2 (1) because of its size.[15] However, a domestic animal of substantial size will only satisfy the requirement of likelihood of severe damage if its size is abnormal. One possible illustration of this principle might be that of the diseased animal, such as a cow with foot and mouth disease, a sheep with scab, or a dog with rabies.[16] It might be said that such an animal was unlikely to cause damage, but equally, if it did happen to cause damage, the damage caused was likely to be severe.

If a dog of a fierce breed attacked the plaintiff, as in the case of attacks by Alsatian and Dobermann Pinscher guard dogs, then it might be said that such a dog was unlikely to cause damage, but that, if it did, such damage was likely to be severe because of the physical characteristics of such an animal, i.e.

---

[15] *Supra*, p. 41.
[16] Provided one can say that infection is a "characteristic" of the infected animal.

size, strength, and aggressive nature.[17] These characteristics
are common to those breeds of dog and there will only be liability under s. 2 (2) if the characteristics indicating that
damage may be severe are abnormal. Once again, one has to
ask whether subdivisions are to be made between breeds and
types of dog. If one looks at the characteristics of dogs in
general, then it might be said that dogs do not normally possess
these characteristics and the plaintiff might recover. If one
looks at the particular characteristics of these breeds of dogs,
then there is no abnormality and the plaintiff will fail.

Finally, one should note that liability under this second head
of s. 2 (2) (a) is based upon the fact that the damage is likely
to be severe. There is no requirement that in the actual
eventuality it was severe, only that it was likely to be so.
There are three miscellaneous issues which are relevant to a
discussion of the kind of damage for which liability is imposed
under s. 2 (2). A definition of "damage" is provided by s. 11
of the Animals Act 1971, as follows: " 'Damage' includes the
death of, or injury to, any person (including any disease and
any impairment of physical or mental condition)".

If the victim of an attack by an animal which is dangerous
within the meaning of s. 2 (2) is injured or killed by that animal
then he or his estate may recover and his dependents will have
a right of action under the Fatal Accidents Acts 1846–1959.[18]
If the plaintiff, or his animals, are infected by the disease
carried by the defendant's animal and this abnormal state is
known to the defendant, then again the defendant will be
liable. Whether a plaintiff could ever recover under s. 2 (2)
for nervous shock is probably unlikely, for few animals of a
non-dangerous species can have abnormal characteristics such
that they are likely to cause nervous shock.[19] Any damage to
the plaintiff's property will fall within the scope of liability
under s. 2 (2).

The second issue relates to causation. There must be a
causative link between the plaintiff's damage and the defen-

---

[17] 312 H.L. Deb. cc. 840–846.
[18] See Animals Act 1971, s. 10, *supra*, p. 46.
[19] *Cf. Gilligan* v. *Robb* 1910 S.C. 856.

dant's animal. For example, in *Bard* v. *O'Connor*,[20] the plaintiff alleged that he had been injured when the defendant's boxer dog had attacked his poodle. When the plaintiff realised the dogs were fighting he ran out, jumped down some steps and fractured his ankle. The Court of Appeal held that the broken ankle could not have been caused by the dogs fighting. On that basis there could not, today, be liability for such a broken ankle under s. 2 (2).

Finally, so far as remoteness of damage is concerned, it is suggested that the rule applicable under s. 2 (2) will be the same as that in relation to s. 2 (1), namely a rule of direct consequences rather than of reasonable foresight.[1]

(iii) Knowledge

The final condition of liability under s. 2 (2) is that provided by s. 2 (2) (c). The keeper of an animal will be liable if the abnormal characteristics of the animal in question:

> "were known to that keeper or were at any time known to a person who at that time had charge of the animal as that keeper's servant or, where that keeper is the head of a household, were known to another keeper of the animal who is a member of that household and under the age of sixteen".

There are, therefore, three situations envisaged here: the knowledge of the keeper himself or his "vicarious knowledge" through either an employee or a member of his household under the age of sixteen. There seems little doubt that what con-stitutes knowledge of the abnormal characteristics will be the same in each case. Furthermore there is no definition of knowledge in the Animals Act 1971. That being so, one may assume that it is an issue left to be resolved by the common law and that the meaning of knowledge for the purposes of liability under s. 2 (2) will be the same as for liability under the *scienter* action for animals *mansuetae naturae*. Before examining the three different instances where a keeper will be considered to have knowledge of the animal's characteristics, the concept

---

[20] [1960] C.L.Y. 86.
[1] *Supra*, pp. 47–48; and see Davis (1945), 18 A.L.J. 338.

of knowledge itself will be discussed in the light of the common law decisions.

The requirement of knowledge will be satisfied in a variety of ways.

(a) Proof that the animal has, to the knowledge of its keeper, actually caused this kind of damage before. Thus, if the keeper knows that his dog has previously bitten a human being, that is adequate knowledge that it has characteristics such that it is likely to do so again.[2] Perhaps the most striking example of this is *Parsons* v. *King*.[3] The plaintiff was a potman in a public house visited by the defendant and his terrier. The dog bit the plaintiff slightly and half an hour later in the street the dog bit the plaintiff more seriously and the plaintiff claimed damages at common law under the *scienter* action. During the half hour the defendant had taken no steps to secure the dog and the plaintiff succeeded for "the action was not for the first bite, but for the second. Half an hour had intervened between them, and during that time it was the duty of the defendant, who knew his dog had just bitten a man, to secure him in some way so as to prevent him from biting again. This he might very easily have done, but had not done."[4]

(b) Proof that the keeper knows that the animal has attempted to do the harm in question even though it has not yet succeeded in so doing. Thus in *Worth* v. *Gilling*[5] the defendants kept a dog chained to its kennel on a seven foot chain, and they knew that whenever anyone passed, it ran out to the limit of its chain, barking and trying to bite. When it succeeded in biting the plaintiff in the arm the defendants were considered to have knowledge of its ferocity, as they knew of its attempts to bite.

(c) Proof that the keeper knows the animal has this vicious characteristic even though it has not yet attempted to cause any injury. In *Barnes* v. *Lucille, Ltd.*[6] the defendant's chow

---

[2] *Charlwood* v. *Greig* (1851), 3 Car. & Kir. 46; *Pacy* v. *Field* (1937), 81 Sol. Jo. 160; *Gladman* v. *Johnson* (1867), 36 L.J.C.P. 153.
[3] (1891), 8 T.L.R. 114.
[4] *Ibid.*, at p. 115.
[5] (1866), L.R. 2 C.P. 1; and see *Wood* v. *Vaughan* (1888), 28 N.B.R. 472.
[6] (1907), 96 L.T. 680.

bitch with pups bit the plaintiff, an employee of the defendants, but it was not clear that the defendants knew that the dog had bitten or attempted to bite anyone before, though they did know that it had a propensity so to do and was dangerous unless guarded. This was sufficient knowledge for

> "It is a misapprehension on the part of many people to suppose that in order to make the owner of a dog liable that the dog must have actually bitten someone before. Nor do I think it is necessary to show that the dog has attempted to bite somebody. What is necessary is that there should be evidence that the dog is a ferocious dog, which means that he would be likely to bite without provocation."[7]

Thus if an owner knows that "his bull would run at anything red" this is evidence that he is aware that it is a dangerous animal.[8] Again, the fact that the defendant had warned people to take care lest her dog bite them has been considered evidence of *scienter*.[9] Yet on the other hand the mere placing of a notice saying "Beware of the dogs" on a front gate does not imply knowledge of a dog's viciousness.[10] The fact that a dog is kept on a running lead does not of itself prove that the keeper knew of its vicious characteristic.[11]

It will be recalled that the keeper of an animal is considered to have knowledge of his animal's abnormal characteristics in three circumstances, as laid down by s. 2 (2) (c). These must now be examined.

(a)   The knowledge of the keeper himself

This is obvious. Whoever is the keeper will be liable if he, himself, knows of the animal's dangerous characteristics. Provided that the keeper has knowledge himself, or through

---

[7] (1907), 92 L.T. 680, 681.
[8] *Hudson* v. *Roberts* (1851), 6 Exch. 697.
[9] *Judge* v. *Cox* (1816), 1 Stark. 285.
[10] *Dolan* v. *Bright,* [1962] C.L.Y. 72; and see *Cruttendon* v. *Brenock,* [1949] V.L.R. 366; *Simpson* v. *Bannerman* (1932), 32 S.R. (N.S.W.) 126, 133.
[11] *Beck* v. *Dyson* (1815), 4 Camp. 198; *Hogan* v. *Sharpe* (1837), 7 C. & P. 755; *McNeill* v. *Frankenfeld* (1963), 44 D.L.R. (2d) 132, 146.

third parties,[12] it does not matter that it was acquired from some other person's statement as to the dangerous nature of the animal,[13] so long as the information was reasonably credible, even though not believed by the keeper.[14]   There is, however, no general rule that the knowledge of one keeper is attributed to another keeper.[15]   So the fact that the possessor of the animal has sufficient knowledge and is liable as a keeper, does not mean that the owner, who is also a keeper,[16] is liable in the absence of knowledge.

(b)   The knowledge of the keeper's servant

The keeper will be deemed to have knowledge of the animal's abnormal characteristics if they "were at any time known to a person who at that time had charge of the animal as that keeper's servant".   There are a number of elements to examine here.   The first is that the person who has the knowledge must be the servant of the keeper.   This might be illustrated by *Baldwin* v. *Casella*.[17]   The defendant's dog was under the care and control of the defendant's coachman and was kept in the stables.   The coachman knew of the dog's propensity to attack people and this knowledge was considered at common law, as it would be under the Animals Act 1971, to be attributable to the master, the keeper, whether it had been communicated to him or not.   Again, knowledge by the defendant's servants that cattle, entrusted to their control to be driven along a highway, were dangerous, has been held to be the knowledge of the master.[18]

---

[12] This can be the knowledge of a servant or member of the keeper's household which is deemed to be that of the keeper, under s. 2 (2) (c), (see (b) and (c) *infra*) ;   or it may be that, because a third party has knowledge, it is assumed that this has been communicated to the keeper, *infra*, pp. 66–68.

[13] *Soames* v. *Barnardiston* (1689), Freem. K.B. 430, 431–432; and see *McIntyre* v. *Carmichael* (1870), 8 Macph. (Ct. of Sess.) 570, 574; *Arnold* v. *Diggdon* (1887), 20 N.S.R. 303.

[14] *Cf. Soames* v. *Barnardiston*, *supra*.

[15] This only applies in the case of a "household" animal, *infra*, pp. 65–66.

[16] Section 6 (3) (a).

[17] (1872) L.R. 7 Exch. 325; and see *Nadeau* v. *City of Cobalt Mining Co.* (1912), 3 D.L.R. 495; *cf. Shelfontuck* v. *Le Page*, [1937] 2 W.W.R. 16, 19; affirmed, [1938] 1 D.L.R. 513.

[18] *Scott* v. *Edington* (1888), 14 V.L.R. 41, 50. It has since been doubted whether this is a true master/servant relationship in the case of drovers: *Queensland Stations Pty., Ltd.* v. *Federal Commissioner of Taxation* (1945), 70 C.L.R. 539.

The requirement that the person envisaged by s. 2 (2) (c) must be the servant of the keeper will both incorporate into the interpretation of this subsection all the common law learning on how to determine whether a person is a servant[19] and exclude anyone who does not fall into that category.   It has been held, in Australia, for example, that if the custody and control of an animal is delegated by the keeper to any third party, such as a friend as well as a servant, then the knowledge of the third party is, as a matter of law, that of the keeper.[20]   This is not the position under the Animals Act 1971.   The knowledge of such a person is not to be attributed to the owner as keeper.

The second element relating to the knowledge of a servant is that the servant must have "had charge of the animal as that keeper's servant".   He must both be in charge of the animal and be so in his capacity as a servant.   It is not, therefore, enough that the person who has the knowledge of the characteristics of the keeper's animal is the keeper's servant unless he has some close relationship of control with the animal. The situation was the same at common law.   Lord COLERIDGE, C.J. has said, "It may be taken to be quite clear that a mere notice to any servant of the owner of the [animal] will not do".[1] This might be exemplified by *Colget* v. *Norris*[2] where the defendant's dog bit the plaintiff, a postman, as he was delivering letters to the defendant's house.   There was evidence that complaints about the dog had been made to the defendant's domestic servants but that they had not been communicated to the defendant.   The action failed because "notice to the domestic servant could not be said to be notice to the master",[3] and the fact that the servant "had taken the dog to the door and had occasionally washed it"[4] was insufficient to place the

---

[19] Atiyah, *Vicarious Liability,* Part II.
[20] *Cruttendon* v. *Brenock,* [1949] V.L.R. 366, 370.
[1] *Applebee* v. *Percy* (1874), L.R. 9 C.P. 647, 655; and see *Stiles* v. *Cardiff Steam Navigation Co.* (1864), 33 L.J.Q.B. 310, 312.
[2] (1886), 2 T.L.R. 414, and 471 (C.A.).
[3] (1886), 2 T.L.R. 471, 472; and see *Stiles* v. *Cardiff Steam Navigation Co., supra,* where knowledge of porters or carters, employed by the defendant company, of the dangerous characteristics of a dog was insufficient to render the company liable as the employees had no control over the business, the premises or the dog in question, even though the dog was kept for guarding and protecting the defendant company's premises.
[4] (1886) 2 T.L.R. 414, 415.

dog in the control of the servant. Equally, such an employee would not be considered to "have charge" of the dog within the meaning of s. 2 (2) (c) of the Animals Act 1971. The same might well be said where the servant's only contact with the animal is that he has merely taken it for a walk,[5] or fed it occasionally.[6] A recent example where the animal was in the charge of one servant but another servant had knowledge of its dangerous characteristics is provided by *Maclean* v. *The Forestry Commission*.[7] The pursuer, an employee of the defenders, was injured by a horse belonging to them. Another of the defenders' employees knew that the horse was dangerous, but he was held not to have charge or control of the horse.[8] The employee who did have charge of it did not know of its dangerous characteristics. The court was not prepared to combine the knowledge of one employee with the control of the other. Lord WHEATLEY went so far as to say:

"If each is to be regarded in his own way as the alter ego of the employers it seems to produce a schizophrenic legal persona, and I cannot imagine that the law leads to such a result."[9]

Not only must the person in charge be a servant but he must be in charge of the animal in that capacity in order for the keeper to be fixed with the employee's knowledge under s. 2 (2) (c). The mere fact of a master/servant relationship does not necessarily lead to the conclusion that the former is fixed with the latter's knowledge of the animal's dangerous characteristics. An example where knowledge would not be attributed might be the case where an animal is kept by the employee for his own purposes as a pet and not on behalf of his employer, as in *Knott* v. *L.C.C.*[10] Here, a school caretaker who lived on the school premises kept a large dog there which he knew to be

---

[5] *Cf. Cleverton* v. *Uffernel* (1887) 3 T.L.R. 509.
[6] *Cf. Cruttendon* v. *Brenock*, [1949] V.L.R. 366, 374.
[7] 1970 S.L.T. 265.
[8] There was some evidence that, at one stage, though not at the time of the accident, the employer who knew of the viciousness was in charge of the horse: 1970 S.L.T. 265, 266–267. That would be enough, under s. 2 (2) (c) of the Animals Act 1971, for the defendants to have imputed knowledge, see *infra*, p. 64. (Though the Animals Act 1971 does not apply to Scotland: see s. 13 (4)).
[9] 1970 S.L.T. 265, 271.
[10] [1934] 1 K.B. 126.

vicious.   The dog bit the plaintiff, a cleaner at the school, who alleged *scienter* on the part of the defendants, the school authority.   They had no knowledge of the existence, let alone the propensities, of the dog.   It was held that the caretaker did not keep the dog as a servant but for his own private purposes and so his knowledge was not to be attributed to the defendants.   As Lord WRIGHT said:

> "The position is not different from that of a chauffeur who keeps his dog in the room over the garage or a groom who keeps his dog in his rooms over the stables."[11]

In such cases there would be no liability placed on the employer by s. 2 (2) of the Animals Act 1971 for the two reasons that the employer is not a keeper of the animal where he is neither owner nor possessor, and the employee is not in charge of the animal as an employee.   There would still be no liability if, although the employer owned the animal and was, therefore, a keeper, the animal was kept by the employee as a pet or was being looked after by the employee during the employer's absence, unless this was done in his capacity as a servant.

The third, and final, element relating to the knowledge of a servant is that of time.   Section 2 (2) (c) speaks of characteristics which "were *at any time* known to a person who *at that time* had charge of the animal as that keeper's servant".[11a] The italicised phrases indicate that for the knowledge of the servant to be deemed that of the master, the servant must have had his knowledge at a time when he was a servant, but that need not have been the time of the plaintiff's injury. Thus, if a servant has charge of an animal which he knows to be dangerous that knowledge will be attributed to the master even though the injury occurs several years later[12] or at a time when the servant is no longer in charge of the animal,[13] nor employed by the master, or even when the servant is dead.[14]

---

[11] [1934] 1 K.B. 126, 140.   [11a] Italics added.

[12] There was a time lag of a year in *Baldwin* v. *Casella* (1872) L.R. 7 Exch. 325; of two years in *Cruttendon* v. *Brenock*, [1949] V.L.R. 366; and there was a four year time lag in *Gladman* v. *Johnson* (1867), 36 L.J.C.P. 153, *infra,* p. 67; a case of a wife's knowledge being evidence of her husband's.

[13] *Cf. Maclean* v. *The Forestry Commission*, 1970 S.L.T. 265.

[14] 306 H.L. Deb. cc. 691–693; 312 H.L. Deb. cc. 846–849; 313 H.L. Deb. cc. 446–447.

(c) *The knowledge of another keeper who is a member of the keeper's household under the age of sixteen*

The keeper will be deemed to have knowledge of the dangerous characteristics of his animal if, "where that keeper is the head of a household, [they] were known to another keeper of the animal who is a member of that household and under the age of sixteen". A number of the factors relevant to this provision in s. 2 (2) (c) were considered earlier when the definition of a keeper was examined. For example, it is necessary that the keeper to whom knowledge is to be attributed should be a head of a household and that the keeper under sixteen should be a member of that household.[15] It is, however, also necessary that the member of the household must either own or possess it. A father will not be fixed with the knowledge of his children under sixteen unless they are keepers of the animal also. This might be illustrated by the decision in *Elliott* v. *Longden*[16] where the owner of a dog was held liable for damage it caused by biting or frightening a horse and causing it to bolt thereby injuring the horse and damaging the carriage it was pulling. The owner of the dog had no knowledge of its dangerous propensities, but his eleven year old son did. That knowledge was enough for the defendant to be held liable in the *scienter* action. It would not be enough under s. 2 (2) (c) unless the child was also a keeper of the dog. Such a keeper must also be under the age of sixteen; there will be no knowledge attributable to the head of a household from the knowledge of a child who is a member thereof over sixteen.[17]

It has been argued that in the case of a family household pet which:

"is freely taken out in public by different members of a household, the knowledge of the propensity should as a matter of equity and general rule be attributed to all."[18]

This argument is not accepted in the Animals Act 1971 and, unless the provisions of s. 2 (2) are satisfied, the knowledge of a

---

[15] *Supra*, pp. 27–28.
[16] (1901), 17 T.L.R. 648; and see *infra*, pp. 186–187.
[17] *Cf. McIntyre* v. *Carmichael* (1870), 8 Macph. (Ct. of Sess.) 570, 574; *Stanford* v. *Robertson*, [1946] 3 D.L.R. 313.
[18] *Flockhart* v. *Ferrier* 1959 S.L.T. (Sh. Ct. Rep.) 2, 4.

child is not attributed to the father as a matter of law, nor is
the knowledge of a spouse ever to be deemed to be that of the
other spouse.

There is also a "time problem" in relation to the knowledge
of a keeper under the age of sixteen being attributed to a
keeper who is the head of a household of which the child is a
member.   It will be recalled that the knowledge of a servant
was attributed to his master whether the servant was still
employed or not at the date of the accident, so long as he was
in charge of the animal as a servant at the time when he
acquired the knowledge.[19]   The position in the present context
is different.   Section 2 (2) (c) stipulates that the keeper who is
the head of a household will be liable if the characteristics of
the animal *"were* known to another keeper of the animal who
is a member of that household and under the age of sixteen."[20]
Here the characteristics may be known to the young keeper at
any time in the past, but he must still be a keeper and a member
of the household and under the age of sixteen at the time when
the damage is caused to the plaintiff by the animal.   If any
of these requisites are not satisfied at the time of the injury,
the head of the household will not be fixed with his knowledge.
The obviously likely case is that where a child who knew of the
characteristics when under sixteen has now reached that age.
When he does, his knowledge ceases to be imputed to the head
of the household.

Finally, it should be mentioned that knowledge is imputed
to the head of household as keeper under s. 2 (2) (c) whether
he is a keeper both by reason of his ownership or possession of
the animal[1] and by reason of his headship of a household wherein
someone under sixteen is also a keeper,[2] or whether he is a
keeper merely by reason of the latter.

This does not necessarily mean that a keeper will not have the
knowledge of a third party attributed to him outside the provisions of s. 2 (2).   There were a variety of circumstances at
common law where the fact that a servant, child or spouse had

---

[19] *Supra*, p. 64.
[20] Italics added.
[1] Section 6 (3) (a).
[2] Section 6 (3) (b).

knowledge of an animal's dangerous characteristics led to a presumption that the master, parent or other spouse had such knowledge. There is nothing in s. 2 (2) to indicate that such decisions will not be relevant to a determination of whether the keeper himself has knowledge; this being an issue quite separate from the issue whether he is fixed with knowledge, which he may manifestly not have, through his servant or young member of his household. It could well be that:

> "the relationship of the defendant to the third party may be such that it is open to the jury[3] to infer, as a matter of probability, that the knowledge would be and was communicated."[4]

In the case of servants, there may be those who do not "have charge" of the animal but nevertheless know of its dangerous characteristics. In such cases, it has been held that:

> "notice to them of the vicious and ferocious nature of a dog kept about the premises . . . was, upon principle and upon authority, evidence fit to be submitted to the jury of a notice to their employer."[5]

Thus, where complaints of the viciousness of the defendant's dog were made to barmen serving in the defendant's public house, the knowledge of the barmen, though not considered as a matter of law to be that of their employer because the barmen were not in control of the dog, was evidence of the employer's *scienter* to be submitted to a jury[6] Under s. 2 (2), the barmen's knowledge would not be deemed to be that of their employer, for they did not "have charge" of the dog, but it is suggested that it would still be evidence of the keeper's own knowledge.

The position is similar in the case of husband and wife. In *Gladman* v. *Johnson*[7] the knowledge by a wife of her husband's dog's vicious propensity acquired four years prior to the incident was attributed to her husband, not as a matter of law, but on the grounds that the jury could infer that the wife had

---

[3] Today, of course, the judge as trier of fact.
[4] *Cruttendon* v. *Brenock*, [1949] V.L.R. 366, 370. It was the view of the Law Commission, Report, § 79, that such inferred knowledge should remain.
[5] *Applebee* v. *Percy* (1874), L.R. 9 C.P. 647, 656.
[6] *Ibid.*
[7] (1867), 36 L.J.C.P. 153; and see *Norton* v. *Fitzgerald*, [1928] 3 D.L.R. 474; *Flockhart* v. *Ferrier* 1959 S.L.T. (Sh. Ct. Rep.) 2.

told her husband of this.   There is no reason why such knowledge of a spouse should not be relevant under s. 2 (2) as evidence of the knowledge of the keeper.   Furthermore, a similar rule should apply to a husband's knowledge raising an inference of communication to his wife.[8]

It should not be forgotten that where a servant, spouse or member of a household is the keeper of an animal jointly with the master, other spouse or head of the household, then his knowledge of the animal's dangerous characteristics will be relevant to his own liability as keeper.[9]

Finally, it should be borne in mind that it is necessary to prove actual knowledge on the part of the defendant[10] or of the third party whose knowledge under s. 2 (2) (c) is deemed to be that of the keeper.   Where the knowledge of a spouse or child is attributed to the keeper it is as evidence of the keeper's own knowledge.   The fact that the keeper *ought to have known* is not enough, but the courts have been prepared to accept very slight evidence of knowledge.[11]   On the other hand, in actions of negligence[12] a defendant may well be liable if he ought to have known of the danger from an animal and he was negligent in failing to take adequate precautions.[13]

(E)   ESCAPE OF A DANGEROUS ANIMAL

Nothing in the Animals Act 1971 alters the general common law rule applicable to the *scienter* action that in the case both of dangerous and non-dangerous animals it was not necessary to prove that the animal escaped from the land on which it was kept.   There may be liability irrespective of where the animal causes the damage.   The law is the same whether the plaintiff is injured or suffers loss on his own land,[14] on the defendant's

---

[8] *Miller* v. *Kimbray* (1867), 16 L.T. 360; Williams, 307–308.
[9] E.g. *Stanford* v. *Robertson*, [1946] 3 D.L.R. 313 (infant); *Duncan* v. *Carleton* (1895), 11 T.L.R. 524 (wife).
[10] E.g. *Mason* v. *Keeling* (1700), 12 Mod. 332, 335.
[11] E.g. *Judge* v. *Cox* (1816), 1 Stark. 285; *cf. Sneddon* v. *Baxter*, 1967 S.L.T. (Notes) 67.
[12] Discussed, *infra*, Chapter 6.
[13] *White* v. *Steadman*, [1913] 3 K.B. 340.
[14] E.g. *Read* v. *Edwards* (1864), 17 C.B.N.S. 245; *Behrens* v. *Bertram Mills Circus, Ltd.*, [1957] 2 Q.B. 1.

land,[15] on a third party's land,[16] on the highway[17] or, even, in a car.[18] The duty of the keeper of the animal both at common law and, now, under s. 2 of the Animals Act 1971 is "to keep that beast so confined as to be incapable of doing damage".[19] A corollary of the proposition that there need be no actual escape from the defendant's animal is that it is irrelevant to liability whether or not the defendant's animal is trespassing.[20]

A vexed issue at common law was whether the animal must have escaped from the defendant's control, even though it did not have to escape from the defendant's land. It was said by Lord WRIGHT that:

"It is not unlawful or wrongful to keep such an animal; the wrong is in allowing it to escape from the keeper's control with the result that it does damage."[1]

Nevertheless, it was quite sufficient for liability at common law for a lion to maul a child through its cage[2] or for a bear kept on a six foot chain to seize someone walking past its house.[3] Such liability is justified by CROWDER, J. in that:

"A person who keeps such an animal is bound so to keep it that it shall do no damage. If it be insufficiently kept, or so kept that a person passing is not sufficiently protected, the owner is liable."[4]

---

[15] E.g. *Besozzi* v. *Harris* (1858), 1 F. & F. 92; *Wyatt* v. *Rosherville Gardens Co.* (1886), 2 T.L.R. 282. There is also the possibility in such cases of an action based on occupiers' liability: e.g. *Gould* v. *McAuliffe*, [1941] 2 All E.R. 527; *Pearson* v. *Coleman Bros.*, [1948] 2 K.B. 359; *McNeill* v. *Frankenfeld* (1963), 44 D.L.R. (2d) 132, 139–140; *infra*, pp. 180–183.

[16] E.g. *Parsons* v. *King* (1891), 8 T.L.R. 114: injury on the employer's premises

[17] E.g. *Hudson* v. *Roberts* (1851), 6 Exch. 697; in these circumstances there may be liability in the absence of negligence, though negligence has for a long time been a usual requirement in actions for injuries on the highway: see Fleming, *Torts*, 4th ed. 306, n. 36.

[18] *Sycamore* v. *Ley* (1932), 147 L.T. 342.

[19] *Pearson* v. *Coleman Bros.*, [1948] 2 K.B. 359, 380; and see *Read* v. *J. Lyons & Co., Ltd.*, [1947] A.C. 156, 171; *Behrens* v. *Bertram Mills Circus, Ltd.*, [1957] 2 Q.B.1, 19.

[20] E.g. *Manton* v. *Brocklebank*, [1923] 2 K.B. 212, 231.

[1] *Knott* v. *L.C.C.*, [1934] 1 K.B. 126, 138.

[2] *Pearson* v. *Coleman Bros.*, [1948] 2 K.B. 359.

[3] *Besozzi* v. *Harris* (1858), 1 F. & F. 92; *Wyatt* v. *Rosherville Gardens Co.* (1886), 2 T.L.R. 282.

[4] *Ibid.*, at p. 93.

However, in *Rands* v. *McNeil*[5] it would appear that the fact that there was no escape was considered significant in denying liability in the *scienter* action.   The defendant kept a bull, known by him to be dangerous, for stud purposes.   The bull was dehorned and kept untethered in a loose box.   The plaintiff, the defendant's employee, entered the loose box without tethering the bull and he was injured when the bull charged at him. His action based on *scienter* failed and one of the reasons given in the Court of Appeal[6] was that the bull had not escaped from the box.   DENNING, L.J. suggested that:

> "In order to impose strict liability even to the public it is essential to prove not only knowledge of the dangerous propensity of the animal, but also to prove that it escaped and did harm."[7]

Insofar as this decision required an actual escape it was out of line with previous authorities, but it could, perhaps, be justified on the grounds that an *escape from control*[8] was necessary. Thus, a bull in a loose box was still within control, whilst a lion in a barred cage was not.[9]   It was, however, difficult to reconcile such a requirement with the fact that failure to control at all could never justify an argument that there was no escape from control.[10]   Furthermore, this requirement of escape from control was unrealistic.   If a dog known to be dangerous is kept chained in such a way that it can injure passers-by, then, though it has not *escaped,* it has been held to have *escaped from control* in that:

> "the control or restraint that one assumes a keeper will put on a vicious dog proves insufficient to prevent the dog doing injury to someone lawfully about."[11]

Despite its obvious disadvantages, the requirement that the defendant should only be liable if there was an escape from

---

[5] [1955] 1 Q.B. 253; noted by Payne (1955) 18 M.L.R. 295; and see *Henderson* v. *John Stuart (Farms) Ltd.,* 1963 S.C. 245.

[6] Another reason was that there could be no such liability between master and servant; see now Animals Act 1971, s. 6 (5), discussed, *infra,* pp. 73–76.

[7] [1955] 1 Q.B. 253, 257; and see at pp. 267, 269–271.

[8] *Christian* v. *Johannesson,* [1956] N.Z.L.R. 664, 666.

[9] *Aliter,* if there is injury when the whole cage is fenced off: *Murphy* v. *Zoological Society of London,* [1962] C.L.Y. 68.

[10] *McNeill* v. *Frankenfeld* (1963) 44 D.L.R. (2d) 132, 134.

[11] *Ibid.,* and see *Christian* v. *Johannesson, supra.*

control was emphasised by DEVLIN, J. in *Behrens* v. *Bertram Mills Circus, Ltd.*,[12] for he stated that:

"It does not follow . . . that if an elephant slips or stumbles, its keeper is responsible for the consequences. There must be a failure of control."[13]

The requirement of escape from control was not accepted by the Law Commission[14] and there is no such requirement in the Animals Act 1971. It has been abolished along with the abolition of the *scienter* action[15] and has not been resuscitated for the purposes of statutory liability under s. 2. If the defendant fails to restrain a dangerous animal or an animal with known dangerous characteristics, he will be liable if it causes injury. The animal need neither escape nor escape from control. It merely needs to injure. Therefore, there will now be liability if an elephant "slips or stumbles" and thereby causes injury, or if someone is injured by a dangerous horse or bull in its stall.[16]

(F) DEFENCES

There are four defences to liability under s. 2 for harm caused by dangerous animals which are provided by the Animals Act 1971. Two are peculiar to liability under s. 2, whilst the other two are more general defences to liability under the Animals Act. The two special defences will be examined first.

(i) Voluntary acceptance of risk

This is really the defence of consent[17] and it is provided by s. 5 (2) of the Animals Act 1971 that:

"A person is not liable under section 2 of this Act for any damage suffered by a person who has voluntarily accepted the risk thereof."

This defence is closely related to those of contributory negli-

---

[12] [1957] 2 Q.B. 1. [13] *Ibid.*, at p. 19.
[14] Law Commission report, s. 19. [15] Animals Act 1971, s. 1.
[16] Subject to any defence of assumption of risk, the fault of the plaintiff or contributory negligence.
[17] For a discussion of the general principles of this defence, see Fleming, *Torts*, 4th ed., Chapter 11; Winfield and Jolowicz, *Tort*, 9th ed., 624–639; Salmond, *Torts*, 15th ed., 664–678; Street, *Torts*, 4th ed., 74–77, 160–165.

gence[18] and the default of the plaintiff.[19] If the plaintiff not only knows of the danger from the defendant's dangerous animal but also agrees, expressly or impliedly, to run the risk of that danger, he could not later complain of his injuries in the *scienter* action[20] nor can he under s. 2.

However, knowledge alone of the dangerous characteristics will not suffice[1] and so the exercise of a right by the plaintiff cannot be prevented simply because the plaintiff knows that the defendant's dangerous animal may be in the vicinity.[2] On the other hand, the plaintiff must not be reckless, for:

> "The pursuit of one's own rights may sometimes be so foolhardy that the reasonable man should desist and seek another remedy. If a man is on the highway and he sees elephants approaching in procession, the law does not require him to elect between turning down a side street or accepting the risk of their misbehaviour if he goes on; but if he sees them stampeding and remains where he is because he considers that he has as much right to the highway as they have, he might fail to recover."[3]

Although it has been suggested that to intervene in a fight between your own and the defendant's dog may amount to consent or assumption of risk if you are bitten,[4] yet such a plaintiff acting in defence of his property ought to be in no worse position than a third party who is injured when attempting to prevent harm being done. The latter is not taken to consent to his injuries if there is some "serious exigency pressing upon him to incur the risk which he did."[5] However, he who climbs a barrier beside a leopard's cage to extinguish a smouldering cigarette-end clearly assumes the risk of being mauled,[6]

---

[18] Animals Act 1971, s. 10, *infra*, pp. 86–89.
[19] *Ibid.*, s. 5 (1), *infra*, pp. 83–86.
[20] *Rands* v. *McNeil* [1955] 1 Q.B. 253, 266; *Behrens* v. *Bertram Mills Circus, Ltd.*, [1957] 2 Q.B.1, 20–21; and see *Stanford* v. *Robertson*, [1946] 3 D.L.R. 313, 316–317; affirmed, [1947] 1 D.L.R. 493; *Carroll* v. *Kehoe* (1927), 61 I.L.T.R. 192.
[1] *Shelfontuck* v. *Le Page*, [1938] 1 D.L.R. 513.
[2] *Tarasoff* v. *Zielinsky*, [1921] 2 W.W.R. 135, 140–141.
[3] *Behrens* v. *Bertram Mills Circus, Ltd.*, [1957] 2 Q.B. 1, 20.
[4] *Smith* v. *Shields* (1964), 108 Sol. Jo. 501.
[5] *Sylvester* v. *G. B. Chapman, Ltd.*, [1935] L.J. C.C.A. 261, 265. Compare *Cutler* v. *United Dairies (London), Ltd.*, [1933] 2 K.B. 297 with *Haynes* v. *Harwood*, [1935] 1 K.B. 146.
[6] *Sylvester* v. *G. B. Chapman, Ltd.*, [1935] 1 L.J.C.C.A. 261.

as does someone who climbs up a lion's cage to reach a notice on top of it.[7]

If a plaintiff claims in negligence, rather than under s. 2 of the Animals Act 1971, for the injuries caused by the defendant's animal, the defence of assumption of risk is equally applicable.[8] There was some opposition to the inclusion of s. 5 (2) in the Animals Act 1971[9] and there is, undoubtedly, a danger that those who keep dangerous animals in zoos and parks will exculpate themselves by notices stating that the members of the public enter at their own risk.

There is a special provision in the Animals Act 1971 to deal with the issue of assumption of risk in the employment context. It is provided by s. 6 (5) that:

"Where a person employed as a servant by a keeper of an animal incurs a risk incidental to his employment he shall not be treated as accepting it voluntarily."

The purpose of this provision would appear to be to alter an anomalous rule of the common law that an employer would only be liable to his employees for *negligently* subjecting them to risk or for providing an unsafe system of work. An employer was not held strictly liable to his employees under the *scienter* action. The leading authority for this rule was *Rands* v. *McNeil*[10] where the plaintiff, the defendant's employee, was injured by a bull kept in a loose box. His claim against his employer based on the *scienter* action failed, *inter alia*, because, as JENKINS, L.J. said,

"I do not think that this doctrine of absolute liability can reasonably be applied as between a farmer and the persons employed by him on his farm in relation to the handling by those persons of an animal such as a bull kept by the farmer for breeding purposes."[11]

---

[7] *Young* v. *Green*, [1958] O.W.N. 426.
[8] *Breen* v. *Slotin*, [1948] 4 D.L.R. 46; *Collins* v. *Richmond Rodeo Riding, Ltd.* (1966), 56 D.L.R. (2d) 428.
[9] 305 H.L. Deb. cc. 1415–1421.
[10] [1955] 1 Q.B. 253, *supra*, pp. 69 70; and see *Henderson* v. *John Stuart (Farms), Ltd.* 1963 S.C. 245, 253; *cf. Brock* v. *Copeland* (1794), 1 Esp. 203 discussed in *Bird* v. *Holbrook* (1828), 4 Bing. 628, 642. *Barnes* v. *Lucille, Ltd.* (1907), 96 L.T. 680, another employment case, is confusing as to whether the action therein was based upon *scienter* or negligence.
[11] [1955] 1 Q.B. 253, 266; and see at p. 257.

This really amounted to an irrebuttable presumption of assumption of risk by the employee.[12]

If, of course, there was evidence of negligence on the part of the employer in his provision of safe working conditions for his employee he would, and will, be liable, as where he keeps a bull in a loose box without providing any means of tethering it before the box is cleaned out.   There will be liability for negligence in such cases even though the employer is unaware of the dangerous nature of the bull, so long as he ought to have known of the dangers.[13]

The denial of any action to an employee in *scienter* in these types of case really amounted to confusion of strict liability under that action with the employer's obligations to provide a safe system of work, a confusion which may well have been avoided in Scotland.[14]   It would appear to be the purpose of s. 6 (5) of the Animals Act 1971 to reverse the effect of *Rands* v. *McNeil,* so that an employee will not always be deemed to have assumed risks incidental to his employment.[15]

When one examines s. 6 (5), however, it may be that it has achieved too much.   In providing that when an employee incurs a risk incidental to his employment he shall not be treated as accepting it voluntarily, it undoubtedly alters the law in the situation where the employee did not, in fact, assume the risk.   *Rands* v. *McNeil* is reversed, and in such a case the employee could succeed under s. 2.   No longer is he deemed to have accepted the risk.   There is also, however, another situation to consider.   There could be situations where an employee both knows of risks from his employer's dangerous animals and agrees to run them, i.e. cases of actual, rather than presumed, assumption of risk.   It has, for instance, been suggested that the custodian of a bull with dangerous pro-

---

[12] It did not serve to protect the employer against a claim by a third party: *Henderson* v. *John Stuart (Farms), Ltd.,* 1963 S.C. 245, 253.

[13] *Ibid.; cf. Beer* v. *Wheeler* (1965), 109 Sol. Jo. 457, another case concerning a bull in a pen where, on the evidence, the plaintiff's employer was not negligent.

[14] There seems to have been an assumption in *Clark* v. *Armstrong* (1862), 24 D. 1315 that an action would lie; and see *Henderson* v. *John Stuart (Farms), Ltd.,* 1963 S.C. 245, 251, 253; *Sneddon* v. *Baxter,* 1967 S.L.T. (Notes) 67; *cf. Daly* v. *Arrol Bros.* (1886), 14 R. 154.

[15] Law Commission Report, §. 20.

pensities may be taken to assume the normal risks of his
employment.[16]   Similarly it has been said that a man employed
as a horse-breaker "must take the risk of being thrown or
injured by a restive or unbroken horse."[17]   It is debateable
whether this type of case has not also been affected by s. 6 (5).
Undoubtedly the employee has incurred a risk incidental to
his employment.   If he has accepted it voluntarily, can he
fall within a provision that "he shall not be treated as accepting
it voluntarily"?   The better interpretation of s. 6 (5) is that
it covers both the case where, at common law, assumption of
risk was presumed, and the case where it was actual.   If that
is so then s. 6 (5) places employees in a privileged position in
relation to their employers' liability under s 2, so that an
employee may sue for damage from a risk which he has actually
assumed.   The only way to avoid such a conclusion would be
to interpret s. 6 (5) as applicable only to cases where there is no
actual assumption of risk, by emphasising that the phrase "he
shall not be *treated* as accepting it voluntarily"[18] refers only
to situations where, but for s. 6 (5), assumption of risk might
have been presumed.   It is suggested that this is an interpretation which hardly accords with the words of the sub-section.
One is left, therefore, with the conclusion that the defence of
assumption of risk is not open to an employer whose employee
claims under s. 2 of the Animals Act 1971,[19] provided that the
risk in question was one incidental to his employment.

If, although the parties are employer and employee, the risk
in question is not incidental to the plaintiff's employment,
than s. 6 (5) is inapplicable.   In *Mansfield* v. *Baddeley*,[20] the
plaintiff was employed by the defendant as a dressmaker.   At
the request of the defendant she visited the defendant's kitchen
where she was bitten by the defendant's dog.   The court
decided that the plaintiff could not recover for risks incidental

---

[16] *Rands* v. *McNeil*, [1955] 1 Q.B. 253, 272.
[17] *Bowater* v. *Rowley Regis Corpn.*, [1944] K.B. 476, 481; *cf. Yarmouth* v. *France* (1887), 19 Q.B.D. 647.
[18] Italics added.
[19] Because the employer should insure against such liability: Law Commission Report, §. 20.
[20] (1876), 34 L.T. 696.

to her employment. Was the visit to the kitchen and the risk
from the dog incidental to her employment? The court
thought it was not. GROVE, J. said:

> "No doubt she cannot recover for risks incidental to the service.
> I think that this risk is not incidental to the service . . . . If the
> plaintiff when she entered her employment knew the character
> of the dog, and that in the ordinary course of her employment she
> would have to go by the place where it was tied up, it might
> perhaps be said she took the risk. But here she was asked to do
> something which was no part of her service, in fact a mere good-
> natured act, it being something *ultra* her service to go to the
> kitchen. The dog then rushes out and bites her. Such a risk
> was not incidental to the service, nor one which by her conduct she
> has undertaken to bear."[1]

Although this case starts from the opposite position from the
present law, i.e. that all risks incidental to employment are
assumed, whereas the present law is that none are, it does
provide some indication of what risks might be considered
incidental to employment. Under s. 5 (2), those which are not
incidental to an employee's employment are ones which he may
assume, so as to relieve his employer from liability.

Finally, it should be mentioned that even if an employee has
actually assumed risks incidental to his employment, although
he is protected by s. 6 (5) from any defence of assumption of
risk raised by his employer, under s. 5 (2), he is not protected
from any claim that his injury is due to his own fault,[2] or a
claim of contributory negligence.[3] This is of some importance
in a case where an employee is injured by an animal which he
knows to be dangerous. His knowledge is deemed to be that
of his employer, the keeper.[4] If the employee has not informed
his employer of the danger, the employer will nevertheless be
liable under s. 2 and cannot rely on the employee's assumption
of risk, but can only rely on the employee's own fault or contributory negligence.

---

[1] (1876) 34 L.T. 696, 697.
[2] Section 5 (1), *infra*, pp. 83–86.
[3] Section 10, *infra*, pp. 86–89.
[4] Section 2 (2) (c).

(ii) Injuries to trespassers

Whilst there is substantial authority for the view that an occupier of premises is not liable in negligence to a trespasser[5] injured on the premises by a dangerous animal unless the occupier intended the injury or acted with reckless d'sregard of the presence of the trespasser,[6] there was very little direct authority[7] at common law on the question whether the fact that the plaintiff was a trespasser afforded a defence to the *scienter* action.[8] However, it has been stated by Lord GREENE, M.R. that:

"If facts established by the plaintiff herself show her to be a trespasser, then the obligations of the defendants must be treated on that footing, and it is impossible to put on them a greater obligation than the law imposes with regard to trespassers on their land."[9]

Under the Animals Act 1971 the issue of liability for injuries to trespassers by dangerous animals is dealt with specifically by s. 5 (3), which provides:

"A person is not liable under section 2 of this Act for any damage caused by an animal kept on any premises or structure to a person trespassing there, if it is proved either—
(a) that the animal was not kept there for the protection of persons or property; or
(b) (if the animal was kept there for the protection of persons

---

[5] The liability of an occupier to trespassers is governed by the common law and not by the Occupiers' Liability Act 1957; see North, *Occupiers' Liability*, Chapter 11.

[6] Williams, 349–352. A number of the "animals" cases concerned with occupiers' liability are concerned primarily with the issue whether the plaintiff was a trespasser or a lawful visitor; e.g. *Lowery* v. *Walker*, [1910] 1 K.B. 173, reversed [1911] A.C. 10; *Gould* v. *McAuliffe*, [1941] 1 All E.R. 515; [1941] 2 All E.R. 527; *Pearson* v. *Coleman Bros.*, [1948] 2 K.B. 359; *cf. Murphy* v. *Zoological Society of London*, [1962] C.L.Y. 68.

[7] See *Pearson* v. *Coleman Bros.*, *supra*, at pp. 370–371, 377; *Murphy* v. *Zoological Society of London*, *supra*. *Sarch* v. *Blackburn* (1830), 4 C. & P. 297 might be such a case, for TINDAL, C.J., at p. 300, refers to the requirement of the defendant's knowledge of the dog's propensity to bite; but, later, at p. 301, he discusses the requirement that the defendant be shown to be negligent.

[8] Though see the discussion of liability to a trespasser under the Dogs Acts 1006 1098, *infra*, pp. 101 104.

[9] *Pearson* v. *Coleman Bros.*, *supra*, at p. 371.

or property) that keeping it there for that purpose was not unreasonable."

Before examining the two specific provisions of s. 5 (3), a number of general issues must be considered. The first is that the sub-section applies to the keeping of an animal "on any premises or structure". These terms are not defined in the Animals Act 1971, but they are very reminiscent of the phraseology used in the Occupiers' Liability Act 1957. That Act applies to liability for injuries to visitors to premises and visitors to "any fixed or moveable structure, including any vessel, vehicle or aircraft".[10] If that analogy may be applied to the Animals Act, then the scope of s. 5 (3) is quite wide. It would apply to dangerous animals kept not only in a house, a farm building or a field,[11] but also in a zoo,[12] or a wild-life park. Furthermore, "structure" would encompass the keeping of such an animal in temporary circus premises,[13] on board a ship or aircraft, or in a car.[14]

Secondly, the plaintiff envisaged by s. 5 (3) is "a person trespassing" on the premises or structure. One assumes that "trespass" has its normal meaning of someone on the premises without permission or lawful authority and against whom an action of trespass to land could lie at the suit of a person with an adequate interest in the land.[15] Thus, the position of the car thief who is bitten by a dog in the car he steals would fall within s. 5 (3). However, s. 5 (3) does not require that the plaintiff be a trespasser *vis à vis* the keeper of the animal against whom his action under s. 2 is being brought. There may be varied instances where the statutory liability under s. 2 is placed upon a keeper who has no interest in the land where the animal is kept and *vis à vis* whom the plaintiff will not be a trespasser. An obvious example would be that where an animal is owned by one person but is in the possession of

---

[10] Occupiers' Liability Act 1957, s. 1 (3).
[11] 305 H.L. Deb. 1424; *cf.* 195 H.C. Deb. 557.
[12] *Cf. Murphy* v. *Zoological Society of London,* [1962] C.L.Y. 68.
[13] *Cf. Pearson* v. *Coleman Bros.,* [1948] 2 K.B. 359.
[14] *Cf. Sycamore* v. *Ley* (1932), 147 L.T. 342.
[15] North, *op. cit.,* pp. 162–170.

another person who is the occupier of the premises where it is kept. Both are keepers within the meaning of s. 6 (3) (a) but the plaintiff would only be a trespasser as against the possessor and not as against the owner. Nevertheless, both keepers can rely on the fact that the plaintiff was a trespasser as against one of them. Indeed where premises are protected by guard dogs supplied with a handler each evening by a security firm then the security firm will be the keeper of the dogs and the occupier of the premises where they roam at night has no responsibility under s. 2 for he is neither owner nor possessor of them.[16] If a trespasser is injured by the dogs, the owner may rely, under s. 5 (3), on the fact that the dogs are kept[17] by him on premises upon which the plaintiff was trespassing even though no trespass is committed against the owner, and the occupier of the premises is not a keeper.

Thirdly, s. 5 (3) provides a defence and so it is for the defendant to satisfy the court that the various elements of the defence laid down in that sub-section are satisfied. No doubt this is right, for the purpose for which the animal is kept[18] is peculiarly within the knowledge of the defendant.

To turn now to the two specific provisions of s. 5 (3), the first states that the defence applies if "the animal was not kept [on the premises] for the protection of persons or property."[19] The vast majority of animals will fall into this category, though there may, of course, be some which fulfil the function of protection although it is claimed that they are not kept for that purpose. A dog may be kept for companionship, but it is very convenient that it will bark when burglars appear. No doubt the courts will have to decide which is the predominant purpose. The consequence of the general provision in s. 5 (3)

---

[16] He may be liable for any injuries caused through his negligence, or he may be liable to a trespasser if he acted recklessly in allowing the dogs to roam his premises at night.

[17] Despite doubts expressed in the House of Lords: 305 H.L. Deb. c. 1426; 306 H.L. Deb. cc. 687, 690; 312 H.L. Deb. cc. 224, 231; there would seem little likelihood that a court would conclude that such dogs were not "kept" on the premises trespassed upon, even though they were only there for a relatively short time. Whilst they are there, they are "kept" there.

[18] Discussed *infra*.

[19] Section 5 (3) (a).

(a) is that if the plaintiff is injured by a bull grazing in a field, no action will lie under s. 2 if the plaintiff is a trespasser for the bull is not kept for the protection of persons or property.[20] Again, any trespasser in a zoo[1] or a circus or a wild-life park will be unable to succeed under s. 2 for there will be little doubt that the animals kept in such places are kept to entertain the public and not for the protection of persons or property.[2]

The second specific provision in s. 5 (3) is that there will be no liability to a trespasser injured by an animal kept on the premises for the protection of persons or property if keeping it there for that purpose was not unreasonable.[3]   There are three factors relevant here.   Was the animal kept on the premises, on which the plaintiff trespassed, for the purpose of the protection of persons or property?   Was it reasonable to keep that animal for that purpose? and Was it reasonable to keep it on the premises or structure in question for that purpose?

The obvious type of case envisaged is the keeping of guard dogs.   There may be other, albeit rare, instances of other dangerous animals, such as snakes or lions, being kept to guard property.   There seems little doubt that, at common law, it was considered wholly reasonable to keep fierce dogs for the purposes of guarding property,[4] and it would be surprising if the law were otherwise under the Animals Act 1971.   On the other hand it is very likely that a court would conclude that the keeping of lions or poisonous snakes for the guarding of property is quite unreasonable.[5]   This will, however, mean that if you

---

[20] The same was true at common law: *Hudson* v. *Roberts* (1851) 6 Exch. 697, 699; *Blackman* v. *Simmons* (1827), 3 C. & P. 138, 140; *Deane* v. *Clayton* (1817), Taunt. 489, 532–533.

[1] *Murphy* v. *Zoological Society of London,* [1962] C.L.Y. 68; and see *Marlor* v. *Ball* (1900), 16 T.L.R. 239.

[2] An unsuccessful attempt to apply s. 5 (3) only to animals not belonging to a dangerous species and to make the keeper of the latter liable to trespassers was made in the House of Lords: 312 H.L. Deb. cc. 852–857.

[3] Section 5 (3) (b).   The burden of proof of reasonableness would appear to rest on the defendant.

[4] *Brock* v. *Copeland* (1794), 1 Esp. 203; *Sarch* v. *Blackburn* (1830), 4 C. & P. 297, 300; *Sycamore* v. *Ley* (1932), 147 L.T. 342, 344; and see *Wilkins* v. *Manning* (1897), 13 W.N. (N.S.W.) 220; *Trethowan* v. *Capron,* [1961] V.R. 460.

[5] Lord GARDINER, L.C. considered that any other conclusion was "unthinkable": 306 H.L. Deb. c. 685; and see *Ibid.*, c. 689.

keep lions merely for entertainment, there will be no liability under s. 2 to a trespasser injured by them, but that if they are kept to protect property liability to a trespasser may ensue. If the keeper of the lions is the occupier of the premises trespassed upon, then under the common law rules relating to an occupier's liability to trespassers, he will only be liable if his conduct in keeping the dangerous animals amounted to an intention to injure the trespasser or to act with reckless disregard of his presence.[6] If, on the other hand, the keeper is not the occupier of the premises trespassed upon, he cannot rely upon the fact that the plaintiff was a trespasser and he will be liable if he has been negligent in the way in which he kept the animals.[7]

It must also be reasonable to keep the dangerous animal on the premises in question for the purpose of protection. It may be reasonable to keep guard dogs in some places but not in others; it might be reasonable for them to guard enclosed buildings, but not open fields.[8] What is, perhaps, a very significant factor in assessing reasonableness, and one not dealt with directly in s. 5 (3), is that of a warning of the presence of the dangerous animal. It may be reasonable to keep a fierce guard dog to protect premises but only if due warning of its presence is given. Otherwise it appears as though it is being kept to injure as well as to protect, and that would be unreasonable.

Finally, it should be borne in mind that s. 5 (3) is not the only provision of the Animals Act which may be relevant to liability under s. 2 for injuries caused to trespassers by dangerous animals. If a trespasser is injured by an animal unreasonably kept for the protection of persons or property then, although no protection is afforded to the keeper by reason of s. 5 (3), it

---

[6] *Robert Addie & Sons (Collieries), Ltd.* v. *Dumbreck*, [1929] A.C. 358; North, *Occupiers' Liability*, Chapter 11. *Murphy* v. *Zoological Society of London*, [1962] C.L.Y. 68 provides an example of this rule in the context of injury to a trespasser by a lion; and see *Marlor* v. *Ball* (1900), 16 T.L.R. 239; (trespasser kicked by a zebra in its stall).

[7] *Cf. Creed* v. *McGeoch & Sons, Ltd.*, [1955] 3 All E.R. 123; North, *op. cit.* pp. 28–31.

[8] 306 H.L. Deb. c. 685.

could be that there is no liability by reason of s. 5 (2).[9]   This
sub-section provides that:

> "A person is not liable under section 2 of this Act for any damage
> suffered by a person who has voluntarily accepted the risk thereof."

If there is a large notice warning that premises are protected by
dangerous snakes, prowling lions or roaming guard dogs where
it would be unreasonable to keep them, there is some common
law authority to support the view that a trespasser on those
premises who is aware of the notice has assumed the risk of all
but intentional injuries.   It was said by BAYLEY, J. in *Ilott* v.
Wilkes[10]:

> "Suppose . . . a person were to give a notice that in his premises
> there is a furious bull, and that it is dangerous for any person to
> enter, and a wrongdoer, who had read this notice, enters, and the
> bull attacks him, it is clear that he could maintain no action for
> the consequences of his own act.   So, also, if a trespasser enters
> into the yard of another, over the entrance to which notice is
> given, that there is a furious dog loose, and that it is dangerous
> for any person to enter in without one of the servants or the owner.
> If the wrongdoer, having read that notice, and knowing, therefore,
> that he is likely to be injured, in the absence of the owner enters
> the yard, and is worried by the dog, . . . it is clear that the party
> could not maintain any action for the injury sustained by the dog,
> because the answer would be . . . that he could not have a
> remedy for an injury which he had voluntarily incurred."[11]

Furthermore, s. 5 (1) provides that a person is not liable under
s. 2 for "any damage which is due wholly to the fault of the
person suffering it",[12] and there is, again, common law authority
suggesting that if a trespasser is injured by an animal on the
premises trespassed against, such injury is the result of his own
fault.   TINDAL, C.J. has said:

> "If a man puts a dog in a garden, walled all round, and a

---

[9] Discussed in more detail, *supra*, pp. 71–76.
[10] (1820) 3 B. & Ald. 304, 313; and see *Ibid.*, at p. 316; *Lowery* v. *Walker*,
[1910] 1 K.B. 173, 198.
[11] Whilst bulls and reasonably kept guard dogs would now be dealt with under
s. 5 (3) of the Animals Act 1971, the principle of assumption of risk here
expounded is relevant whatever the animal.
[12] Discussed in more detail, *infra*, pp. 83–86.

wrongdoer goes into that garden, and is bitten, he cannot complain in a Court of Justice of that which was brought upon him by his own act."[13]

This principle could apply where a trespasser is injured by a dangerous animal unreasonably kept for the guarding of premises, at least where the trespasser is warned of its presence. There is also no reason why the defences under s. 5 (1) and s. 5 (2) should not operate in the case of a trespassing plaintiff, claiming under s. 2, whether or not the defendant, the keeper of the animal in question, was occupier of the premises trespassed upon.

It should be reiterated, in conclusion, that the strict liability of a keeper of a dangerous animal to a trespasser based on s. 2 of the Animals Act 1971 is based on principles different from other heads of liability to trespassers. What may be a defence to liability under s. 2 is not, necessarily, relevant to a claim based on the negligence of a keeper who is not an occupier of the premises trespassed upon or to a claim based on the liability of an occupier, as such, to a trespasser injured on his premises by a dangerous animal.[14]

(iii)   Damage due wholly to the fault of the plaintiff

At common law, if the plaintiff's own conduct was the cause of his injury, then he could not claim damages for it.[15]   This is equally true under the Animals Act 1971, for s. 5 (1) provides that:

"A person is not liable under sections 2 to 4 of this Act for any damage which is due wholly to the fault of the person suffering it."

This defence is, of course, applicable not only to claims for injuries caused by dangerous animals, under s. 2, but also to claims for damage caused by a dog injuring or killing livestock,

---

[13] *Sarch* v. *Blackburn* (1830), 4 C. & P. 297, 300; and see *Brock* v. *Copeland* (1794), 1 Esp. 203, 203–204; *Marlor* v. *Ball* (1900), 16 T.L.R. 239, 240.
[14] General liability at common law for injuries caused by animals is examined in Chapter 6.
[15] E.g. *Filburn* v. *People's Palace and Aquarium Co., Ltd.* (1890), 25 Q.B.D. 258, 260.

under s. 3,[16] and to claims for damage done by straying live-stock, under s. 4.[17]

One general problem is that it is not always easy to determine in what circumstances the plaintiff is to be considered to have brought his injury upon himself. If the plaintiff goes up to zebras in a stall to stroke them, then probably he cannot complain if one kicks him and the other bites him,[18] or, indeed, if he so shouted at a horse that it kicked him.[19] On the other hand, a plaintiff could claim in *scienter* and, presumably, still can claim under s. 2 (2) of the Animals Act 1971 when bitten by a strange dog which he had patted on the head.[20] A small boy who put his arm round a dog and kissed it to induce it to play was considered to be the cause of his own injury when the dog bit him;[1] but another small boy who lay down beside a dog and put his arms round its neck was able to recover.[2] Both were cases involving the *scienter* action but both seem relevant to liability under s. 2 (2). Again, when a child, a lawful visitor, chose to relieve herself near a lion's cage, the defendants, the proprietors of a circus, were held liable when the child was mauled by the lion. The child, who was only five years old, was not considered to be the cause of her own injury.[3]

It has been held not to be default on the part of the plaintiff merely to walk near where a dangerous animal is kept,[4] at least if the plaintiff is unaware of the existence of the animal. If the plaintiff is aware of the existence of an animal of a dangerous species then he may also be taken to know that it is

---

[16] *Infra*, pp. 190–191.
[17] *Infra*, pp. 110–111.
[18] *Marlor* v. *Ball* (1900), 16 T.L.R. 239; see also *Young* v. *Green*, [1958] O.W.N. 426. Nor could a plaintiff complain if he foolishly tried to take some smouldering straw out of a leopard's cage and was mauled by the leopard: *Sylvester* v. *G. B. Chapman, Ltd.*, [1935] L.J.C.C.A. 261 (also briefly reported in (1935) 79 Sol. Jo. 777) for "he was bringing the trouble upon himself". (at p. 264).
[19] *Dowler* v. *Bravender* (1968), 67 D.L.R. (2d) 734.
[20] *Gordon* v. *Mackenzie* 1913 S.C. 109.
[1] *Lee* v. *Walkers* (1939), 162 L.T. 89.
[2] *Charlwood* v. *Greig* (1851), 3 Car. & Kir. 46; and see *Smith* v. *Pelah* (1747), 2 Stra. 1264.
[3] *Pearson* v. *Coleman Bros.*, [1948] 2 K.B. 359.
[4] *Besozzi* v. *Harris* (1858), 1 F. & F. 92.

dangerous. Indeed, in *Besozzi* v. *Harris*,[5] where the plaintiff was injured by a bear, it was suggested that "if the plaintiff, with knowledge that the bear was there, put herself in a position to receive the injury, she could not recover". In such a case the injury is due to the fault of the plaintiff because the animal is of a dangerous species. Probably, however, in the case of animals which do not belong to a dangerous species the plaintiff must be aware both of the existence of the animal and of its dangerous characteristics[6] before it can be said that his injury is due to his own fault. Indeed, one can argue that that should always be the case where the plaintiff is injured by such an animal,[7] unless he provokes it. If the plaintiff actually provokes or teases the animal he would have had no claim in *scienter*[8] if injured,[9] and his injury would appear to be due wholly to his own fault within the meaning of s. 5 (1) of the Animals Act 1971. On the other hand, an earlier teasing will not justify a later attack.[10]

Section 5 (1) of the Animals Act 1971 refers to damage which is due "wholly to the fault of the person suffering it". "Fault" is defined[11] as having the same meaning as in the Law Reform (Contributory Negligence) Act 1945. Under s. 4 of the 1945 Act, fault is defined as:

"negligence, breach of statutory duty or other act or omission which gives rise to a liability in tort or would, apart from this Act, give rise to the defence of contributory negligence."[12]

In order for the defence under s. 5 (1) to be nefit the defendant

---

[5] (1858), 1 F. & F. 92, 93; and see *Young* v. *Green*, [1958] O.W.N. 426; *cf. Wyatt* v. *Rosherville Gardens Co.* (1886), 2 T.L.R. 282, where the plaintiff recovered in *scienter* though he had gone into an inner gallery close to a bear's den. That case might be distinguished, today, as one of contributory negligence and not of the plaintiff's default.

[6] E.g. *Sycamore* v. *Ley* (1932), 147 L.T. 342.

[7] *Cf. Lee* v. *Walkers* (1939), 162 L.T. 89.

[8] Or under the Dogs Acts 1906–1928; see *Elliott* v. *Longden* (1901), 17 T.L.R. 648, 649, *infra*, pp. 190–191. It appears, however, that a claim in negligence might lie: *Jones* v. *Perry* (1796), 2 Esp. 482, as cited in Peake, *Law of Evidence*, (1822) 5th ed. 313; Williams, 343.

[9] *Behrens* v. *Bertram Mills Circus, Ltd.*, [1957] 2 Q.B. 1, 19; and see *Simpson* v. *Bannerman* (1932), 47 C.L.R. 378, 384.

[10] *Brown* v. *Stewart* (1824), 3 S. 127; and see *Smith* v. *Pelah* (1747), 2 Stra. 1264.

[11] Animals Act 1971, s. 11.

[12] E.g. breach of contract: *Quinn* v. *Burch Bros.*, [1966] 1 Q.B. 370.

the plaintiff's injuries must be due *wholly* to his fault.   This
requirement must be read subject to some limitations.   The
injury must have been caused by an animal but the fact that
the animal caused it must have been wholly attributable to
the fault of the plaintiff and in no way to the fault, i.e. the
negligence, breach of statutory duty or the like, of the defendant.
If a visitor to a wild life park ignores the many notices warning
him not to get out of his car or open its windows in an enclosure
full of lions, his mauling by the lions would be due wholly to
his own fault.

(iv)   Contributory negligence

The connection between contributory negligence and the
previous defence of the default of the plaintiff is obvious.
However, the differentiation between the two defences is made
here[13] because if the plaintiff is the cause of his own injury he
cannot recover at all, but if he is contributorily negligent his
damages will be apportioned under the Law Reform (Contributory Negligence) Act 1945 according to his degree of responsibility for his own injuries;   though, of course, the plaintiff
may still be held fully responsible.[14]

The defence of contributory negligence was applied to
scienter actions at common law,[15] and it was the view of the
Law Commission[16] that contributory negligence should provide
a defence to liability under s. 2 of the Animals Act 1971.
Section 10 of the Animals Act 1971 provides that:

> "For the purposes of . . . the Law Reform (Contributory Negli-
> gence) Act 1945 . . . any damage for which a person is liable under
> sections 2 to 4 of this Act shall be treated as due to his fault."

This provision has then to be read against the provisions of the

---

[13] *Cf. Chittenden* v. *Hale*, [1933] N.Z.L.R. 836, 847;   *Rands* v. *McNeil*, [1955] 1
Q.B. 253, 266.
[14] *Beer* v. *Wheeler* (1965), 109 Sol. Jo. 457.
[15] Just as it had been applied to ordinary actions of negligence based on
injury by animals, e.g. *Flett* v. *Coulter* (1903), 5 O.L.R. 375.
[16] Law Commission Report, §. 21.   The Law Commission doubted whether
public opinion would accept the stricter rule that a defendant should be
wholly liable irrespective of the negligence of the plaintiff.

Law Reform (Contributory Negligence) Act 1945, s. 1 (1) of which states:

"Where any person suffers damage as the result partly of his own fault and partly of the fault of any other person or persons, a claim in respect of that damage shall not be defeated by reason of the fault of the person suffering the damage, but the damages recoverable in respect thereof shall be reduced to such extent as the court thinks just and equitable having regard to the claimant's share in the responsibility for the damage."[17]

The effect of all this in the context of liability under s. 2 of the Animals Act 1971 is that, although liability under s. 2 is strict, yet if a plaintiff is injured partly as the result of his own negligence or breach of statutory duty and partly as the result of the defendant's breach of his statutory obligations under s. 2, the defence of contributory negligence is open to the defendant.

No doubt decisions under the *scienter* action will be relevant in indicating what type of conduct by a plaintiff amounts to contributory negligence. At common law, it was considered that the issue of contributory negligence was raised when the plaintiff went into an inner gallery close to a bear's den[18] and again when the plaintiff patted a strange dog on the head in the street.[19] The defence has been allowed where two cats were killed by the defendor's dog in or near the pursuer's shop, for:

"to allow an animal liable within common knowledge to be attacked by other domestic animals to be at large in a public place where these other animals may legitimately be is contributory negligence."[20]

---

[17] See Williams, *Joint Torts and Contributory Negligence, Part II*.

[18] *Wyatt* v. *Rosherville Gardens Co.* (1886), 2 T.L.R. 282, 283.

[19] *Gordon* v. *Mackenzie* 1913 S.C. 109; *cf. Simpson* v. *Bannerman* (1932), 47 C.L.R. 378.

[20] *Brown* v. *Soutar* 1914 2 S.L.T. 399, 400; and see Williams, 317–318. This should not prevent a cat, in such circumstances, from being allowed to act in self defence; Williams, 333.

Again, in *Rands* v. *McNeil*,¹ the case of injury by a bull in a loose box, the issue raised by the fact that the plaintiff actually went into the box was considered by DENNING, L.J.:

> "I realise, of course, that [a third party] and the plaintiff were both at fault. They ought not to have gone into the box at all, because they must have known it was a dangerous thing to do and that they ought not to do it; but their fault does not excuse the farmer from his share of the responsibility, if he also was at fault. It is only a ground for reducing the damages."²

Very common situations where the issue of contributory negligence has arisen are those where the plaintiff is driving a dangerous animal off his land. If the animal is known by its keeper to be dangerous the plaintiff's action for injuries caused to him by the animal will only be defeated if he acts unreasonable and negligently in the way he drives the beast off.³ If the plaintiff hits the animal to drive it off this will not amount to contributory negligence, provided it was reasonable in the circumstances to do so.⁴ The mere fact that one knows that the defendant's dangerous animal is on one's land does not require one either to remain indoors until it has gone or face the defence of contributory negligence if one is injured whilst working the land.⁵

Mere knowledge alone of the fierce or dangerous nature of the defendant's animal does not, of itself, amount to contributory negligence, as where a postman was bitten by the defendant's dog, which the postman knew to be dangerous, when delivering a telegram to the defendant.⁶

In cases where there is a warning or notice of the dangerous characteristics of the animal, this does not automatically indicate contributory negligence on the part of a plaintiff

---

¹ [1955] 1 Q.B. 253, *supra*, pp. 69–70; and see *McNeill* v. *Frankenfeld* (1963), 39 D.L.R. (2d) 332; varied on appeal: (1963) 44 D.L.R. (2d) 132—a decision on the British Columbia Contributory Negligence Act 1960.
² [1955] 1 Q.B. 253, 259; and see *Ibid,* at pp. 266, 269. See also *Behrens* v. *Bertram Mills Circus, Ltd.,* [1957] 2 Q.B. 1, 19–20.
³ E.g. *Jacobson* v. *Schneider,* [1927] 2 W.W.R. 257, 259; and see *Dawson* v. *Warren* (1884), 2 N.Z.L.R. 255.
⁴ *Blackman* v. *Simmons* (1827), 3 C. & P. 138; *Shelfontuck* v. *Le Page,* [1937] 2 W.W.R. 16, 19; affirmed (1938) 1 D.L.R. (2d) 513, 519.
⁵ *Tarasoff* v. *Zielinsky,* [1921] 2 W.W.R. 135, 140.
⁶ *Carbury* v. *Measures* (1904) 4 S.R. N.S.W. 569.

who goes near the animal, especially if the defendant's conduct leads the plaintiff to believe that the animal is safe.[7] All the more is this true if the notice in question is inadequate to convey awareness of the danger to the plaintiff. A painted notice has been considered to be an inadequate warning to a plaintiff who could not read.[8] The warning, to be effective, must be such as to warn against the danger which actually occurred.[9]

Where contributory negligence is a defence, the court must apportion damages as between the plaintiff and the defendant on such basis "as the court thinks just and equitable having regard to the claimant's share in the responsibility for the damage."[10] Where liability is strict, as under s. 2 and especially under s. 2 (1), there may be little or no blameworthiness on the part of the defendant, but the court must nevertheless attempt to apportion the damage rather than impose it all on the negligent plaintiff. The two main factors of causative potency and relative blameworthiness have to be considered by the court in a flexible manner in cases of strict liability.[11]

(v) Inapplicable defences

Two possible defences to liability under the *scienter* action will not apply to liability under s. 2 of the Animals Act 1971. The first is Act of God. The more acceptable view was that this defence was applicable to common law liability.[12] There is no provision for such a defence in the Animals Act 1971. To take an example given by BRAMWELL, B.,[13] the law now is that "if a man kept a tiger, and lightning broke his chain,

---

[7] *Curtis* v. *Mills* (1833), 5 C. & P. 489; *cf. Dolan* v. *Bright*, [1962] C.L.Y. 72; and see *Forbes* v. *M'Donald* (1874), 7 A.L.T. 62; *O'Dolan* v. *Burke* (1962), 96 I.L.T.R. 285.

[8] *Sarch* v. *Blackburn* (1830), 4 C. & P. 297, 300–301; *Pearson* v. *Coleman Bros.*, [1948] 2 K.B. 359, 370.

[9] *Pearson* v. *Coleman Bros, supra*, at pp. 369–370.

[10] Law Reform (Contributory Negligence) Act 1945, s. 1 (1).

[11] Williams, *Joint Torts and Contributory Negligence*, 326–328.

[12] *Baker* v. *Snell*, [1908] 2 K.B. 825, 834, 836; *Rands* v. *McNeil*, [1955] 1 Q.B. 253, 266; *Williams*, 336; Law Commission Report, §. 24.

[13] *Nichols* v. *Marsland* (1875), L.R. 10 Exch. 255, 260. See also *Barker* v. *Herbert*, [1911] 2 K.B. 633, 647.

and he got loose and did mischief" the keeper of the tiger would be liable under s. 2 (1).

The second inapplicable defence is that of act of a third party. It was debatable whether such a defence to an action of *scienter* existed. Whilst there was Scottish authority favouring such a defence,[14] the preponderance of English authority indicated that no such defence existed.[15] The Law Commission was of the opinion that there should be no such defence to liability under s. 2 of the Animals Act 1971, for "the act of a third party is one of the circumstances against which the person creating the risk should take precautions."[16] If the plaintiff is injured by the defendant's dangerous animal it will be no defence that the injury was caused by the negligence or the wilful misconduct of a third party. In *Baker* v. *Snell*,[17] the plaintiff, who was the defendant's housemaid, was injured when the defendant's dog, known to be dangerous, was brought by the defendant's potman into the kitchen and was incited to attack her by the potman saying: "Go it Bob." Such conduct would, today, impose liability on the defendant under s. 2 (2) of the Animals Act 1971.

---

[14] *Fleming* v. *Orr* (1857), 2 Macq. 14.
[15] *Baker* v. *Snell*, [1908] 2 K.B. 825, 833, 834; *Behrens* v. *Bertram Mills Circus, Ltd.*, [1957] 2 Q.B. 1, 21–25.
[16] Law Commission Report, §. 24.
[17] [1908] 2 K.B. 825.

3

STATUTORY LIABILITY FOR STRAYING LIVESTOCK

The common law action of cattle trespass[1] provided that if animals, within the description of cattle, strayed from A's land on to B's then A was strictly liable *per se*. He would be held responsible for any damage done to the land,[2] to chattels thereon or to the occupier.[3]

In its examination of this head of liability the Law Commission took the view:

"that the retention of strict liability for cases of cattle trespass can only be justified if it provides a clear rule as to liability for trespassing cattle, enabling disputes to be settled normally without recourse to litigation".[4]

Rather than recommend piecemeal alterations to the existing law, the Law Commission proposed a restatement of the principles of strict liability for straying animals to replace the law of cattle trespass. The essential provisions of this restatement, as now embodied in the Animals Act 1971, are:

(1) The statutory abolition of liability for cattle trespass;[5] and

(2) Its replacement by a new head of liability for damage

---

[1] Williams, Part 2; Delany (1952), 10 N.I.L.Q. 135, 137–145; Davis, (1964), 1 N.Z.U.L.R. 206, 213 222.
[2] *Sutcliffe* v. *Holmes*, [1947] K.B. 147.
[3] *Wormald* v. *Cole*, [1954] 1 Q.B. 614.
[4] Law Commission Report, §. 63.
[5] Section 1 (1) (c).

caused by straying livestock. It is provided by section 4 of the Animals Act 1971 that:

"(1) Where livestock belonging to any person strays on to land in the ownership or occupation of another and—

(a) damage is done by the livestock to the land or to any property on it which is in the ownership or possession of the other person; or

(b) any expenses are reasonably incurred by that other person in keeping the livestock while it cannot be restored to the person to whom it belongs, or while it is detained in pursuance of section 7 of this Act[6] or in ascertaining to whom it belongs;

the person to whom the livestock belongs is liable for the damage or expenses, except as otherwise provided by this Act.

(2) For the purposes of this section any livestock belongs to the person in whose possession it is."

There are a number of elements in this statutory tort which should be considered separately:

(A) THE ANIMALS IN QUESTION MUST FALL WITHIN THE
DEFINITION OF "LIVESTOCK"

The action of cattle trespass, a mediaeval cause of action, was based on liability for animals falling within the term "avers". This included most, if not all, domestic productive farm animals, namely, oxen, cows, sheep, goats, pigs, horses, asses, hens, geese, ducks and, probably, turkeys.[7] It was extended to include deer;[8] but it excluded dogs,[9] cats.[10] bees[11] and, probably, domestic pigeons.[12] All wild animals were

---

[6] Discussed *infra*, pp. 115–123.

[7] *Cf. Fettiplace* v. *Bates* (1624), Benl. 143.

[8] *Brady* v. *Warren*, [1900] 2 I.R. 632; Williams, 147–148.

[9] *Beckwith* v. *Shordyke* (1767), 4 Burr. 2092; *Brown* v. *Giles* (1823), 1 C. & P. 118; *Sanders* v. *Teape and Swan* (1884), 51 L.T. 263; *Buckle* v. *Holmes*, [1926] 2 K.B. 125, 128–129, 130; *Tallents* v. *Bell & Goddard*, [1944] 2 All E.R. 474; *cf. Doyle* v. *Vance* (1880), 6 V.L.R. (L) 87.

[10] *Buckle* v. *Holmes*, [1926] 2 K.B. 125; *Toogood* v. *Wright*, [1940] 2 All E.R. 306, 308.

[11] *O'Gorman* v. *O'Gorman*, [1903] 2 I.R. 573; *cf. McStay* v. *Morrissey* (1949), 83 I.L.T.R. 28 on liability for the negligent keeping of bees. On the whole question of liability for bees, see Paton, (1939) 2 Res Judicatae 22; Frimston, *Bee-Keeping and the Law* (1966); Swan, *A Receiver of Stolen Property* (1956).

[12] Williams, 148; *cf. Brady* v. *Warren*, [1900] 2 I.R. 632, 645.

excluded from the law of cattle trespass and therefore there was no such liability for rats,[13] rabbits,[14] or pheasants[15] which bred on A's land then strayed and caused damage to B's land or crops, though there may be liability for nuisance[16] or negligence[17] in such cases.[18]

Liability under the statutory action is for the straying of "livestock", rather than "cattle". The former is defined, for the purposes of s. 4, as: "cattle, horses, asses, mules, hinnies,[19] sheep, pigs, goats and poultry, and also deer not in the wild state."[20] There is a further sub-definition of poultry as: "the domestic varieties of the following, that is to say, fowls, turkeys, geese, ducks, guinea-fowls, pigeons, peacocks and quails".[1] This would seem to be little different from the common law definition of "cattle". Dogs and cats, as well as wild animals, are still excluded, as are bees.

The one possible change in the law made by the Animals Act 1971 is that domestic pigeons are included in the definition of poultry. The definition of poultry appears to make the owner of pigeons liable if they stray and cause damage.[2] As pigeons are very capable of both straying and of causing damage by eating crops,[3] this provision may strike terror into the hearts of pigeon fanciers. The addition of peacocks and quails to the categories of creatures for whose straying their owner will be liable takes account of the growing number of farms for the commercial breeding of such creatures. Nevertheless, as pheasants, partridges and grouse are excluded from the

---

[13] *Stearn* v. *Prentice Bros.*, [1919] 1 K.B. 394.
[14] *Boulston's Case* (1597), 5 Co. Rep. 104b; *Brady* v. *Warren*, [1900] 2 I.R. 632.
[15] *Seligman* v. *Docker*, [1949] 1 Ch. 53; *cf. Robson* v. *Marquis of Londonderry* (1900), 34 I.L.T.R. 88; *Foley* v. *Berthoud* (1903), 37 I.L.T.R. 123.
[16] See, e.g. *Farrer* v. *Nelson* (1885), 15 Q.B.D. 258; *Bland* v. *Yates* (1914), 58 Sol. Jo. 612; *Pratt* v. *Young* (1952), 69 W.N. (N.S.W.) 214.
[17] *Cf. McStay* v. *Morrissey* (1949), 83 I.L.T.R. 28.
[18] Discussed *infra*, chapter 6.
[19] The converse of mules.
[20] Section 11.
[1] Section 11. It is a little difficult to see why quails when bred commercially are within the general definition of livestock but that pheasants, partridge and grouse when bred in captivity are not; see H.C. Standing Committee A, March 18th 1971, cc. 79–81.
[2] Thus affirming the view of JOHNSON, J. in *Brady* v. *Warren*, [1900) 2 I.R. 632, 645.
[3] Discussed, *infra*, pp. 101–102.

definition of livestock for the purposes of s. 4, the domestic breeder can still let them stray on to his neighbour's land without liability under that section.[4]   The common law of nuisance will, however, still provide protection to the neighbour.[5]

(B)   PARTIES TO THE ACTION

(i) Plaintiff

Under the law of cattle trespass[6] the plaintiff had, as in all cases of trespass to land, to be in possession of the land trespassed against at the time of the trespass.[7]   This excluded a person who had merely a right of common,[8] a passer-by on the highway,[9] the servant of the occupier or possessor,[10] or any other person such as a relative[11] or guest who was not in occupation.   Included however in the categories of persons able to sue in cattle trespass were a licensee[12] and the buyer of a growing crop damaged by the trespassing animals.[13]   Possibly the agent of the occupier could have been able to sue, if injured whilst driving off a trespassing animal on the occupier's behalf.[14]

The statutory liability under s. 4 is no longer based upon a technical trespass, for it would *seem* to depend upon the fact that livestock have *strayed*.   The reason for the qualification

---

[4] They are only included as livestock, under s. 11, for the purposes of s. 3 and s. 9, i.e. the liability of the keeper of a dog for killing or injuring livestock and the right to kill or injure such a dog; see chapter 7.

[5] Discussed, *infra*, pp. 172–174.

[6] Williams, 175–178.

[7] Except perhaps in cases of "depasturing of chattels": Williams, 152–156.

[8] *Cox* v. *Burbidge* (1863), 13 C.B.N.S. 430, 435–436.

[9] See *infra*, pp. 166–167.

[10] *Wormald* v. *Cole*, [1954] 1 Q.B. 614, 623, 627, 631; and see *Child* v. *Hearn* (1874), L.R. 9 Exch. 176; *cf. Bradley* v. *Wallaces, Ltd.*, [1913] 3 K.B. 629.

[11] *Cf. Waugh* v. *Montgomery* (1882), 8 V.L.R. 290; *Whalley* v. *Vandergrand* (1919), 44 D.L.R. 319 where the successful plaintiff was both the son of, and an employee of, the occupier; and see *Street* v. *Craig* (1920), 56 D.L.R. 105.

[12] *Rutherford* v. *Hayward* (1877), 3 V.L.R. (L) 19.   It is hard to see how such a licensee has an adequate interest to maintain trespass to land when, e.g. a person whose livestock are on the land trespassed upon by the defendant's bull, under a contract of agistment, does not have such an interest: *Edwards* v. *Rawlins*, [1924] N.Z.L.R. 333.

[13] *Wellaway* v. *Courtier*, [1918] 1 K.B. 200; *cf. Wiseman* v. *Booker* (1878), 3 C.P.D. 184.

[14] *Waugh* v. *Montgomery* (1882), 8 V.L.R. 290; *cf. Winters* v. *Owens*, [1950] I.R. 225, 230.

of that statement is that although s. 1 abolishes liability for cattle trespass, the marginal note to s. 4 states "Liability for damage and expenses due to trespassing livestock.[15] There is some indication from that that "straying" means "trespassing". On the other hand it is, perhaps, proper to assume that had it been intended that s. 4 should apply to "trespassing" livestock that phrase would have been used in the actual section.[16] That is why it is suggested, therefore, that liability under s. 4 is based on "straying" rather than on "trespassing". This being so, then the class of possible plaintiffs does not need to be limited to those in possession of the land strayed upon.

The Law Commission proposed[17] that the owner out of occupation of the land strayed upon should also be able to sue, in so far as the "trespass" had injured his interest in the land or chattels thereon, i.e. strict liability for injury to his reversionary interest. The example is given of damage to a cottage and garden leased by a farmer, for a short term, to a holidaymaker.[18] However, s. 4 is drafted in wider terms than this, for it talks of livestock straying on to land "in the ownership or occupation of another". By inference, this allows an action to be brought by the owner out of occupation for damage done to the land or property owned by him, irrespective of whether this constitutes an injury to his reversionary interest.[19] This would seem, therefore, to include the long lease as well as the short lease; for s. 4 (1) (a) refers to damage to the land and not to the owner's interest in the land.

One question of interpretation is whether both owner and occupier can sue for actual damage, for s. 4 indicates clearly who may be liable[20] but is not explicit on the question of the circumstances in which the owner or the occupier may sue. It

---

[15] Similarly, the heading and marginal note to s. 7 refer to "trespassing livestock", see *infra*, p. 117.
[16] It should be pointed out that "modern cases . . . are clear that marginal notes can afford no legitimate aid to construction": Craies, *Statute Law*, 7th ed. 196–197.
[17] Law Commission Report, §. 66.
[18] *Ibid.*, §. 66, n. 96.
[19] *Cf.* Winfield & Jolowicz, *Tort*, 9th ed. 403.
[20] Section 4 (2), *infra*, pp. 96–98.

appears clear from s. 4 (1) (a) that an action will lie if damage is done to any property on the land which is in the ownership or possession of the plaintiff. Thus, if straying horses damage the landlord's car when parked in the drive of a house he has leased to a third party, an action will lie at the suit of the landlord; but if the landlord has not only leased his house to a tenant, but has allowed the latter to use a bicycle owned by the landlord, then if the bicycle is damaged by straying livestock, an action will lie at the suit of both landlord, as the owner of the bicycle, and the tenant as the possessor thereof.

There is still, however, no liability for injuries done to someone, or his property, who has no interest in the land arising from ownership or occupation, e.g. the servant or spouse of the owner or occupier.

(ii) Defendant[1]

Liability is imposed on the person to whom the livestock belongs. Such a person is defined by s. 4 (2): "For the purposes of this section any livestock belongs to the person in whose possession it is." This means that the only possible defendant under s. 4 will be the same person who was the normal defendant in an action of cattle trespass, namely the possessor of the livestock which have strayed.[2] He will also, normally, be the occupier of the land from which they have strayed.[3] The possessor of the animals is liable even though he is not the owner of the animal, as where he has possession under a contract of agistment[4] or even from his wife.[5] In such circumstances the owner out of possession is not liable;[6] nor will he be liable if he is a bailor, for he has no possession of the

---

[1] Liability may be imposed on the Crown: Animals Act 1971, s. 12, discussed *supra*, pp. 33–34.
[2] *Dawtry* v. *Huggins* (1635), Clay. 32; and see *Winters* v. *Owens*, [1950] I.R. 225.
[3] On the liability for cattle straying from common land, see Harris & Ryan, *The Law Relating to Common Land*, 63.
[4] *Hammond* v. *Mallinson*, [1939] L.J.C.C.R. 357; and see *Dawtry* v. *Huggins* (1635), Clay. 32, 33.
[5] *Broderick* v. *Forbes* (1912), 5 D.L.R. 508.
[6] Williams, 177–178; *Hammond* v. *Mallinson*, [1939] L.J.C.C.R. 357; *Hickey* v. *Cosgrave* (1854), 6 Ir. Jur. N.S. 251; *Dalton* v. *O'Sullivan*, [1947] Ir. Jur. Rep. 25.

animal.[7] Similarly when livestock is acquired under a hire purchase arrangement, the technical owner of the livestock during the running of the arrangement will not be liable, but the hirer, the farmer, will be for he is the possessor of the livestock.

The requirement that the proper defendant should be the possessor of the livestock will exclude from liability those who have an interest less than possession. If livestock are in the possession of a farmer then his cowman, as an employee, will merely have custody of the livestock in his charge and the cowman will not be held liable under s. 4 if the livestock stray.

At common law it was a debatable issue whether the occupier or owner of the *land* could be liable in cattle trespass for cattle straying from his land, though he was not in possession or control of the animals. In the Irish case of *Noonan* v. *Hartnett*[8] the defendant was the owner and occupier of land which he let to a third party for grazing, and the latter undertook to maintain the fences and herd the cattle. Some of the cattle which were on the land pursuant to the grazing contracts strayed on to the plaintiff's land and damaged his crops. The plaintiff's action in cattle trespass succeeded against the defendant, the owner of the land, though the cattle in question were neither owned by him nor under his occupation or control: for they were on his land in pursuance of a contract made with him.[9] Notwithstanding this decision, it was generally thought that liability in cattle trespass ought to depend on control of the animal, rather than occupation of the land from which it strayed.[10]

When one turns to the statutory liability under s. 4, it is

---

[7] If the owner of cattle under a grazing letting does retain some control over them then he is still liable provided the control is enough to amount to possession; *cf. Winters* v. *Owens,* [1950] I.R. 225. A contract of sale may pass possession, and thus liability, to the buyer even before actual delivery: *Alsop* v. *Lidgerwood* (1916), 22 Argus L.R. (N) 13.

[8] (1950), 84 I.L.T.R. 41.

[9] It is difficult to accept the reliance on the principles of *Rylands* v. *Fletcher* here for pasturing cattle would seem to be a natural user of land; see *infra,* pp. 174–176.

[10] Williams, 176–178; 198–199; *Manton* v. *Brocklebank,* [1923] 2 K.B. 212; *cf. Hammond* v. *Mallinson,* [1939] L.J.N.C.C.R. 357, 360–361; *Dalton* v. *Sullivan,* [1947] Ir. Jur. Rep. 25, 27; *Winters* v. *Owens,* [1950] I.R. 225, 229.

clear that there is no liability on either the owner out of possession of the livestock in question nor on the owner or occupier of the land from which the animals strayed. Liability is placed only on the person in possession of the livestock. Is this wholly desirable? We are told that liability is to be imposed solely on the possessor of the straying livestock on the ground that the object of a simple rule of strict liability is to ensure speedy settlement of disputes between neighbours.[11] One can see that such a justification explains the exclusion of the liability of the owner out of possession or control of the animals in question, as was the law of cattle trespass;[12] but if the speedy settlement of disputes between neighbours justifies strict liability, then is not the relevant issue that the parties are neighbours, and not that one is the possessor of the livestock in question? Naturally, most possessors of animals occupy the land on which the animals are pastured or kept; but s. 4 excludes the liability, as such, of the occupier of the land (the neighbour) from which the cattle have strayed.[13]

(C)   SCOPE OF THE ACTION

(i)   Place on to or from which the livestock strays

1.   *General Rule*

Any owner or occupier of land may sue under s. 4 if livestock stray on to land owned or occupied by him.

2.   *Exceptions*[14]

(a) If livestock stray on to the highway, only the owner or occupier thereof may sue, and not a passer-by.[15]

(b) If livestock lawfully using a highway stray from the highway on to adjoining property, then it is provided by s. 5 (5) of the Animals Act 1971 that there is no statutory liability under s. 4. The only liability that will exist will be that which,

---

[11] Law Commission Report, §. 63.
[12] *Supra*, p. 96.
[13] *Cf. Noonan* v. *Hartnett* (1950), 84 I.L.T.R. 41, *supra*, p. 97.
[14] More apparent than real.
[15] See the discussion of liability for animals straying on to the highway, *infra*, pp. 166–167.

at common law, emanates from negligence on the part of the person in control of the livestock.[16] If livestock are not lawfully on the highway then there will be liability under s. 4 if they stray from the highway on to land owned or occupied by the plaintiff.[17]

(c) There was, at common law, normally no obligation to prevent cattle from straying from common land. Indeed there was, and presumably still is, often an obligation on the adjoining occupier to "fence against the common". Thus in *Barber* v. *Whiteley*[18] this is justified by COCKBURN, C.J. who said:

> "The purpose of enclosing lands is that they may be used as cultivated land, and since such a use of them, beneficial to the person to whom it is permitted, makes it the more necessary that the land should not be open indifferently to grazing animals, it is more likely that the obligation of preventing such a trespass was imposed on the occupier than on the tenants of the manor, who had rights of common on the waste, formerly exercisable without such risks of distress, and who were a varying and uncertain body. Therefore, granting it to be a principle of law that where no obligation to fence is shown upon either of two adjoining landowners, each must take care his cattle do not stray; yet a different legal relation arises where . . . there is, on the one hand, a person inclosing from common land, and, on the other a body of persons entitled by law to exercise commonable rights on the land adjacent".[19]

No express provision is made in the Animals Act 1971 to deal with animals straying from common land. If, however, there was an obligation on the adjoining occupier to fence against the common, failure to fence constituted a defence to an action of cattle trespass and this defence is continued in the 1971 Act.[20] In the absence of such a fencing obligation s. 4 would appear to

---

[16] *Tillett* v. *Ward* (1882), 10 Q.B.D. 17; *Gayler and Pope, Ltd.* v. *B. Davies & Son, Ltd.*, [1924] 2 K.B. 75; *Goldston* v. *Bradshaw*, [1934] L.J.N.C.C.R. 355; Williams, 369; *cf. Timothy Whites, Ltd.* v. *Byng*, [1934] L.J.N.C.C.R. 47, which would seem to be incorrectly decided.

[17] See *infra*, pp. 112–114.

[18] (1865), 13 W.R. 774, 775.

[19] *Cf. Coaker* v. *Willcocks*, [1911] 2 K.B. 124; Hunt, *Boundaries & Fences*, 6th ed. 98–99; Harris & Ryan, *op. cit.*, 63.

[20] Animals Act 1971, s. 5 (6), *infra*, pp. 135–148; *cf. Crow* v. *Wood*, [1971] 1 Q.B. 77.

cover the situation and thus impose liability where animals which belong to a commoner stray on to a neighbour's land.   It is suggested, however, that there should be no liability in such circumstances, as it is unlawful for the commoner to erect fences to contain his animals unless he has obtained the consent of the Secretary of State for the Environment.[1]

(ii)   Kinds of damage recoverable

There was little doubt that damages in an action of cattle trespass[2] could be recovered for damage to the plaintiff's land and crops.[3]   Damages could also be recovered for injury to the plaintiff's animals on the land trespassed against.   Thus, if the trespassing animals kicked[4] or bit[5] the plaintiff's horse or killed his cow[6] damages were recoverable.   Again where the plaintiff's animals became infected by disease carried by the defendant's animals the defendant would be liable.[7]   Special problems arose when animals of different sexes were put in proximity through a trespass.   If a bull trespassed into a field containing cows the owner of the cows could recover damages for the fact that his cows were served by the bull[8] or even that there was no guarantee that they had not been.[9]   If cows strayed into land containing a bull then the owner of the latter could recover damages for injuries to the bull in trying to serve the cows.[10] If the trespassing animals ate all the grass on the land so that the plaintiff's sheep died of starvation then such loss was actionable.[11]   An action in cattle trespass would also lie where the defendant's animals injured inanimate chattels on the

---

[1] Law of Property Act 1925, s. 194 (1).

[2] Williams, 157–173; on the measure of damages, see Williams, 164.

[3] *Park* v. *J. Jobson & Son*, [1945] 1 All E.R. 222; *Sutcliffe* v. *Holmes*, [1947] K.B. 147; *Wormald* v. *Cole*, [1954] 1 Q.B. 614; and see *Brady* v. *Warren*, [1900] 2 I.R. 632; *Noonan* v. *Hartnett* (1950), 84 I.L.T.R. 41.

[4] *Lee* v. *Riley* (1865), 18 C.B.N.S. 722; *Holgate* v. *Bleazard*, [1917] 1 K.B. 443; *Whalley* v. *Vandergrand* (1919), 44 D.L.R. 319.

[5] *Ellis* v. *Loftus Iron Co.* (1874), L.R. 10 C.P. 10.

[6] *Messenger* v. *Stevens* (1910), 9 E.L.R. 91.

[7] *Anderson* v. *Buckton* (1719), 11 Mod. 304; *Earp* v. *Faulkner* (1875), 34 L.T. 284, 286; *Theyer* v. *Purnell*, [1918] 2 K.B. 333.

[8] *McLean* v. *Brett* (1919), 49 D.L.R. 162, and cases cited in Williams, 166, n. 8; and see *Daniel Logan & Son* v. *Roger*, 1952 S.L.T. (Sh. Ct. Rep.) 99; *Dobbie* v. *Henderson* 1970 S.L.T. (Sh. Ct. Rep.) 27; 305 H.L. Debates, cc. 1394–1395.

[9] *Halstead* v. *Mathieson*, [1919] V.L.R. 362.

[10] *Eustace* v. *Eyre*, [1947] L.J.N.C.C.R. 106.

[11] *Challoner* v. *McPhail* (1877), Knox 157 (N.S.W.).

plaintiff's land, such as machinery[12] or vehicles.[13]   A dramatic example of such recovery provided by *Cooper* v. *Railway Executive*.[14]   The plaintiff's cattle strayed on to the defendants' railway line and a claim for injury to the cows failed as the defendants were not in breach of their duty to fence.[15] However, the cows caused a train to be derailed by the impact of hitting them and the defendants' counter-claim for damages for repair to the train and the track was successful.

Finally, despite arguments to the contrary,[16] it appeared that, in England at least, damages could be recovered in cattle trespass for personal injuries.   In *Wormald* v. *Cole*[17] the defendant's cattle strayed into the plaintiff's garden.   The plaintiff was knocked down and injured by a heifer and the Court of Appeal allowed recovery of damages for her personal injuries.   It was, however, essential that there should have been a trespass, however technical,[18] to the plaintiff's land.[19]

Under the Animals Act 1971, liability for straying livestock applies, under s. 4 (1) (a), to the case where "Damage is done by the livestock to the land or to any property on it which is in the ownership or possession of the other person".   This is, in many respects, a statutory enactment of the heads of damage for cattle trespass.   Thus the damage which is actionable under this subsection will extend, as at common law, to damage to the land, including crops and buildings thereon, and chattels on the land, which will include, presumably, animals[20] and other chattels such as trains[1] and other vehicles.[2]   The Law Commission rejected[3] as impractical any attempts to limit the

---

[12] *Moon* v. *Stephens* (1915), 23 D.L.R. 223.
[13] *Welch* v. *Dominion Transport Co.* (1922), 69 D.L.R. 588.
[14] [1953] 1 All E.R. 477.
[15] Discussed *infra*, pp. 129–130.
[16] Williams, 168–173.
[17] [1954] 1 Q.B. 614.
[18] *Ellis* v. *Loftus Iron Co.* (1874), L.R. 10 C.P. 10.
[19] *Cox* v. *Burbidge* (1863), 13 C.B.N.S. 430; *Bradley* v. *Wallaces, Ltd.*, [1913] 3 K.B. 629; and see *Theyer* v. *Purnell*, [1918] 2 K.B. 333, 338; *Manton* v. *Brocklebank*, [1923] 2 K.B. 212.   See also Williams, 152–157.
[20] As in, e.g. *Lee* v. *Riley* (1865), 18 C.B.N.S. 722; and see 305 H.L. Deb. cc. 1392–1393.
[1] *Cooper* v. *Railway Executive*, [1953] 1 All E.R. 477.
[2] E.g. *Welch* v. *Dominion Transport Co.* (1922), 69 D.L.R. 588.
[3] Law Commission Report, §. 65.

property in question to agricultural property, and there is no such limitation in the Act.   There is, however, no liability for personal injuries under this head of statutory liability; so the decision in *Wormald* v. *Cole*[4] has been abrogated.[5]   Of course, there can still be liability for such personal injuries on proof of negligence.[6]

It is, perhaps, relevant to note that s. 4 (1) (a) deals with the situation where straying livestock cause *damage*, rather than cause *loss*.   This may be illustrated by the case of the straying of diseased or potentially diseased animals.   If a diseased cow strays from the defendant's land on to the plaintiff's and there infects the plaintiff's cows with the disease in question, there is no doubt that damage has been caused to the plaintiff's property, in that his cow has become diseased and an action will lie under s. 4.[7]   If, however, the defendant has a cow found to be suffering from foot and mouth disease and that cow strays on to the plaintiff's land, then even though no cow of the plaintiff's can be proved to have been infected it may well be that an order restricting the movement of the plaintiff's cattle could be imposed by the Minister of Agriculture.   The consequence would be that the plaintiff would suffer financial loss in being unable to take his cattle to market at the proper time even though none has been infected or damaged.   Such loss is not actionable under s. 4, though it might be actionable on proof of negligence on the part of the defendant.[8]   A similar situation would arise if a cow from the defendant's herd, not being brucillosis free, strayed on to the plaintiff's land, the latter having a brucillosis free herd.[9]   Even though none of the

---

4 [1954] 1 Q.B. 614.
5 This is so even though "damage" is defined in the Animals Act 1971, s. 11, so as to include the death of or injury to a person.   The wording of s. 4 (1) (a) would appear to confine liability thereunder to damage to land or property. That being so, it is rather strange to find that, by reason of s. 10 of the Animals Act 1971, the Fatal Accidents Acts 1846–1959 are held to be applicable to claims under s. 4.
6 See Chapter 6, *infra*.
7 *Cf. Theyer* v. *Purnell*, [1918] 2 K.B. 333.
8 *Cf. Weller & Co.* v. *Foot and Mouth Disease Research Institute*, [1966] 1 Q.B. 569; and see Chapter 6.
9 This was a problem that led to much debate during the passage of the Animals Act: 305 H.L. Deb. cc. 559, 1393–1400, 1409–1414; 306 H.L. Deb. cc. 659–665, 677–684; 815 H.C. Deb. c. 611.

plaintiff's cattle were proved to be infected, he would cease to be an accredited brucillosis free farmer and thereby suffer consequential financial loss. As with the foot and mouth example, he could only recover under s. 4 if his cows became infected or, possibly, under the common law if the straying was due to the negligence of the defendant.[10]

Some instances of financial loss were, however, recoverable at common law in cattle trespass. A plaintiff could claim not only for actual damage to his land or property caused by trespassing cattle but also for the cost of maintaining animals which had strayed on to his land,[11] and for the extra cost of feeding his own animals; in short for "any loss naturally following from the trespass".[12]

Similar provision is made under the Animals Act 1971, s. 4 (1) (b). Even though no damage is done to the plaintiff's land or to the property on it, the plaintiff may claim for any expenses which are reasonably incurred by him in keeping the defendant's livestock while it cannot be restored to him or while it is being detained in pursuance of s. 7 of the Act,[13] or for expenses reasonably incurred in ascertaining to whom it belongs.

At common law, in order for an action of cattle trespass to lie, the damage done by the animal had to be "natural to the species of the animal." Whilst there was no doubt that there was liability for, for example, damage caused by the spread of disease, this being regarded as a natural consequence of diseased animals straying,[14] damage which did not result from the natural behaviour of the animal would appear to have been irrecoverable.[15] Thus it was suggested that it was not natural for a horse to kick human beings[16] though in *Wormald* v.

---

[10] *Cf. Weller & Co.* v. *Foot and Mouth Disease Research Institute, supra*; and see Chapter 6.

[11] *Theyer* v. *Purnell*, [1918] 2 K.B. 333, 336–337.

[12] *Ibid*, at p. 341; *Buckle* v. *Holmes*, [1926] 2 K.B. 125, 130; *Wormald* v. *Cole*, [1954] 1 Q.B. 614, 627.

[13] Which replaces the law of distress of animals damage feasant; see Law Commission Report, §§. 69–72; and *infra*, pp. 115–123.

[14] *Theyer* v. *Purnell*, [1918] 2 K.B. 333; and see the explanation at pp. 339–340; *cf. Cooke* v. *Waring* (1863), 2 H. & C. 332.

[15] The burden of proof of abnormality of behaviour appeared to rest on he who alleged it: *McCabe* v. *Delany*, [1951] Ir. Jur. Rep. 10.

[16] *Cox* v. *Burbidge* (1863), 13 C.B.N.S. 430, 437; *Bradley* v. *Wallaces, Ltd.*, [1913] 3 K.B. 629.

Cole[17] doubt was cast on the assumption that there would be no liability if a horse *attacked* a human being[18] for Lord GODDARD stated:

> "I leave open the question whether it follows that if a trespassing animal attacks the occupier he can recover, though I incline to the opinion that he can".[19]

There is no indication in s. 4 of the Animals Act 1971 that the damage in question must be natural to the species of the animal. Liability will exist whether or not this is so, provided the damage is to land or property thereon.[20]   The exclusion of liability for personal injuries will, in fact, greatly minimise the circumstances where straying livestock cause "non-natural" damage, for the area at common law where difficulty arose was that of personal injuries.   Nevertheless an action will now lie under s. 4 for any damage caused to land or property thereon by straying livestock even though of a kind unusual for the animal in question.

(D) STRICT LIABILITY

There was no doubt that cattle trespass[1] was a tort of strict liability and was independent of proof of negligence.[2]   It has been held

> "again and again, that there is a duty on a man to keep his cattle in, and if they get on another's land it is a trespass; and that is irrespective of any question of negligence whether great or small".[3]

It is equally true that liability under s. 4 is strict.   No proof is required of fault on the part of the possessor of livestock who

---

[17] [1954] 1 Q.B. 614.
[18] Rather than another horse, as in *Lee* v. *Riley* (1865), 18 C.B.N.S. 722; *Ellis* v. *Loftus Iron Co.* (1874), L.R. 10 C.P. 10.
[19] [1954] 1 Q.B. 614, 625; *cf. Ibid.* at pp. 632–633; and see *Hennigan* v. *M'Vey* (1882), 9 R. 411—trespassing boar; *cf. Mark* v. *Barkla,* [1935] N.Z.L.R. 347.
[20] Though see the discussion of remoteness of damage, *infra,* pp. 107–108.
[1] Williams, 185–194.
[2] *E.g. Cox* v. *Burbidge* (1863), 13 C.B.N.S. 430, 438; *Fletcher* v. *Rylands* (1868), L.R. 1 Exch. 265, 280.
[3] *Ellis* v. *Loftus Iron Co.* (1874), L.R. 10 C.P. 10, 12, *per* Lord COLERIDGE, C.J.; and see at p. 13, *per* BRETT, J.

allows them to stray on to land owned or occupied by the plaintiff.   In fact, the continued existence of strict liability for this conduct was one good reason for not allowing claims hereunder for personal injuries.[4]   As the defendant is liable though not at fault, his ability to prove lack of fault is irrelevant unless, perhaps, he can prove that the straying was involuntary.[5]

(E) ACTIONABILITY

There was no doubt that cattle trespass like other forms of trespass to land was actionable without proof of damage.[6] However, proof of a technical trespass was necessary before there could be an award of damages for consequential injury.[7] This may be illustrated by *Ellis* v. *Loftus Iron Co.*[8]   The plaintiff's mare was injured when the defendants' horse bit and kicked her.   The two horses were each on their owners' own land but the defendants' horse did the injury through the fence. That being so it was clear to Lord COLERIDGE, C.J.:

> "that some portion of the defendants' horse's body must have been over the boundary.   That may be a very small trespass, but it is a trespass in law".[9]

The technical trespass having been proved, the plaintiff recovered.

Here a change has been made by s. 4 of the Animals Act 1971, for the statutory head of liability thereunder is not actionable *per se*.   There must be proof of actual damage or the incurring of reasonable expenses.   This makes little substantial alteration;   for the rule that cattle trespass, as a form of trespass to land, was actionable *per se* was only of importance where there had been a possibly doubtful technical trespass to land, followed by actual damage to property thereon.[10]   However, the new statutory liability is not, in so many words, based upon

---

[4] Law Commission Report, §. 65.
[5] *Cf. Mitten* v. *Faudrye* (1626), Poph. 161.
[6] Except, perhaps, in the case of "depasturing of chattels";   Williams, 150.
[7] *Ellis* v. *Loftus Iron Co.* (1874), L.R. 10 C.P. 10;   *Wiseman* v. *Booker* (1878), 3 C.P.D. 184;   Williams, 150.
[8] (1874), L.R. 10 C.P. 10.
[9] *Ibid.* at p. 12.
[10] E.g. *Ellis* v. *Loftus Iron Co., supra.*

a technical trespass to land.[11] The Animals Act 1971 talks of
livestock straying on to land *"in the ownership or occupation* of
another"[12] and the owner out of occupation cannot maintain an
action for trespass to land.[13]   Liability is now to be based upon
actual injury to the land and property thereon or actual
expenses incurred as a consequence of the straying.   What is
not clear is whether *Ellis* v. *Loftus Iron Co.*[14] would still be
decided in the same way today.   Whilst there was no doubt
of the injury to the property, the mare, on the plaintiff's land,
can it be said that a horse which puts its head over a fence
"strays on to the land?"[15]

Some possible light is thrown on this question by *Wiseman* v.
Booker.[16]   The defendant's horses had put their heads over the
inadequate fence between the land of the defendant and
adjoining land rented by the plaintiff's father from a railway
company.   The horses had eaten vegetables growing on the
land, which growing vegetables had been sold to the plaintiff by
his father.   The defendant alleged that there was a statutory
obligation on the railway company to maintain the fence
thereby protecting the land "from trespass or the cattle of the
owners or occupiers thereof from straying thereout."[17]   In
other words, the railway company was under an obligation to
fence out the defendant's horses.   If that fencing obligation
had been broken then the defendant would be relieved from
liability.   So the main issue was really whether horses which
put their heads over or through a fence had strayed.   LINDLEY, J.
held that the action failed.   As the railway company was in
breach of its duty to the defendant to maintain the fences, the
defendant could not be made responsible to the railway
company's tenant for injury resulting from breach of the
fencing obligation.   In the course of his judgment, LINDLEY, J.

---

[11] Section 4 (1), italics added.
[11] The problem arising from the fact that the marginal note to s. 4 refers to
"trespassing livestock" is considered, *supra,* p. 95.
[12] Section 4 (1), italics added.
[13] E.g. *Cooper* v. *Crabtree* (1882), 20 Ch.D. 589.
[14] (1874), L.R. 10 C.P. 10.
[15] In their Report the Law Commission recommend that liability should be
based upon a "trespass".   This led to their recommendation that there
should cease to be liability for "depasturing chattels"; Report, §. 68.
[16] (1878), 3 C.P.D. 184.
[17] Railways Clauses Consolidation Act 1845, s. 68.

stated: "The structure is to be sufficient to keep the cattle of the adjoining owners from straying on to the land of the company. *The horses here were straying within the fair meaning of those words*; and this it was the duty of the company to prevent."[18]

Whilst one must always be chary of applying decisions interpreting one statute to the interpretation of another, it would appear that this case provides persuasive authority for liability being imposed under s. 4 of the Animals Act 1971 in the *Ellis* v. *Loftus Iron Co.* situation. If, of course, the defendant's livestock are lawfully on the land where they cause damage, as under a contract of agistment,[19] they cannot be said to have strayed and there will be no liability under s. 4. There is, however, the problem of livestock which was lawfully on the plaintiff's land but then outstays its welcome by remaining on the land longer than the permitted period. Such conduct constitutes a trespass and could well have given rise to liability for cattle trespass.[20] It is difficult to see, however, how such livestock can be said to have strayed.

(F) REMOTENESS OF DAMAGE

Though it has been argued that cattle trespass should have ceased to be a tort of strict liability,[1] it did remain such a tort. Thus it fell within the general statement that the test of remoteness of damage based on reasonable foresight, as laid down in *The Wagon Mound*,[2] is not intended to apply to torts of strict liability.[3] It would seem clear that statutory liability under s. 4 of the Animals Act 1971, being strict

---

[18] (1878), 3 C.P.D. 184, at p. 188, italics added.
[19] E.g. *Manton* v. *Brocklebank*, [1923] 2 K.B. 212; and see *Mathieson* v. *G. Stuckey & Co., Ltd.*, [1921] V.L.R. 637, 641.
[20] *Stodden* v. *Harvey* (1608), Cro. Jac. 204; Williams 150–152.
[1] Williams (1961), 77 L.Q.R. 179, 211–212; and see Dias, [1962] C.L.J. 178, 195–196.
[2] [1961] A.C. 388.
[3] *Ibid.*, at pp. 426–427; and see Mayne & McGregor, *Damages*, 12th ed., §. 73a; *cf. Brook* v. *Cook* (1961), 105 Sol. Jo. 684 and see *ibid.*, at p. 1095; though in *The Wagon Mound (No. 2)*, [1967] 1 A.C. 617 such a remoteness rule was applied to the whole of the law of nuisance, including elements of strict liability though, apparently, excluding the "cases like *Wringe* v. *Cohen*", [1954] 1 K.B. 229; see Lord Reid: [1967] 1 A.C. 617, 639.

liability, is likewise not subject to the test of remoteness of damage based upon reasonable foresight. So cattle trespass decisions will be relevant to the remoteness problems which may arise under s. 4. If the test is not that of reasonable foresight, then it is one of direct consequences,[4] and it has been held that if a trespassing horse kicks or bites the plaintiff's horse this damage is the "natural and direct consequence of the trespass committed".[5] The same can be said if the defendant's diseased sheep, trespassing on the plaintiff's land, infect the latter's sheep,[6] and if a trespassing cow gores and kills the plaintiff's horse.[7]

The issue of whether or not damages can be recovered if the injury is not natural to the species has been discussed[8] but the application of that rule to cattle trespass meant that all damage natural to the species was recoverable, and one could say that other damage was irrecoverable because it was too remote.[9] If damage not natural to the species was regarded as too remote for the purposes of the law of cattle trespass, the same might well be true of liability under s. 4 of the Animals Act 1971.[10] In practice, if liability is restricted to injuries natural to the species of the straying animal this will come very close to a test of liability for consequences which the defendant ought to have foreseen.[11] With the abolition of liability for personal injuries caused by straying livestock, the problem may well be academic.

(G) DEFENCES

The abolition by the Animals Act 1971 of the common law action for cattle trespass carries with it the corollary of the

---

[4] *Re Polemis and Furness Withy & Co.,* [1921] 3 K.B. 560; and see Williams, 157–173.
[5] *Ellis* v. *Loftus Iron Co.* (1874), L.R. 10 C.P. 10, 12; and see *Lee* v. *Riley* (1865), 18 C.B.N.S. 722; or if a trespassing cow injures the plaintiff's cow: *Ryan* v. *Glover,* [1939] Ir. Jur. Rep. 65.
[6] *Theyer* v. *Purnell,* [1918] 2 K.B. 333, 336, 340–341.
[7] *McCabe* v. *Delany,* [1951] Ir. Jur. Rep. 10; and see *Wormald* v. *Cole,* [1954] 1 Q.B. 614; *cf. Bradley* v. *Wallaces, Ltd.,* [1913] 3 K.B. 629; but see *Harrison* v. *Armstrong* (1917), 51 I.L.T.R. 38—apparently a negligence case.
[8] *Supra,* pp. 103–104.
[9] E.g. *Cox* v. *Burbidge* (1863), 13 C.B.N.S. 430, 436–437, 438; *Manton* v. *Brocklebank,* [1923] 2 K.B. 212, 223, 225.
[10] See Winfield & Jolowicz, *Tort,* 9th ed., 404–406.
[11] Fleming, *Torts,* 4th ed., 301.

abolition of all the defences thereto. It would appear, there-fore, that the only defences available to an action under s. 4 are those provided by the Animals Act 1971. This object is achieved by the provision in s. 4 (1) that the possessor of the straying livestock shall be liable "except as otherwise provided by this Act". No defences apply other than those laid down in the Act. There appear to be *four* such defences:

(i) Contributory negligence of the plaintiff

It was stated, by the Law Commission,[12] that contributory negligence on the part of the plaintiff should remain a defence as under the law of cattle trespass. This is achieved in the Act by what may be recalled[13] as a rather involved process. Section 10[14] provides that:

"For the purpose of . . . the Law Reform (Contributory Negligence) Act 1945 . . any damage for which a person is liable under sections 2 to 4 of this Act shall be treated as due to his fault."

Thus, although the liability under s. 4 is, in fact, strict liability, yet the defence of contributory negligence as provided by the 1945 Act will be available. It would seem that decisions under the law of cattle trespass will be relevant still in examining allegations of contributory negligence in claims brought under s. 4. There was no doubt that contributory negligence could constitute a defence to cattle trespass.[15] Thus if the plaintiff is licensed to build a haystack on the defendant's land,[16] and the defendant's cattle eat the hay, the failure of the plaintiff to fence off his haystack is evidence of his contributory negligence.[17]

If an occupier finds livestock straying on his land he should take steps to drive them out and if, in the process, he suffers damage to his land or property on it, the possessor of the

---

[12] Law Commission Report, §. 67 (ii).
[13] *Supra*, pp. 86–89.
[14] Which has been described as "a rather inelegant piece of legislation by reference".: 312 H.L. Deb. c. 201.
[15] Williams, 178–180; Williams, *Joint Torts & Contributory Negligence*, 209, 286.
[16] Of course the plaintiff will fail under s. 4 (1), unless he is shown to be an occupier of the land.
[17] *Cf. Plummer* v. *Webb* (1619), Noy. 98.

straying livestock will not be able to plead that the conduct of the plaintiff in driving the cattle out was, in itself, evidence of contributory negligence.[18]

(ii)   Damage due wholly to the fault of the plaintiff

This defence, which is similar in nature to that of contributory negligence, is provided by s. 5 (1):

> "A person is not liable under sections 2 to 4 of this Act for any damage which is due wholly to the fault of the person suffering it."

As "fault" is defined[19] by reference to the definition in the Law Reform (Contributory Negligence) Act 1945,[20] this means that the plaintiff is unable to sue for damage done by straying livestock if it has been caused wholly by his own negligence, breach of statutory duty, breach of contract[1] or any other act or omission which would give rise to the defence of contributory negligence.[2]   This is wider than the recommendation by the Law Commission[3] that the defence shall apply where the plaintiff was solely responsible for the damage "by reason of his negligence".

At common law there was a defence to an action of cattle trespass if the damage was done by the "leave and licence" of the plaintiff.   Thus in *Park* v. *J. Jobson and Son*[4] the defendants' cattle strayed on to the plaintiff's allotment and it was argued that the allotment fence had been damaged by the allotment holders of whom the plaintiff was one and that therefore the plaintiff had licensed the presence of the cattle on his allotment.   The defence failed as the defendants failed to prove that the plaintiff's act had caused the cattle to stray and they failed, therefore, to prove any licence by the plaintiff. Nevertheless, the Court of Appeal accepted that the defence of

---

[18] Williams, 179–180; *cf. Waugh* v. *Montgomery* (1882), 8 V.L.R. 290.
[19] Section 11.
[20] Section 4 of the 1945 Act.
[1] See *Quinn* v. *Burch Bros. (Builders), Ltd.,* [1966] 2 Q.B. 370.
[2] Williams, *Joint Torts & Contributory Negligence,* p. 318.
[3] Law Commission Report, §. 67 (ii).
[4] [1945] 1 All E.R. 222; discussed *infra.,* Chapter 4 pp. 136–138, on the question of who is liable for failure to fence.

consent was applicable to cattle trespass in appropriate circumstances for Lord GREENE, M.R. said:

> "I do not think the proposition is likely to be disputed that a person who gives leave, expressly or impliedly, to his neighbours' cattle to trespass on his land cannot complain, and that such leave and licence can be inferred from the circumstances of a particular case."[5]

Whether the leaving open of a gate or other such gaps in the fencing was leave and licence was difficult to assess, for generally there is no duty to fence out your neighbour's cattle. To leave a gap is not necessarily to license cattle to come through it.[6]

It will be necessary to determine what circumstances which fell under the common law defence now fall within s. 5 (1). The likeliest situation is that where the plaintiff leaves a gate open or leaves gaps in his fences through which the livestock stray. Whilst it was debatable at common law whether leaving such a gap amounted to a licence for cattle to come through it, such straying would seem normally to be due wholly to the fault of the plaintiff, within the meaning of s. 5 (1).

(iii) The plaintiff's failure to fence

This statutory defence is provided by s. 5 (6) which states that "In determining whether any liability for damage under section 4 of this Act is excluded by subsection (1) of this section the damage shall not be treated as due to the fault of the person suffering it by reason only that he could have prevented it by fencing;[7] but a person is not liable under that section where it is proved that the straying of the livestock on to the land would not have occurred but for a breach by any other person, being a person having an interest in the land, of a duty to fence."

This statutory defence is discussed in Chapter 4.[8]

---

[5] [1945] 1 All E.R. 222, 224.
[6] *Swift* v. *Ellis*, [1939] L.J.N.C.C.R. 384, 389; *cf. Wellaway* v. *Courtier*, [1918] 1 K.B. 200, 203; Williams, 180–181.
[7] "Fencing" includes "the construction of any obstacle designed to prevent animals from straying"; s. 11.
[8] *Infra*, pp. 135–148.

(iv) Straying from the highway

It is provided by s. 5 (5) that:

" A person is not liable under section 4 of this Act where the livestock strayed from a highway and its presence there was a lawful use of the highway."

This defence is dependent upon the use of the highway[9] by the livestock being lawful. If the livestock had been turned out to graze on the highway this would constitute a trespass against the occupier of the highway;[10] the user would be unlawful; and there would be liability for damage done when the livestock strayed off the highway. Again, if the livestock strayed on to the highway in the first place, their presence thereon is not a lawful use of the highway[11] for in these circumstances an action under s. 4 could have lain at the suit of the owner or occupier of the highway.

Lawful user of a highway is based upon a right of passage and repassage.[12] However,

"the right of the public to pass and repass on a highway is subject to all those reasonable extensions which may from time to time be recognised as necessary to its exercise in accordance with the enlarged notions of people in a country becoming more populous and highly civilised".[13]

Such reasonable user has been given quite a liberal interpretation by PHILLIMORE, J. in *Hadwell* v. *Righton*,[14] a case concerned with chickens straying on to the highway.

---

[9] No definition of "highway" is provided by the Animals Act 1971 and it is suggested that the meaning of "highway" for the purposes of s. 5 (5) is the general common law meaning of "all portions of land over which every subject of the Crown may lawfully pass": Pratt and Mackenzie, *Law of Highways*, 21st ed., 3. This will include not only ordinary roads but also footpaths, bridleways and driftways.

[10] *Stevens* v. *Whistler* (1809), 11 East 51.

[11] E.g. *Manchester, Sheffield and Lincolnshire Rail. Co.* v. *Wallis* (1854), 14 C.B. 213; *Luscombe* v. *Great Western Rail. Co.*, [1899] 2 Q.B. 313; *Creasy* v. *Abell*, [1945] L.J.R.C.C. 148; *Morris* v. *Curtis*, [1947] L.J.N.C.C.R. 284; and see *Rayner* v. *Shearing*, [1926] S.A.S.R. 313.

[12] *Dovaston* v. *Payne* (1795), 2 Hy. Bl. 527; *R.* v. *Pratt* (1855), 4 E. & B. 860; *Mayhew* v. *Wardley* (1863), 14 C.B.N.S. 550; *Harrison* v. *Duke of Rutland*, [1893] 1 Q.B. 142; *Hickman* v. *Maisey*, [1900] 1 Q.B. 752.

[13] *Hickman* v. *Maisey*, [1900] 1 Q.B. 752, 757–758; and see, e.g. *Randall* v. *Tarrant*, [1955] 1 All E.R. 600.

[14] [1907] 2 K.B. 345, 348.

"In the first place, I think that members of the public, in addition to using it *eundo et redeundo*, are also entitled to use it *morando* for a short time. And I doubt whether, even with that addition, the lawful uses are thereby exhausted. For instance, if fowls are kept near a highway, and there is a corn stubble belonging to their owner on the other side of the road to which they might naturally and properly go, I am not prepared to say that to allow them to go there by themselves would be an unlawful use of the highway by their owner simply because they might while so doing run or fly into someone who was riding a bicycle."

If an animal has strayed on to the highway so that its presence is unlawful, then once the owner takes control of it to drive it home along the highway, such user becomes lawful.[15] It may even be that it is lawfully on the highway before it is recaptured, provided its owner is in pursuit.[16]

If the act of a third party is not to be a defence to the statutory action under s. 4,[17] this strengthens the authority of those decisions at common law[18] which indicated that cattle were not lawfully on the highway even though their straying thereon resulted from the act of a third party in, for example, leaving a gate open. This defence does not, of course, exclude liability for negligence in appropriate circumstances.

There is no limitation to be placed on the defence under s. 5 (5) dependent on the site of the plaintiff's land. It does not matter whether the plaintiff's land adjoins the highway or not.[19] This is justified on the grounds that if animals get on to the plaintiff's land from the highway, the plaintiff occupies such land as imposes upon him the burden of assuming the risk of accidental trespass.[20] This means that in a country like England with a complex road network the majority of occupiers are considered to accept the risk of such straying. There is no requirement in this statutory defence, similar to that which

---

[15] *Midland Rail. Co.* v. *Daykin* (1855), 17 C.B. 126; *cf. Street* v. *Craig* (1920), 56 D.L.R. 105.
[16] *Cf. Spurr* v. *Dominion Atlantic Rly.* (1903), 40 N.S.R. 417.
[17] *Infra*, p. 115.
[18] *Manchester, Sheffield and Lincolnshire Rail Co.* v. *Wallis* (1854), 14 C.B. 213; approved, albeit reluctantly, by Lord ESHER, M.R. in *Charman* v. *South Eastern Rail. Co.* (1888), 21 Q.B.D. 524, 527–528.
[19] Law Commission Report, §. 67, n. 97.
[20] Williams, 375.

may have existed in the common law defence, that the drover of the animals should have pursued them within a reasonable time.[1]

This defence is the statutory replacement of a similar defence to an action of cattle trespass. That common law defence was justified on the ground that occupiers accept the risk of accidental injury caused by cattle straying from a highway.[2] It is worth noting that although the continued existence of such a defence can only be justified on the basis of assumption of risk, the Law Commission did not recommend the retention of the general defence of consent or "leave and licence"[3] except and in so far as circumstances falling within that head could also be classed as circumstances where the plaintiff is wholly responsible by his fault for his injuries.[4]   It should be stressed that the defence under s. 5 (5) is only applicable where the livestock are lawfully using the highway before they stray.   If they may be regarded as trespassers thereon, then liability will exist under s. 4.

(v) Inapplicable defences

It is significant that a number of other defences applicable to cattle trespass will not now apply under the Animals Act 1971 to liability under s. 4.

The defence of Act of God, though still a defence to a common law action based upon a failure to fence,[5] does not provide a defence to an action under s. 4,[6] nor does the defence of consent save in so far as it falls within s. 5 (1).[7]

---

[1] *Cf. Goodwyn* v. *Cheveley* (1859), 4 H. & N. 631, *infra*, pp. 163–165; Williams, 374–375.

[2] E.g. *Fletcher* v. *Rylands* (1866), L.R. 1 Exch. 265, 286; *River Wear Commissioners* v. *Adamson* (1877), 2 App. Cas. 743, 767; *Tillett* v. *Ward* (1882), 10 Q.B.D. 17, 20; *Gayler and Pope, Ltd.* v. *B. Davies and Son, Ltd.*, [1924] 2 K.B. 75, 82–84; *Wormald* v. *Cole*, [1954] 1 Q.B. 614, 626.

[3] It is retained for liability under s. 2; see s. 5 (2), *supra*, pp. 71–76.

[4] *Supra*, pp. 110–111.

[5] *Lawrence* v. *Jenkins* (1873), L.R. 8 Q.B. 274, 278; see Chapter 4, pp. 131–134, *infra*.

[6] Though it probably did provide a defence to an action of cattle trespass: *Fletcher* v. *Rylands* (1866), L.R. 1 Exch. 265, 279–280; *Nichols* v. *Marsland* (1875), L.R. 10 Exch. 255; and see *Sharp* v. *Harvey*, [1935] L.J.N.C.C.R. 261, 265; *Poupart* v. *Brazil*, [1941] L.J.C.C.R. 223, 224.

[7] *Supra*, pp. 110–111.

The defence of act of third party, although accepted in both England[8] and Ireland[9] as a defence to an action of cattle trespass, is inapplicable to a claim under s. 4. Thus if a third party who, for example, has a right of way over the defendant's land leaves a gate open so that the defendant's livestock stray on to the plaintiff's land, that act of a third party is no defence to an action under s. 4.[10] If, however, a third party *drove* the defendant's livestock on to the plaintiff's land, then it is suggested that there would be no liability on the part of the defendant, for his livestock had not "strayed". The third party might well be liable in such a case for trespass to land.[11]

It is provided by s. 5 of the Statute of Limitations 1623 that, *inter alia*, an action for cattle trespass provided it is not intentional can be met by a tender of sufficient amends before the action was brought.[12] Although this provision remains unrepealed after the passage of the Animals Act 1971, it cannot provide a defence to a claim under s. 4[13] for the statute of 1623 applies to actions of trespass quare clausum fregit and cattle trespass as a variety thereof has been abolished.[14]

(H) DETENTION OF STRAYING LIVESTOCK

At common law if the plaintiff had distrained the defendant's trespassing cattle damage feasant[15] then any action for cattle trespass by the plaintiff was barred.[16] This only applied to the actual animals distrained[17] and the action revived if the cattle

---

[8] *Sutcliffe* v. *Holmes*, [1947] K.B. 147; and see *Sharp* v. *Harvey*, [1935] L.J.N.C.C.R. 261; *Morris* v. *Curtis*, [1947] L.J.N.C.C.R. 284, 287; see also *Singleton* v. *Williamson* (1861), 7 H. & N. 410, 416; *cf. Cooke* v. *Skinner* (1948), 98 L.Jo. 38.

[9] *McGibbon* v. *McCurry* (1909), 43 I.L.T.R. 132; *Moloney* v. *Stephens*, [1945] Ir. Jur. Rep. 37.

[10] *Cf. Ibid.*; and also *Park* v. *J. Jobson & Son*, [1945] 1 All E.R. 222, 225. Nor would there be any defence if the defendant's livestock were stampeded on to the plaintiff's land through fright from low-flying aircraft. See 305 H.L. Deb. c. 1450.

[11] See Chapter 6, *infra*, pp. 170–172.

[12] Williams, 196.

[13] A similar statutory defence is provided, however, under s. 7 (3) (b), *infra*, pp. 117–118.

[14] Animals Act 1971, s. 1 (1) (c).

[15] Williams, 195; on the general law of distress damage feasant, see Williams, Part I.

[16] *Vaspor* v. *Edwards* (1702), 12 Mod. Rep. 658; and see *Boden* v. *Roscoe*, [1894] 1 Q.B. 608.

[17] *Vaspor* v. *Edwards*, *supra*, at p. 660.

distrained died, escaped or were stolen without the fault of the distrainor.[18]

Under s. 7 (1) of the Animals Act 1971, the right to seize and detain any animal by way of distress damage feasant is abolished. This constitutes abolition of the right of distress damage feasant in the case of *all* animals and not just those falling within the head of "cattle" or "livestock", though one must agree with the Law Commission that the exercise of the right in the case of other animals "has fallen into complete desuetude".[19]   A new right to detain livestock is created by s. 7 (2):

> "Where any livestock strays on to any land and is not then under the control of any person the occupier of the land may detain it, subject to subsection (3) of this section, unless ordered to return it by a court."[20]

The restriction of this new right to cases of straying livestock is likely to be of any significance only in the case of cats and dogs. There is no statutory right to detain them and the common law right of distress with regard to them has been abolished.[1]

One or two points should be made about this provision. The only person entitled to detain straying livestock is the occupier of the land on to which they strayed.   This is so even though the owner out of occupation of the land is also able to maintain an action under s. 4.   At common law, there is some evidence to suggest that an owner out of occupation could distrain animals damage feasant, at least if there was injury to his reversionary interest.[2]   So far as the new statutory right is concerned, provided the owner out of occupation has a right to enter the property on to which the animals strayed, it would seem desirable to have allowed him to detain livestock and, if necessary, to sell them and offset the price against any claim *he* might have under s. 4.

---

[18] *Williams* v. *Price* (1832), 3 B. & Ad. 695.   The position where these events occurred as a result of the plaintiff's negligence is unclear: Williams, p. 195.
[19] Law Commission Report, §. 69, n. 104.
[20] Under R.S.C. O. 29, r. 6 and C.C.R. O. 13, r. 9, the court may order the return of property on payment into court of the sum against which it is held.
[1] Section 9 deals with a person's rights to kill or injure dogs which are worrying livestock; see *infra*, Chapter 7.
[2] *Hoskins* v. *Robins* (1671), 2 Saund. 324, 328.

The right to detain under s. 7 (2) is dependent upon the livestock not being under the control of any person. This reiterates the common law view as to distress in that an animal actually in use might not be distrained, in order to avoid possible breaches of the peace. So a horse which is being ridden at the time the damage is caused[3] falls outside the provision. It might also be argued that where a horse and rider enter the plaintiff's land, the horse can hardly be said to have "strayed" thereon and so both s. 4 and s. 7 (2) would be inapplicable on that ground. A difficulty may arise if the defendant drives his livestock on to the plaintiff's land. It seems most desirable that the plaintiff should have a right to detain it, but this will only be so if the phrase "where any livestock *strays*"[4] is given a broad enough interpretation to include an intentional trespass. This then raises an issue as to the scope of s. 7 similar to the problem, already considered,[5] of the scope of s. 4. The general heading of, and marginal note to, s. 7 refer to "Detention and sale of trespassing livestock."[6] Section 7 (2), the main substantive subsection, refers, as has been seen, to the situation "where any livestock *strays* on to land."[7] If "stray" means "trespass" then it is surprising that the latter well-known technical phrase was not used; but unless "stray" does mean "trespass" it is hard to see how s. 7 can cover the case of the person who intentionally drives his livestock on to the detainor's land.

When livestock has been detained under s. 7 (2) the right to detain it ceases after forty eight hours unless within that time notice of the detention is given to the police, and, if known, to the person to whom the livestock belongs.[8] The right to detain ceases also if there is a tender of amends to the person detaining the livestock sufficient to satisfy a claim based, under

---

[3] *Storey* v. *Robinson* (1795), 6 Term Rep. 138; *Field* v. *Adames* (1840), 12 Ad. & El. 649.
[4] Section 7 (2), italics added: and see s. 4 (1).
[5] *Supra*, pp. 94–95.
[6] Whilst marginal notes may not be used in the construction of an Act, headings of parts of an Act may be so used: Craies, *Statute Law*, 7th ed., 195–197, 210–212.
[7] Italics added.
[8] Section 7 (3) (a).

s. 4, on the straying of the livestock.[9]   If the person detaining
has no claim[10] the right to detain ceases when the animals are
claimed by the person entitled to their possession.[11]

After the detention of livestock for not less than fourteen
days[12] the person detaining has a power of sale under s. 7 (4).
The sale must be at a market or a public auction.[13]   Furthermore, no such sale may take place if proceedings are pending for
damages under s. 4 for their straying, or for the return of the
livestock.   This latter situation might be illustrated by an
action of detinue in the case of livestock whose straying gives
rise to no valid claim under s. 4.   If the detainor is in breach
of an obligation to fence owed to the possessor of the livestock
he may detain any livestock that stray on to his land but he
must, under s. 7 (3) (c), release them when claimed by their
possessor.   If the detainor refuses to release them and the
possessor claims them in detinue, then such proceedings will
bar any right of sale under s. 7 (4).

A general effect of s. 7 (2) and s. 7 (3) is that the right to
claim damages for straying livestock is not to be barred by the
exercise of the right of detention, whereas an action for cattle
trespass was barred by distraint.   The justification for allowing
an action under s. 4 even though the livestock is being detained,
rather than only after it has been sold, is that:

> "it would seem unreasonable to compel [the plaintiff] to proceed to
> sale if, for example, he knows that the damage caused far exceeds
> the value of the animal."[14]

If, however, the detainor does choose to exercise his power of

---

[9] Section 7 (3) (b) ; *cf.* tender of amends, discussed *supra*, p. 115.

[10] This could be, e.g. because the person on to whose land they strayed was in
breach of a duty to fence: s. 5 (6).

[11] Section 7 (3) (c).

[12] The question whether the period should be 3, 14 or 21 days caused a great
deal of debate during the passage of the Animals Act 1971: 305 H.L. Deb.
c. 536; 317 H.L. Deb. c. 595; H.C. Standing Committee A, 18 March 1971
cc. 14–15, 16–19, 21–22; 815 H.C. Deb. cc. 600–602, 606–607, 608–609.

[13] Despite a fear that farmers would create a "ring" at markets or auctions,
private sales were excluded because sale in a market or at an auction would
ensure publicity so that a fair price would be obtained and a balance struck
between the interests of the owner of the livestock and of the seller.   H.C.
Standing Committee A, March 18th 1971 cc. 15–16, 18–19, 22–26; 810 H.C.
Deb. cc. 761–762.

[14] Law Commission Report, §. 72.

sale then the proceeds of sale must be disposed of in accordance with s. 7 (5) which provides that:

> "Where any livestock is sold in the exercise of the right conferred by this section and the proceeds of the sale, less the costs thereof and any costs incurred in connection with it, exceed the amount of any claim under section 4 of this Act which the vendor had in respect of the livestock, the excess shall be recoverable from him by the person who would be entitled to the possession of the livestock but for the sale."

In the normal case this is quite straightforward. Where the plaintiff in an action for straying livestock under s. 4 chooses to detain and sell the livestock he may apply the proceeds to any claim he may have under s. 4. If the amount realised by the sale is greater than that required to satisfy his claim he must pay the excess over to the original possessor of the livestock less any costs of the sale. There are, however, at least two other situations involving sale of straying livestock for which express provision does not appear to have been made. The first is the case where the detainor has a right of action under s. 4 for straying livestock but the damage done is greater than the value of the livestock detained. It has been seen that this situation has been used to justify the conclusion that the detainor may sue under s. 4 even whilst detaining, but what happens if he sells the livestock? Although he cannot do this if proceedings are pending under s. 4,[15] he may not wish to bring proceedings under s. 4 until he discovers what the proceeds of sale are. If he sells the livestock and then decides to bring proceedings under s. 4, no provision is made in s. 7 either for the disposal of the proceeds of sale or to determine whether the detainor may still claim under s. 4. The only provision in s. 7 relating to the proceeds of sale is s. 7 (5) which deals with the specific case of the proceeds exceeding any claim under s. 4. Where the proceeds are less than the damages claim under s. 4, the desirable solution would be to allow the plaintiff to claim under s. 4 such sum as amounts to his total loss, less the net proceeds of sale, having deducted the costs of sale.

---

[15] Section 7 (4).

The second situation to consider here is that of the detainor who has no claim under s. 4 at all because, for example, the damage is due wholly to his own fault.[16] There is no doubt that s. 7 confers on him a right to detain and sell straying livestock, for s. 7 (3) (c) envisages detention by a person with no claim under s. 4.[17] Such a detainor may choose to exercise his power of sale under s. 7 (4) as in the case where livestock have strayed on to his land as a result of his failure to fence and he does not know to whom they belong. Once he has detained them for fourteen days and the owner has not been found, the detainor will want to be rid of them as soon as possible. If they are then sold at a market or a public auction, what happens to the proceeds? Again no provision is made in s. 7 (5), for that subsection envisages sale by a person who has a claim under s. 4. It would appear that the seller, the detainor, ought to hold the proceeds to the use of the original owner who ought to be able to claim restitution of the proceeds of the sale. Whether the seller can deduct the costs of the sale or any costs for looking after the livestock once a reasonable period has elapsed for the original owner to reclaim them is just not considered in s. 7. The common law is of no assistance for the law of distress damage feasant is abolished by s. 7 (1) and, in any event, did not permit distress by someone who had no right of action. The most reasonable solution would appear to be to require the detainor in such cases to pay over the gross proceeds of sale unless the original owner has delayed unreasonably in claiming his livestock. In that latter event the detainor should deduct the costs of sale and of maintaining the livestock after such a period has elapsed. It must not be forgotten that there is no statutory warrant for such conclusions, but as s. 7 gives such a person a power of sale, the common law will have to decide what is to be done with the proceeds.

It will be recalled that the right to bring an action for straying livestock under s. 4 is not affected by the fact that the plaintiff has detained the livestock. It appears that such an

---

[16] Section 5 (1).
[17] Notwithstanding the use of the phrase "trespassing livestock" in the heading to s. 7.

action for straying livestock is not affected by the fact that the
livestock detained either has died or has escaped through the
negligence of the plaintiff.[18]   However, the defendant may be
able to counterclaim for any loss which stems from the plaintiff's
failure to take reasonable care of the livestock detained, for
s. 7 (6) provides:

> "A person detaining any livestock in pursuance of this section is
> liable for any damage caused to it by a failure to treat it with
> reasonable care and supply it with adequate food and water while
> it is so detained."

Any references in s. 7 to a claim for damages for straying
livestock under s. 4 do not include any claim under s. 4 for
damage done or expenses incurred in respect of the livestock
before the straying in connection with which it is detained
under s. 7.[19]   Thus, if the defendant's livestock have strayed
onto the plaintiff's land on several occasions, the plaintiff cannot, when seizing the animals on their last intrusion, sell them
under the powers given by s. 7 (4) and then, under s. 7 (5), set
the proceeds of sale off against his claims under s. 4 for all the
different acts of straying.   He can only deduct from the sale
price damages due for damage or expenses incurred during the
straying incident in which the detention was made.

It should not be forgotten that if a detainor chooses not to
exercise his power of sale, no change in the ownership of the
livestock takes place.   The livestock still belongs to the original
owner; though the longer the period before the latter reclaims,
the greater the claim for the expenses of the livestock's keep,
under s. 4 (1) (b), he can expect to face.

The varied provisions of s. 7 raise some difficulty with regard
to the general scope of the right to detain straying livestock.
It has been seen, already, that it is a right to detain "livestock"
and not "animals" as was the case under the common law of
distress damage feasant.   Another comparison is that the
common law right to distrain applied to causes of action other

---

[18] The effect of this on a plaintiff's position in an action of cattle trespass was
quite unclear: Williams, 195.
[19] Section 7 (7).

than cattle trespass,[20] though some cause of action had to be open and probably one relating to infringement of rights over land. It would apply, for example, to cases of nuisance.[1] This was relevant where the distrainor had insufficient interest to maintain cattle trespass but could maintain the latter. The new provision under s. 7 is drafted in terms applicable specifically to the statutory right of action under s. 4. However, it also applies where there is no claim under s. 4 and so it would appear to apply in all cases where livestock stray on to another's land irrespective of the cause of action thereby created or whether there is any cause of action at all. Nevertheless, it should be borne in mind that the right to detain is only open to the occupier of the land[2] and so it is most unlikely that anyone with a right to detain would wish to utilise it in the context of an action other than one under s. 4.

In conclusion, the practical implications of the inter-relation of s. 4 and s. 7 might be considered. It is a tidy theoretical proposition to state that if another's livestock stray on to your land you may detain them provided the police are notified and that if they are not claimed within 14 days you may sell them and apply the proceeds of sale to any damage you may have suffered. Undoubtedly this is a sensible and practical proposition where the livestock stray on to the land of another farmer who has the facilities for detaining and feeding them. The position is very different if a sheep or a pony strays into a suburban garden and there does a good deal of damage. If the damage is greater than the value of the livestock its owner will keep quiet and not claim it. The victim of the straying is, in such a case, protected by s. 7 but he must catch, secure and feed the animal for 14 days before he can sell it to recoup some of his loss. This will, all too often, be quite impracticable. It is better to drive the unidentified beast out and away with little hope of any redress. The nature of the problem has been exemplified thus:

> "If a man who owns a terrace house finds that his garden has been completely ruined as a result of the entry of a sheep which is still

---

[20] Williams, 65–76.
[1] *Ibid.*, pp. 65–66.
[2] Section 7 (2).

in his garden, can it be reasonable to suggest that he—in a garden of very small proportions and totally lacking in the facilities which a farmer would have—having notified the police, should be required to keep that sheep tethered in his back garden, if he has one? Many terraced houses have no garden. Often the sheep is not merely in the garden; it has come in and caused damage in the outbuildings and the house itself."[3]

The problem is really one of balancing the two interests at stake—to provide security for the person who has suffered the damage and to protect the property interest of the owner of the straying livestock. It appears that the Act does this quite well in the case of neighbouring farmers but it may well be that a right to detain is, in the case of the urban plaintiff, of very little practical value.[4] If he knows whose animal it is, he will claim rather than detain. It is only where the owner is unknown that he will want the right to detain but then he has nowhere to keep the animal.

---

[3] H.C. Standing Committee A, March 16th 1971, c. 14; and see 810 H.C. Deb. cc. 747–748, 773.
[4] The remedy under s. 7 has been described as "cumbersome and unrealistic in practice"; Powell-Smith (1971) 121 N.L.J. 584, 585.

4

FENCING AND STRAYING ANIMALS[1]

A common reason for animals, and particularly livestock, straying on to another's land is that of a defective fence. The obligation to one man to fence his land is relevant in a number of ways to tortious liability affecting animals. Failure to fence may both provide a cause of action to one party and a defence to another. Before examining the effects of a failure to fence, the nature of the obligation itself must be considered.

(A) THE OBLIGATION TO FENCE

The obligation to fence may be placed on the plaintiff in various ways. It can be by agreement[2] although this has given rise to debate as to whether an "easement of fencing"[3] is thereby created or whether the obligation is personal to the parties.[4] This problem appears to have been resolved in *Jones* v. *Price*[5] where the Court of Appeal held that a con-

---

[1] Williams, Part III.
[2] Hunt, *Law of Boundaries, Walls and Fences*, 6th ed., 97–98; e.g. *Holgate* v. *Bleazard*, [1917] 1 K.B. 443; *Park* v. *J. Jobson & Son*, [1945] 1 All E. R. 222. It is significant to note the inference from these two cases that the contractual obligation binds only the parties to it and cannot be relied on by a third party.
[3] Gale on *Easements*, 13th ed., 33–34, on the nature of the obligation to fence; and see Megarry & Wade, *Law of Real Property*, 3rd ed., **875**.
[4] Williams, 210–211; *cf.* Gale, *op. cit.*, 34.
[5] [1965] 2 Q.B. 618.

tractual obligation to maintain a boundary fence bound only the parties to the contract and did not run with the land.[6]

More commonly the obligation, described as a "quasi-easement"[7] or a "spurious easement",[8] will be created by prescription.[9] Thus in *Lawrence* v. *Jenkins*[10] the plaintiff's cow strayed on to the defendant's land through a gap in the fence caused by the defendant's felling a tree. The cow died through eating yew tree leaves on the defendant's land. As there was a prescriptive obligation on the defendant, acquired over the previous forty years, to repair the fence, the plaintiff was able to recover for the loss of his cow and would also have been able to resist a claim in cattle trespass and would now be able to resist a claim based on statutory liability for straying livestock under section 4 of the Animals Act 1971. To maintain a claim to a prescriptive right it must be shown that the fence or hedge has been maintained and repaired by the occupier[11] of the "quasi-servient" tenement as a matter of obligation and not just in his own interests of containing his own animals.[12] The best method of proof of this, though perhaps not the only method of proof,[13] is to show that the repairs were done at the request of the occupier of the "quasi-

---

[6] [1965] 2 Q.B. 618, 633, 639, 644–647, on the authority of *Austerberry* v. *Oldham Corpn.* (1885), 29 Ch.D. 750; *Hilton* v. *Ankesson* (1827), 27 L.T. 519; and see *E. & G.C., Ltd.* v. *Bates* (1935), 79 L.Jo. 203. See, however, Report of the Committee on Positive Covenants affecting Land (1965) Cmnd. 2719, and also Law Reform Committee, Fourteenth Report, Acquisition of Easements & Profits by Prescription (1966) Cmnd. 3100.

[7] *Jones* v. *Price*, [1965] 2 Q.B. 618.

[8] *Lawrence* v. *Jenkins* (1873), L.R. 8 Q.B. 274, 279; *Coaker* v. *Willcocks*, [1911] 2 K.B. 124, 131; and see *Crow* v. *Wood*, [1971] 1 Q.B. 77, 84–85, 86. It was described as "anomalous" in the Report of the Committee on Positve Covenants affecting Land (1965) Cmnd. 2719, §. 8 (v).

[9] Williams, 203–210; Hunt, *op. cit.*, 100–109.

[10] (1873), L.R. 8 Q.B. 274. See also *Anon* (1675), 1 Vent. 264; *Star* v. *Rookesby* (1710), 1 Salk. 335; *Rooth* v. *Wilson* (1817), 1 B. & Ald. 59; *Boyle* v. *Tamlin* (1827), 6 B. & C. 329; *Powell* v. *Salisbury* (1828), 2 Y. & J. 391; *Coaker* v. *Willcocks*, [1911] 2 K.B. 124.

[11] The obligation is on the occupier and not on the owner out of occupation: *Cheetham* v. *Hampson* (1791), 4 Term Rep. 318.

[12] *Jones* v. *Price*, [1965] 2 Q.B. 618, 634–636; Hunt, *op. cit.*, 109; *cf.* Williams, 203–208.

[13] *Boyle* v. *Tamlin* (1827), 6 B. & C. 329; *Barber* v. *Whiteley* (1865), 34 L.J.Q.B. 212; *Jones* v. *Price*, [1965] 2 Q.B. 618, 636.

dominant" tenement.[14]   The obligation to fence can only be
created by prescription in the cases of adjoining owners.   It
does not arise where all the lands in question have, until
recently, been held in common ownership.[15]

It would thus seem that the right to an "easement of fencing"
may be acquired by immemorial user,[16] by presumption of lost
grant[17] and by grant.[18]

This last situation was considered by the Court of Appeal in
Crow v. *Wood*.[19]   A large Yorkshire moor had, with adjoining
farms, remained in common ownership for many years.   The
tenants of the various farms had been granted the right to
stray their sheep on the moor and the tenants agreed to
maintain their fences and walls in good repair.   One of these
farms was sold to the plaintiff and another to the defendant's
landlord.   The plaintiff did not let any sheep stray on the moor
and she did not maintain her fences so as to keep out the sheep
of other farmers pastured on the moor.   Some of the defendant's sheep strayed from the moor on to the plaintiff's
land causing damage for which the plaintiff claimed damages in
cattle trespass.   The defendant argued that his sheep strayed
because the plaintiff had failed in her duty to fence them out.
Was there such an obligation upon which the defendant could
rely?   The Court of Appeal concluded that:

> "a right to have your neighbour keep up the fences is a right in the
> nature of an easement which is capable of being granted by law so
> as to run with the land and to be binding on successors.   It is a

---

[14] *Lawrence* v. *Jenkins* (1873), L.R. 8 Q.B. 274; *cf. Hilton* v. *Ankesson* (1872),
27 L.T. 519; *Jones* v. *Price*, [1965] 2 Q.B. 618, 645 *per* WILLMER, L.J.

[15] *Kilgour* v. *Gaddes*, [1904] 1 K.B. 457; *Crow* v. *Wood*, [1971] 1 Q.B. 77, 83.

[16] *Lawrence* v. *Jenkins* (1873), L.R. 8 Q.B. 274; *Jones* v. *Price*, [1965] 2 Q.B.
618, 634–636.

[17] *Barber* v. *Whiteley* (1865), 34 L.J.Q.B. 212 and see *Boyle* v. *Tamlin* (1827),
6 B. & C. 329; *Sharp* v. *Harvey*, [1935] L.J.C.C.R. 261, 266.   *Cf. Sutcliffe*
v. *Holmes*, [1947] 1 K.B. 147; *Jones* v. *Price*, [1965] 2 Q.B. 618, 636–637.
WILLMER, L.J., at [1965] 2 Q.B. 618, 647, suggested that the earlier cases
"are in a special category"; and see Hunt, *op. cit.*, 103–104; Williams, 209.
The "special circumstances" may well be based upon the original enclosure
of the land from the common: Gale, *op. cit.*, 34.

[18] *Crow* v. *Wood*, [1971] 1 Q.B. 77, 84, 87; Megarry & Wade, *op. cit.*, 875; *cf.
Jones* v. *Price, supra*, at p. 640.

[19] [1971] 1 Q.B. 77; P.V.B. (1971), 87 L.Q.R. 13; Wilkinson (1971), 34
M.L.R. 223.

right which lies in grant and is of such a nature that it can pass under section 62 of the Law of Property Act 1925".[20]

Each farmer adjoining the moor had the right to pasture his sheep thereon and the duty to fence against the moor. These were rights and advantages, under s. 62, which had been enjoyed by the previous owner of the defendant's farm and which passed on conveyance of the farm; and so the plaintiff failed. This decision indicates, quite clearly, that an "easement of fencing" can be created by grant, either express or implied.

There are also a number of cases where the obligation to fence is placed upon an occupier by common law rules, as with the obligation of mine and quarry owners or licensees to fence off their property.[1] In the case of the occupier of property adjoining the highway, he does not have an obligation to fence against the highway such that he can be made responsible for the erection or maintenance of fences; but he cannot succeed in an action for damage done by straying livestock if livestock stray on to his land from the highway,[2] provided their presence on the highway was a lawful use thereof, and he cannot lawfully resist the entry on to his land of the driver of the cattle to retake his animals.[3] On the other hand, the occupier will not be held responsible for injury to animals which stray on to his property from the highway.[4]

Finally, the obligation to fence may be created by statute[5] as

---

[20] [1971] 1 Q.B. 77, 84–85. Section 62 (1) of the Law of Property Act 1925 provides: "A conveyance of land shall be deemed to include and shall by virtue of this Act operate to convey, with the land, all . . . easements, rights and advantages whatsoever, appertaining or reputed to appertain to the land, or any part thereof, or, at the time of conveyance, demised, occupied, or enjoyed with, or reputed or known as part or parcel of or appurtenant to the land or any part thereof."

[1] Williams, 211–212; Hunt, *op. cit.*, 109–113; *Churchill* v. *Evans* (1809), 1 Taunt. 529; *Groucott* v. *Williams* (1863), 4 B. & S. 149; *Hawken* v. *Shearer* (1887), 56 L.J.Q.B. 284; and see *M'Morrow* v. *Layden*, [1919] 2 I.R. 398; *Harrison* v. *M'Culvey* (1840), 2 Craw. & D. 1.

[2] Animals Act 1971, s. 5 (5); *supra*, pp. 112–114.

[3] Williams, 372.

[4] *Blithe* v. *Topham* (1607), Cro. Jac. 158; Williams, 373. *Cf.* the general rule, discussed *infra*, pp. 131–133.

[5] Hunt, *op. cit.*, 113–118; Powell-Smith, *The Law of Boundaries and Fences*, pp. 77–82.

in the case of the obligation of railways[6] to fence adjoining land and level crossings, and mines and quarries legislation.[7]   It may also be created by an enclosure award[8] but not by custom.[9]

(B)   STANDARD OF THE OBLIGATION

The duty to fence "is only to keep reasonable fences to prevent the escape of ordinary cattle in ordinary circumstances",[10] for the obligation is now one to fence against ordinary livestock, rather than other animals or children.   The obligation is, however, not only to prevent the livestock of the owner of the "quasi-servient" tenement from straying on to the "quasi-dominant" tenement, but also to prevent the latter's livestock from straying on to and being injured on the former's land.[11]

The fences must be maintained, by any means, in such a way as to make them proof against livestock in ordinary circumstances.   Thus, the duty is broken if a hole is left in a hedge through which sheep could pass[12] or if a gate is left open.   If the fence is defective it does not matter whether this is as a result of the positive act of the "quasi-servient" tenant[13] or the result of neglect.[14]

If the animals in question are peculiarly prone to straying or act in an unusual manner then, provided there are reasonable

---

[6] Railway Clauses Consolidation Act 1845, s. 68; see, e.g. *Ricketts* v. *East and West India Docks etc. Rail. Co.* (1852), 2 C.B. 160; *Dawson* v. *Midland Rail. Co.* (1872), L.R. 8 Exch. 8; *Child* v. *Hearn* (1874), L.R. 9 Exch. 176; *Wiseman* v. *Booker* (1878), 3 C.P.D. 184; *Dixon* v. *Great Western Rail. Co.,* [1897] 1 Q.B. 300; and see Hunt, *op. cit.,* 113–115; Williams, 212, 219 n. 5; *cf. Cooper* v. *Railway Executive,* [1953] 1 All E.R. 477.   It has been held that the nature of the fencing obligation imposed by the 1845 Act is the same as it would be at common law under a prescriptive obligation to fence: *Ricketts* v. *East and West India Docks etc. Rail. Co., supra; Manchester, Sheffield and Lincolnshire Rail. Co.* v. *Wallis* (1854), 14 C.B. 213, 223–224.

[7] Hunt, *op. cit.,* 116–118; Williams, 212.

[8] *Singleton* v. *Williamson* (1861), 7 H. & N. 410.

[9] *Polus* v. *Henstock* (1670), 1 Vent. 97; *Jones* v. *Price,* [1965] 2 Q.B. 618, 639, 646–647; *Crow* v. *Wood,* [1971] 1 Q.B. 77, 83–84.   For extinction of the obligation, see Williams, 212–213.

[10] Williams, 214.

[11] Hunt, *op. cit.,* 100.

[12] *Bessant* v. *Great Western Rail. Co.* (1860), 8 C.B.N.S. 368; and see *Page* v. *Great Eastern Rail. Co.* (1871), 24 L.T. 585.

[13] E.g. *Lawrence* v. *Jenkins* (1873), L.R. 8 Q.B. 274.

[14] E.g. *Barber* v. *Whiteley* (1865), 34 L.J.Q.B. 212.

fences, there is no obligation if the animals break through them. Thus, in the case of a pig the obligation is to erect "such a fence that a pig not of a peculiarly wandering disposition, nor under any excessive temptation, will not get through it".[15] In *Coaker* v. *Willcocks*[16] the defendant occupied a farm which had been enclosed from land forming part of the Forest of Dartmoor and it was agreed that the defendant was bound to fence his land against moorland sheep. The defendant seized some of the plaintiff's sheep which had strayed on to his land from the commonable land. It was held that though there was an obligation on the defendant to fence against commonable animals this did not extend to the plaintiff's peculiar Scottish sheep, for as DARLING, J. said:[17]

"these Scotch sheep are of a peculiarly wandering and saltative disposition, straying and jumping in a way which distinguishes them from sheep which have hitherto been turned on to the unenclosed land, wandering as other sheep do not and jumping as other sheep cannot. In my judgment the defendant was not bound to fence his land from sheep of this description; it was the duty of the plaintiff, if he chose to own such sheep, to keep them from trespassing on the defendant's land."

Apart from the relevance of the disposition of the animal in question, the fence need only be reasonably secure; for the courts have not decreed:

"that there must be a fence so close and strong that no pig could push through it, or so high that no horse or bullock could leap it."[18]

In *Cooper* v. *Railway Executive*[19] the plaintiff's cattle broke through a railway fence on to the defendants' railway line and three of them were killed when hit by a train which was itself derailed. The defendants were under a duty to fence[20] and the plaintiff alleged breach of that duty and claimed damages for

---

[15] *Child* v. *Hearn* (1874), L.R. 9 Exch. 176, 182.
[16] [1911] 1 K.B. 649. See also *Spry* v. *Mortimore*, [1946] L.J.C.C.R. 83, 86.
[17] *Ibid.*, at p. 654.
[18] *Child* v. *Hearn* (1874), L.R. 9 Exch. 176, 181–182.
[19] [1953] 1 All E.R. 477, and see *Dobbie* v. *Henderson* 1970 S.L.T. (Sh. Ct. Rep.) 27.
[20] Under the Railways Clauses Consolidation Act 1845, s. 68.

the death of his cattle, but the defendants counter-claimed alleging cattle trespass.   The cattle were in a state of excitement because the calves had been separated from the cows and the court found that the fence

"was as strong as any ordinary farm fence could be to offer protection against the ordinary behaviour of cattle.   Indeed, it was a great deal stronger, being made of concrete posts and strong chain link fencing."[1]

As the fence was strong enough to "prevail against the ordinary forcible behaviour of cattle in ordinary circumstances" the defendants had satisfied the obligation to fence and succeeded in their counter-claim for cattle trespass.   A fence which allows animals to put their heads over the top and cause damage or be injured, e.g. by eating yew tree leaves,[2] would be insufficient.[3]

It seems probable that the obligation to fence is strict in that no enquiry should be made into the reasonableness of the conduct of the servient tenant so far as maintenance is concerned.   This has been considered to apply even in the case of an action for damages brought by the dominant tenant for injury to his cattle on the servient tenement.[4]   It can be argued that the defences of Act of God,[5] act of third party,[6] and inevitable accident should be open to the servient tenant in such cases.[7]

(c)   EFFECTS OF THE FAILURE TO FENCE[8]

(i)   Repair of the fence

The dominant tenant can compel the repair of the fence by the servient tenant.   This obligation used to be enforced by the old writ *de curia claudenda,*[9]

---

[1] [1953] 1 All E.R. 477, 479.
[2] E.g. *Lawrence* v. *Jenkins* (1873), L.R. 8 Q.B. 274; *cf. Wilson* v. *Newberry* (1871), L.R. 7 Q.B. 31.
[3] *Cf. Wiseman* v. *Booker* (1878), 3 C.P.D. 184, 188.
[4] *Lawrence* v. *Jenkins* (1873), L.R. 8 Q.B. 274, 278.
[5] *Ibid.,* at p. 278.
[6] Williams, 223, 225; *cf. Sutcliffe* v. *Holmes,* [1947] K.B. 147; and see *Singleton* v. *Williamson* (1861), 7 H. & N. 410, 416.
[7] Williams, 225.
[8] Williams, pp. 215–225.
[9] See Williams (1938), 54 L.Q.R. 405; Hunt, *op. cit.,* 100; *Lawrence* v. *Jenkins* (1873), L.R. 8 Q.B. 274, 279.

"which lay for the tenant of the freehold against another tenant of land adjoining to compel him to make a fence or wall, which he ought, by prescription, to make between his land and the plaintiff's."[10]

The writ was abolished by the Real Property Limitation Act 1833, s. 36. It appears that the obligation is now normally enforced by an action on the case which is not to be limited to obligations of fencing created by prescription alone. Such remedy, however, is adequate only to provide damages but will not compel the servient tenant to erect or maintain his fence. The enforcement of that obligation must be by way of mandatory injunction.[11] The action lies between adjoining possessors of land[12] rather than between adjoining freeholders.[13] It does not, apparently, lie at the suit of a commoner,[14] though this restriction seems difficult to justify. There can be no obligation on the servient tenant to maintain a hedge on the dominant tenement, not forming the boundary between the two.[15]

(ii)   Injury to livestock

The dominant tenant can recover damages for injury to his livestock suffered on the servient tenement.[16] When the dominant tenant's cattle died through eating yew tree leaves on the servient tenant's land to which they had escaped through a gap in the fence, the servient tenant was held liable for the loss.[17] The result would be the same if the livestock had been

---

[10] *Pomfret* v. *Ricroft* (1669), 1 Saund. 321, 322 n. (c).
[11] P.V.B. (1971), 87 L.Q.R. 13, 15. For the principles for the award of mandatory injunctions, see *Redlands Bricks, Ltd.* v. *Morris*, [1970] A.C. 652.
[12] E.g. *Cheetham* v. *Hampson* (1791), 4 Term Rep. 318.
[13] As with the writ *de curia claudenda: Cheetham* v. *Hampson, supra; Russell* v. *Shenton* (1842), 3 Q.B. 449.
[14] *Smith* v. *Burton* (1674), 1 Freem. K.B. 145.
[15] *Jones* v. *Price*, [1965] 2 Q.B. 618, 623, 642.
[16] If the defect in the fence is such that decayed pieces thereof fall on to the dominant tenement and are there eaten by the dominant tenant's cattle, an action will lie for the consequent death of the cattle: *Firth* v. *Bowling Iron Co.* (1878), 3 C.P.D. 254.
[17] *Lawrence* v. *Jenkins* (1873), L.R. 8 Q.D. 274, 275, *cf. Ponting* v. *Noakes*, [1894] 2 Q.B. 281.

M.L.A.—6

killed by, for example, a falling haystack,[18] through falling into
a ditch,[19] by being hit by a passing train,[20] by drinking con-
taminated water in a mine,[1] by hitting its head against a
viaduct[2] or through falling into a quarry.[3]   Furthermore, if the
dominant tenant's livestock stray on to the servient tenement
and then on to a third person's land where they are injured, the
servient tenant will be liable.[4]   Where the animals on the
dominant tenement are lawfully there but do not belong to the
dominant tenant, the latter may maintain an action for injury
done to them on the servient tenement if he is responsible to
their owner for their safety, as where he is a bailee.[5]   It would
appear, furthermore, that when such animals lawfully on the
dominant tenement stray onto the servient tenement as the
result of the servient tenant's failure to fence, the latter will be
liable to the owner for any injuries to the animals suffered on
the servient tenement even though the owner is not the
dominant tenant.[6]   If, however, the animals were unlawfully
on the dominant tenement and they then stray on to and are
injured on the servient tenement they are regarded as being
unlawfully on the servient tenement even though the servient
tenant is in breach of an obligation to fence owed to the
dominant tenant.   That being so the servient tenant can resist
any action for injury to the animals on his land.[7]   Furthermore, if animals stray from A's land to B's land as a result of
A's defective fences and then they stray on to C's land as a
result of C's failure to fence against B, A cannot recover for

---

[18] *Powell* v. *Salisbury* (1828), 2 Y. & J. 391.
[19] *Anon.* (1675), 1 Vent. 264; and see *Rooth* v. *Wilson* (1817), 1 B. & Ald. 59;
  Corry v. *Great Western Rail. Co.* (1881), 7 Q.B.D. 322.
[20] E.g. *Dawson* v. *Midland Rail. Co.* (1872), L.R. 8 Exch. 8; *Bessant* v.
  Great Western Rail. Co. (1860), 8 C.B.N.S. 368; *Luscombe* v. *Great Western
  Rail. Co.*, [1899] 2 Q.B. 313; *Saunders & Son* v. *Railway Executive*, [1947–
  1951] C.L.C. 8233; and see *Symons* v. *Southern Rail. Co.* (1935), 153 L.T. 98.
[1] *Harrison* v. *M'Culvey* (1840), 2 Craw. & D. 1.
[2] *Dixon* v. *Great Western Rail. Co.*, [1897] 1 Q.B. 300.
[3] *Williams* v. *Groucott* (1863), 4 B. & S. 149; *Hawken* v. *Shearer* (1887), 56
  L.J.Q.B. 284; *M'Morrow* v. *Layden*, [1919] 2 I.R. 398.
[4] *Singleton* v. *Williamson* (1816), 7 H. & N. 410, 416.
[5] *Rooth* v. *Wilson* (1817), 1 B. & Ald. 58.
[6] E.g. *Dawson* v. *Midland Rail. Co.* (1872), L.R. 8 Exch. 8; and see *Anon.*
  (1675), 1 Vent. 264.
[7] *Manchester, Sheffield and Lincolnshire Rail. Co.* v. *Wallis* (1854), 14 C.B. 213;
  Luscombe v. *Great Western Rail. Co.*, [1899] 2 Q.B. 313.

injuries to his animals suffered on C's land, because the animals were unlawfully on B's land.[8]

(iii) Damage to the land

The dominant tenant may claim damages for damage to his land caused by animals straying on to it from the servient tenement. This would seem to be an action separate from cattle trespass and from the new statutory liability under the Animals Act 1971 for straying livestock. It lies not only if the livestock are in the possession of the servient tenant[9] but also, probably, even if they are not.[10] This head of liability does not affect any other possible liability on the part of the owner of the animals.[11] It appears, therefore, that the servient tenant will be liable in damages for failure to repair his fences if animals straying on to his land then strayed on to the dominant tenement through the defective fence. This is so even though no statutory action under section 4 of the Animals Act will lie at the suit of the dominant tenant against the servient tenant in such circumstances because of the servient tenant's lack of control of the livestock. It may be recalled that for the statutory action to lie the livestock must "belong" to the defendant and for the purposes of section 4 "any livestock belongs to the person in whose possession it is".[12]

It would also appear that if the dominant tenant suffers loss when, because of defective fences, livestock stray from his land on to the servient tenement and then stray through the servient tenement onto other land belonging to the dominant tenant, an action for damages will lie against the servient tenant if that other land of the dominant tenant is damaged by the incursions thereon of his own livestock.[13] Furthermore, if as a result of

---

[8] *Ricketts* v. *East and West India Docks etc. Rail. Co.* (1852), 12 C.B. 160.
[9] *Star* v. *Rookesby* (1710), 1 Salk. 335. No doubt the statutory action for straying livestock would lie here also.
[10] Williams, 216 n. 12; and see *Winter* v. *Charter* (1829), 3 Y. & J. 308. *Cf.* liability under the Animals Act 1971, s. 4, *supra*, pp. 96–98.
[11] Hunt, *op. cit.*, 249.
[12] Animals Act 1971, s. 4 (2).
[13] *Brox* v. *Edmonton, Yukon and Pacific Rail. Co.* (1909), 2 Alta. L.R. 379; Williams, 217.

the servient tenant's failure to fence, the dominant tenant's livestock stray on to the land of a third party, the dominant tenant may well be statutorily liable to that third party under the Animals Act 1971, s. 4, for any damage to that third party's property.[14]   In such a case the dominant tenant ought to be able to claim an indemnity from the servient tenant.[15]

(iv)   Recapture of straying livestock

The dominant tenant may enter the servient tenement to recapture his straying animals, provided they strayed as a result of the defective fences;[16] though there is no general right to enter another's land to reclaim straying animals.   The servient tenant onto whose land the animals have strayed has the right to eject them, but this is coupled with an obligation to return them to the land from which they have strayed,[17] and it is not a right just to turn them out onto the highway.   If, however, the occupier of the land on to which the animals stray is under no obligation to repair his fences then he is permitted to drive the straying animals out of his land[18] even on to the highway.[19]   Where animals stray as a result of a failure to fence then it is arguable that the dominant tenant has an obligation to retake his animals within a reasonable time of notice of their escape, or he may find himself liable to the servient tenant, despite the latter's failure to fence, for any damage suffered by the servient tenant from the delay in recovery of the animals.[20]

---

[14] No defence is provided in such circumstances by the Animals Act 1971, s. 5 (6).
[15] Williams, 222–223.
[16] Williams, 180, 217; *Baker* v. *Andrews* (1652), Style 357; *Sorlie* v. *McKee*, [1927] 1 D.L.R. 249, 251, 254.
[17] *Carruthers* v. *Hollis* (1838), 8 Ad. & El. 113; Hunt, *op. cit.* 248–249.
[18] *Tyrringham's Case* (1584), 4 Co. Rep. 36b, 38b.
[19] Williams, 90–92.   One might query whether this does not constitute trespass to the highway, as to which the possessor of the straying animals should be liable to indemnify the person on to whose land they originally strayed; see *supra*.
[20] Williams, 223–224.   The statutory right to detain straying livestock, under the Animals Act 1971, s. 7, is discussed, *supra*, pp. 115–123.

(v) Defence to an action under the Animals Act 1971

The dominant tenant may resist a statutory action for straying livestock which may be brought by the servient tenant under the Animals Act 1971, s. 4, if the former's livestock have strayed on to the latter's land through the defective fences[1] or even if the straying livestock have damaged other land belonging to the servient tenant.[2] This defence to an action under s. 4 of the Animals Act 1971 is provided as a result of the combined effects of s. 5 (1) and s. 5 (6) of that Act. The first subsection provides that a person is not liable for any damage which is due wholly to the fault of the person suffering it. It is then provided by s. 5 (6) that:

> "In determining whether any liability for damage under section 4 of this Act is excluded by subsection (1) of this section the damage shall not be treated as due to the fault of the person suffering it by reason only that he could have prevented it by fencing;[3] but a person is not liable under that section where it is proved that the straying of the livestock on to the land would not have occurred but for a breach by any other person, being a person having an interest in the land, of a duty to fence."

The effect of these subsections is to embody two principles:

(i) If there is no obligation on the plaintiff, in an action for straying livestock, to fence his neighbour's livestock out, the plaintiff is not at fault within the meaning of s. 5 (1) if he fails to do so even though such fencing could have prevented the straying; he may still maintain the statutory action; and

(ii) there is to be no liability if the defendant's livestock strayed on to the plaintiff's land as the result of a breach of an obligation to fence by any person other than the defendant, provided that person had an interest in the land strayed upon.

Although, as has been seen, the general law of fencing is quite

---

[1] E.g. *Wiseman* v. *Booker* (1878), 3 C.P.D. 184.
[2] *Singleton* v. *Williams* (1861), 7 H. & N. 410, 416.
[3] Fencing includes "the construction of any obstacle designed to prevent animals from straying": Animals Act 1971, s. 11. This will mean that fencing will include not only fences but also, for example, ditches though only where the purpose of the ditch is to contain livestock and not where its sole purpose is to carry away water.

complex,[4] the provisions of s. 5 (6) would seem to affect only that part of it which is relevant to an action for straying livestock and they leave untouched that which relates to the other effects of the failure to fence.[5] This singling out of only part of the law of fencing for treatment in the Animals Act 1971 causes no difficulty where the dominant tenant's livestock stray on to the servient tenant's land as a result of the latter's breach of the duty to fence; these will be the majority of cases of liability for straying livestock. Problems do arise, however, where the parties between whom the obligation to fence exists are not the same as those in the action for straying livestock.

In order to understand how the Animals Act 1971 has affected the situation in this context it is necessary to examine the common law position as well as that under the 1971 Act and to examine them both in relation to a number of separate problems. There are three main issues to be considered here. Two arise from the fact that nothing is said in s. 5 (6) as to the person to whom the duty to fence must be owed in order for the defence of failure to fence to be applicable.[6] The third is concerned with an obligation owed to the defendant but by a person other than the plaintiff. Finally, certain problems arising from multiple fencing obligations will be considered.

(1) *A fencing obligation owed by the plaintiff to a person other than the defendant from whose land the livestock have strayed*

Whilst the normal fencing obligation will be owed by a servient tenant to a neighbouring dominant tenant, this will not

---

[4] The Law Commission Report, §. 67, n. 98, expressly declined to examine fencing obligations other than in the context of the provision of a defence to liability for straying livestock. During the House of Lords debates on the Act, Lord DENNING indicated that it was a defect in the Act that nowhere did it indicate what the duty to fence is. Indeed he thought the law relating to the obligation to fence was so complex that that was why the Law Commission had not stated it: 312 H.L. Deb., c. 228, and see 810 H.C. Deb., c. 765.

[5] *Supra*, pp. 130–134.

[6] A suggestion was made in the House of Lords that the duty should be owed to a person with an interest in the land from which the livestock strayed. This amendment was withdrawn after considerable debate and opposition: 312 H.L. Deb., cc. 203–205, 227–231, 857–863; 313 H.L. Deb., cc. 447–452; 810 H.C. Deb., cc. 739–740.

always be the case. Two examples will be considered:

(*a*) *Tenancies*. A tenant of a farm may owe a contractual obligation to his landlord to erect and maintain the farm fences. This may have nothing whatsoever to do with any obligation owed by either the landlord or the tenant to a neighbouring occupier of land. Indeed there may well be no such obligation. This situation may be illustrated by the common law decision in *Park* v. *J. Jobson & Son.*[7] Here, tenants of allotments which adjoined a farm agreed with their landlord to maintain the fences against the farm. In fact their landlord was also the landlord of the farm but this is not significant for present purposes. When cattle from the farm strayed on to the allotments the tenant of one of the allotments sued the farmer in cattle trespass. The fence was in disrepair and the livestock would not otherwise have strayed. Could the defendant farmer resist an action for cattle trespass on the ground that the plaintiff was in breach of his fencing obligations?

This was, therefore, a case where the plaintiff was under an obligation to fence but the obligation was owed to a third party and not to the defendant. As the plaintiff's obligation to fence was a contractual one owed to his landlord, his breach of that obligation was no defence to an action of cattle trespass against the farmer from whose land the cattle had strayed. The latter could not rely on a fencing obligation owed by the plaintiff to a third party. As has been said by RIDLEY, J.:

> "The obligation [to fence] upon the plaintiff . . . is a secondary one and is an obligation as between himself and the landlord, but there is an obligation upon the defendant if he brings cattle upon his land to keep them from straying, and he cannot take advantage of the plaintiff's breach of contract with the landlord by claiming a right to let his cattle escape through the gaps in the fence and trespass on the plaintiff's land."[8]

Could a tenant of the allotments succeed to-day in an action

---

[7] [1945] 1 All E.R. 222; and see *Holgate* v. *Bleazard*, [1917] 1 K.B. 443, which was not cited in the former case.

[8] *Holgate* v. *Bleazard, supra*, at p. 447. On the question of the failure of a third party to fence, see *Sutcliffe* v. *Holmes*, [1947] K.B. 147, *infra*, pp. 144–145.

for straying livestock under s. 4 of the Animals Act 1971 or
could the farmer successfully raise the defence of failure to
fence under s. 5 (6)? The plaintiff was an occupier of the
allotment and so satisfied s. 4. It is assumed that he let the
fence get into disrepair and so was in breach of his fencing
obligation, owed to his landlord. The livestock would not have
strayed but for the breach by the plaintiff of his duty to fence.
The fact that it is owed to his landlord and not to the defendant
is, within the meaning of s. 5 (6), irrelevant. That being so the
defence of failure to fence is made out and the decision would
now be different from that at common law.[9]

(b) *Fencing against common or unenclosed land.* It is often
the case where a farm adjoins open moorland that there is an
obligation on the farmer to fence his land against the moor and
to fence out the livestock of those who have rights to pasture
such livestock on the moor. This might be illustrated by *Crow*
v. *Wood*.[10] It may be recalled that a large sheep moor in Yorkshire and its adjoining farms had been held in common ownership. One of the farms was sold to the plaintiff along with
rights to pasture sheep on the moor, which rights she never
exercised. A neighbouring farm with similar sheep rights over
the moor had earlier been sold to a third party and the rights,
appurtenant to that farm, to pasture sheep on the moor were let
by the new owners of the farm to the defendant. The plaintiff
in recent years had failed to maintain her fences against the
moor and the defendant's sheep, straying on the moor, strayed
on to the plaintiff's land. The plaintiff claimed damages for
cattle trespass and the defendant pleaded as a defence that the
plaintiff was in breach of her obligations to fence against the
moor. Much of the judgments in the Court of Appeal are
concerned with the question whether the plaintiff was under any
obligation to fence against the moor. The Court concluded
that there was a right to have the occupier of the plaintiff's
farm maintain the fences against the moor and that right had
passed to the owners of the neighbouring farm.[11] As Lord

---

[9] Similarly abrogated is the decision on this point in *Holgate* v. *Bleazard,
supra.*
[10] [1971] 1 Q.B. 77, *supra,* pp. 126–127.
[11] By reason of the Law of Property Act 1925, s. 62 (1). This aspect of the
decision is discussed *supra,* pp. 126–127.

DENNING, M.R. said:

"All the tenants of the common owner had previously enjoyed this right. The custom of the moor was that each farmer enjoyed this right. It was obviously enjoyed with the land and reputed to appertain to it. The result is that, in my opinion, each farmer next to Bilsdale West Moor had, on the one hand, a right to put so many sheep on the moor to stray: and each farmer, on the other hand, was under a duty to keep up his own walls and fences so as to keep the sheep of the other owners out."[12]

Having decided that the plaintiff was in breach of her fencing obligation, the Court of Appeal had no hesitation in finding for the defendant. There is an assumption in the judgments that the defendant could rely on the breach of the plaintiff's fencing obligation owed to the owner of the farm from whom the defendant had acquired his rights to stray sheep on the moor.

This position is unaltered by the Animals Act 1971. There is no requirement in s. 5 (6) that the person to whom the fencing obligation is owed should be the defendant or should be a person who has any interest in the land from which the livestock have strayed.[13] So long as the plaintiff is in breach of the fencing obligation, whether or not owed to the defendant, the defence under s. 5 (6) is available.

The general conclusion to be drawn is that the decision not to indicate in s. 5 (6) *to* whom the obligation to fence must be owed, provided it is owed *by* a person with an interest in the land strayed upon, will mean that a defendant can claim the benefit of a breach of a contractual or other fencing obligation to which he is not a party.

(2) *A fencing obligation owed by the plaintiff to the dominant tenant but relied on by a third party*

The basic situation to consider here is that where livestock other than those belonging to the dominant tenant are on the dominant tenement and stray from there on to the servient

---

[12] [1971] 1 Q.B. 77, 85.
[13] It was disputed in the House of Lords debates on s. 5 (6) whether the defendant in *Crow* v. *Wood, supra,* did have any such interest: 312 H.L. Deb. cc. 858–860; 313 H.L. Deb. cc. 449–451.

tenement. Furthermore, it is assumed that straying is as a result of the servient tenant's breach of his fencing obligation owed to the dominant tenant. Does that breach of the fencing obligation affect the servient tenant's right of action under s. 4 of the Animals Act 1971 against the possessor of the livestock ? It is proposed to examine the cases where the livestock is either lawfully or unlawfully present on the dominant tenement and to look, briefly, at the common law position before examining the effects of the Animals Act 1971.

(*a*) *Livestock lawfully present on the dominant tenement with the consent of the owner thereof.* If his livestock are lawfully present on the dominant tenement, the owner would appear, at common law, to be able to rely on the fencing obligations owed by the servient tenant to the dominant tenant.[14] Lawful presence includes various instances of the right to put livestock on the dominant tenement, such as the rights of the tenant of that land,[15] the person who has a right of common over it,[16] the rights of a licensee on the land[17] and the lawful user of a highway.[18]

Such a person may resist a statutory action for straying livestock under s. 4 of the Animals Act 1971 if his livestock, lawfully on the dominant tenement, stray onto the servient tenement as a result of the servient tenant's failure to fence.   A valid defence exists under s. 5 (6), for that subsection merely requires that the plaintiff's fencing obligation be owed *by* a person with an interest in the land strayed upon.   There is no requirement that the obligation be owed to the defendant or to a person with an interest in the land from which the livestock strayed.

(*b*) *Livestock unlawfully present on the dominant tenement.*
(*i*) *At common law.*   It was the case at common law that a

---

[14] *Pomfret* v. *Ricroft* (1669), 1 Saund. 321, 322 (c) ;   *Ricketts* v. *East and West India Docks etc. Co.* (1852), 12 C.B. 160, 174, 176.
[15] *Faldo* v. *Ridge* (1605), Yelv. 74, 75.
[16] *Sir Francis Leke's Case* (1579), 3 Dyer 365a.
[17] *Dawson* v. *Midland Rail. Co.* (1872), L.R. 8 Exch. 8; and see *Sir Francis Leke's Case, supra,* at p. 365b.
[18] E.g. *Dovaston* v. *Payne* (1795), 2 Hy. Bl. 527; *Midland Rail. Co.* v. *Daykin* (1855), 17 C.B. 126; the lawfulness of user of the highway is discussed in Chapter 3, *supra,* pp. 112–114.

servient tenant on to whose land cattle, trespassing on the dominant tenement, had strayed as a result of the servient tenant's breach of his obligation to fence could maintain an action of cattle trespass against the owner of such cattle. The defendant could not rely on the servient tenant's breach of his obligation to fence for it was not owed to him nor to anyone under whom he claimed.[19]   The position was summed up by WILMOT, C.J.:

> "If a man turn his cattle into Blackacre, where he has no right, and they escape and stray into my fields for want of fences, he cannot excuse himself, or justify for his cattle trespassing in my field."[20]

(ii) The effect of the Animals Act 1971.   It will be recalled that nothing is said in s. 5 (6) as to the person to whom the duty to fence must be owed in order for the defence of failure to fence, i.e. the defence under s. 5 (1) that the damage was due wholly to the fault of the plaintiff, to operate.   It will also be recalled that so far as the defendant in an action for straying livestock is concerned, s. 4 refers to the liability of the possessor of the livestock.   He may be either the dominant tenant, or he may be a third party whose livestock are either lawfully on[1] or are trespassing on the dominant tenement.   Under the common law of cattle trespass, as has been seen, the first two but not the third could rely on the breach by the servient tenant of his fencing obligation to the dominant tenant as a defence.   The Animals Act 1971 is silent on this matter.   It cannot be resolved by reference to the specific fencing provisions of s. 5 (6) save to suggest that, as there is no indication in that subsection of to whom the fencing obligation must be owed, a trespasser can shelter behind it.

It may be, however, that s. 5 (1) takes the matter further. Can it be said that damage is due wholly to the fault of the plaintiff, the servient tenant who is in breach of his obligation

---

[19] This may have been because the obligation existed, at least originally, only between neighbouring and contiguous tenements: *King* v. *Rose* (1673), Freem. K.B. 347; and see *Ibid.*, p. 356; *Right* v. *Baynard* (1674), Freem. K.B. 379; *Sutcliffe* v. *Holmes*, [1947] K.B. 147, 154,
[20] *Anon* (1770), 3 Wils. 126; and see *Dovaston* v. *Payne* (1795), 2 Hy. Bl. 527.
[1] Discussed, *supra*, p. 140.

to fence owed to the dominant tenant, when the livestock which stray from the dominant tenement are those which are there unlawfully?   If not, then s. 5 (1) will provide a defence. However, the lawfulness of the presence of the defendant's livestock on the dominant tenement would appear to be quite irrelevant to the fault of the servient tenant in failing to maintain his fences.   The livestock would have strayed through the defective fences whether they were lawfully or unlawfully present on the dominant tenement.   If that argument is accepted, then the Act has produced a change in the common law and a person with no interest in, or lawful presence on, the dominant tenement may rely on the servient tenant's failure to fence against the dominant tenement as a defence to liability for straying livestock.   In other words, the defence does not operate against the dominant tenant but against any possessor of livestock which stray from the dominant tenement.   This is difficult to justify in the case of so unmeritorious a defendant as the person whose livestock are unlawfully present on the dominant tenement.   This conclusion can only be avoided in such a case by holding that the plaintiff's injury is not due wholly to his own fault within the meaning of s. 5 (1).

Finally, it has been assumed so far that it is clear when livestock are unlawfully on the dominant tenement.   Any livestock present without the consent of the dominant tenant or without some other lawful authority would seem to fall within the above discussion.   One case worthy of special mention concerns common land.   If a commoner has a right to turn out a fixed number of animals on to the common he is liable at the suit of other commoners if he turns out more than his allotted number and surcharges the common land.[2]   If he turns out too many animals and some then stray on to a neighbour's land as a result of that neighbour's failure to fence, the excessive number of animals on the common are not considered to be there unlawfully *vis à vis* the plaintiff.[3]

---

[2] See Harris & Ryan, *The Law Relating to Common Land,* pp. 68–70.
[3] *Vivian* v. *Dalton* (1896), 41 Sol. Jo. 129; this was, in fact, a case of cattle trespass and distress damage feasant.

(3) *A fencing obligation owed to the dominant tenant by a person other than the plaintiff*

(i) At common law. Not only did breach of an obligation to fence by the occupier of the servient tenement provide a defence to an action of cattle trespass but breach of such an obligation by the owner out of occupation could also have this effect. If, as in *Wiseman* v. *Booker*,[4] a landlord was under an obligation to fence, then if this obligation was broken his tenant could not maintain an action of cattle trespass against the occupier of the dominant tenement whose horses "trespassed"[5] on to the servient tenement occupied by the tenant and there damaged his crops. The tenant could be in no better position than the landlord.[6]

If, however, the plaintiff was an employee upon whose employer the obligation to fence was placed then the former could not maintain an action of cattle trespass against the owner of pigs which strayed through the defective fence on to his employer's property and there injured him.[7] The employee had no interest in the land such as to maintain an action of cattle trespass;[8] but an action might lie against his employer or the owner of the pigs on proof of negligence.[9]

(ii) The effect of the Animals Act 1971. It is provided by s. 5 (6) that the defence of failure to fence thereunder depends upon "a breach by any other person, being a person having an interest in the land, of a duty to fence". There are two conditions contained herein. First, the person who is in breach of his fencing obligation must be someone other than the defendant, but there is no requirement that it must be the plaintiff. Secondly, that other person must both have a duty to fence and have an interest in the land whereon he is to fence.

The first comment to make on this provision is the obvious

---

[4] (1878), 3 C.P.D. 184, *supra,* pp. 106–107.
[5] This was no more than a technical trespass for the horses just put their heads over the fence.
[6] (1878), 3 C.P.D. 184, 188.
[7] *Child* v. *Hearn* (1874), L.R. 9 Exch. 176.
[8] *Supra,* Chapter 3, pp. 94–96.
[9] Common law liability is discussed, *infra,* Chapter 6.

one that breach of an obligation to fence by the occupier of the servient tenement, the duty to fence being owed by him, will bar his right to bring an action under s. 4 if the dominant tenant's livestock stray on to the servient tenement. Assuming that the duty to fence is placed on the owner of the servient tenement, it must, secondly, be asked what the position of his tenant is. Can the tenant bring an action if the dominant tenant's livestock stray on to the servient tenement? It would appear that he cannot. There has been a breach of a duty to fence by a person, other than the defendant, who has an interest in the land strayed upon, i.e. the owner of the servient tenement. It appears, therefore, that a landlord's breach of his obligation to fence will deprive his tenant of a right of action under s. 4, and the common law position as exemplified by *Wiseman* v. *Booker*[10] is unaltered.

Of course, s. 5 (6) does not apply just to the situation where the servient tenant is a landlord and the actual occupier of the land is his tenant, but that is the likeliest situation where land is occupied by someone other than the person upon whom the fencing obligation is placed. It should not be forgotten that an action under s. 4 can only lie at the suit of the owner or occupier of the land upon which the animals stray.[11]

A case which might be considered in this context is *Sutcliffe* v. *Holmes*.[12] The defendants' livestock strayed from the defendants' land on to that of a local authority as a result of the latter's failure to fence. They went from that land on to the plaintiff's land, the plaintiff being under no fencing obligation. The plaintiff's action for cattle trespass, at common law, would have failed on the basis of the defence of act of third party had the Court of Appeal not held that the defendants should have foreseen and guarded against it. That defence is not available, in any event, under s. 4. Is the statutory "fencing" defence under s. 5 (6) available? There was a duty to fence owed to the person, the defendant, from whose land the livestock strayed

---

[10] (1878), 3 C.P.D. 184, *supra*, pp. 106–107, 143.
[11] Hence an employee will still be unable to sue under s. 4.
[12] [1947] K.B. 147; and see *Redfern & Son, Ltd.* v. *Storey*, [1969] N.Z.L.R. 945.

but no duty to fence was owed by the plaintiff on to whose land the livestock eventually strayed. Within the meaning of s. 5 (6) there was a breach of a fencing obligation by a person other than the defendant and that person had an interest in the land he was obliged to fence. However, the phrase in s. 5 (6) "a person having an interest in the land" must be taken to refer to "the land of the plaintiff's which has been strayed upon".[13] In that case the defence under s. 5 (6) will not apply to facts such as those in *Sutcliffe* v. *Holmes* nor will it apply to any case where the fencing obligation is broken by a third party.[14]

Finally, one general comment should be made on the scope of the defence provided by s. 5 (6). It is only operative where it is proved that the straying would not have occurred but for a breach of a fencing obligation. What of the situation where the plaintiff is under an obligation to fence which he satisfies by the provision of a reasonable fence[15] and yet the defendant's livestock stray on to his land? In this case the defendant is liable under s. 4. If the plaintiff is in breach of his fencing obligation but the circumstances are such that even had he fenced as required he could not have kept the defendant's particular livestock out, as where they are sheep "of a peculiarly wandering and saltative disposition,[16] then the failure to fence does not appear to constitute a defence. The position seems to be the same as that where there was an adequate fence and yet, nevertheless, the livestock strayed, for in such a case they would have strayed even without the breach by the plaintiff of his fencing obligation.

It should not be forgotten that if neither of the occupiers of adjoining land is under an obligation to fence then both occupiers owe a duty to prevent their livestock from straying,[17] and neither can recover for injuries to their livestock on the other's land.[18]

---

[13] This is because s. 5 (6) is dependent upon s. 4 which refers to the plaintiff as the person in occupation of the land strayed upon.

[14] E.g. *Sharp* v. *Harvey*, [1935] L.J.C.C.R. 261; and see *Cooke* v. *Skinner* (1948), 98 L. Jo. 38.

[15] *Supra*, pp. 128–130.

[16] *Coaker* v. *Willcocks*, [1911] 1 K.B. 649, 654, *supra,* p. 129.

[17] *Cf.,* e.g. *Kempston* v. *Butler* (1861), 12 I.C.L.R. 516.

[18] *Ponting* v. *Noakes*, [1894] 2 Q.B. 281; and see *Roberts* v. *Great Western Rail. Co.* (1858), 4 C.B.N.S. 506.

(4)   *Multiple obligations to fence*

The situation envisaged here is that where Blackacre, Whiteacre and Greenacre are contiguous. G, the owner of Greenacre, is bound to fence against Whiteacre and W, the owner of Whiteacre is bound to fence against Blackacre. Livestock belonging to B, the owner of Blackacre, stray on to Whiteacre as a result of W's failure to fence[19] and then, as a result of G's failure to fence, they stray on to Greenacre. What are the consequences of this straying as between B and G ?

(a) B is not statutorily liable for straying livestock. Although there was authority at common law to support the view that B could not rely on G's failure to fence as a defence to an action for cattle trespass because the duty to fence was owed to W and not to B,[20] the statutory position would appear to be that B can rely on the breach of a fencing obligation owed to a third party.   B's livestock would not have strayed on to Greenacre but for the breach of his fencing obligation by G.   As G is a person who has an interest in the land strayed upon, the conditions of s. 5 (6) appear to be satisfied and B has a good defence.   There is no requirement in s. 5 (6) that the fencing obligation which has been broken should have been owed to the defendant.

(b) B may be unable to sue G for injury done to his livestock on Greenacre.   Such a conclusion would follow if the cases at common law holding B liable for cattle trespass[1] are to be applied by analogy here.   This is an undesirable result for, as Williams has pointed out in the cattle trespass context,[2] it may well be that B can sue W for the consequences of W's failure to fence and W may then sue G for the damages paid to B, this latter action being based upon G's breach of his fencing obligation to W.   Circuity of action would be avoided by allowing B to sue G for the damage done to B's livestock.   If

---

[19] The situation where they stray as a result of B's failure to fence has already been discussed, *supra*, pp. 140–142.
[20] *Anon* (1482), Jenk. 161; *Right* v. *Baynard* (1674), Freem. K.B. 379; and see *Harvey* v. *Gulson* (1604), Noy. 107; these decisions are criticised by Williams, pp. 220–221.
[1] See *supra*, N.20.
[2] Williams, p. 221.

G's obligation to fence is to fence against livestock lawfully on Whiteacre it is hard to classify cattle thereon as a result of W's failure to fence other than as being lawfully there.

A variation of this general problem of multiple fencing obligations might properly be considered here. Again, Blackacre, Whiteacre and Greenacre are contiguous. W, the owner of Whiteacre, is obliged to fence against Blackacre but G, the owner of Greenacre, is not obliged to fence against Whiteacre. Livestock belonging to B, the owner of Blackacre, stray from Blackacre on to Whiteacre as a result of W's defective fences. They then stray from there on to Greenacre. What are B's rights and obligations in this type of case?

(a) If B's livestock are injured on Greenacre, B can claim damages from W; for the animals would not have strayed in the first place but for W's breach of his fencing obligations to B.[3] No liability based on breach of an obligation to fence exists between G and B.

(b) If B's livestock cause damage to Greenacre and G sues B under s. 4 of the Animals Act 1971, can B rely on the protection of s. 5 (6)? There is no doubt that the livestock strayed in the first instance as the result of the breach of a duty to fence owed by W to B. However, B cannot claim under s. 5 (6) that the straying would not have occurred but for a breach of a fencing obligation by a person who has an interest in Greenacre, and so B would be liable to G under s. 4.

Furthermore B is unable under the Animals Act 1971 to plead the common law defence of act of third party[4] in that the livestock would not have strayed on to Greenacre but for W's failure to fence them out of Whiteacre. There does, then, remain the question whether B can obtain some redress from W for his statutory liability to G. There is authority both academic[5] and judicial[6] to support a claim by B against W for

---

[3] *Singleton* v. *Williamson* (1861), 7 H. & N. 410, 416.
[4] See Chapter 3, *supra*, p. 115; *cf. Sutcliffe* v. *Holmes*, [1947] K.B. 147; and see also *Sharp* v. *Harvey*, [1935] L.J.C.C.R. 261.
[5] Williams, pp. 222–223.
[6] E.g. *Holbach* v. *Warner* (1623), Cro. Jac. 665; *Right* v. *Baynard* (1674), Freem. K.B. 379, 380; and see *Dunlop* v. *Troy*, [1915] V.L.R. 639 where, however, the action had a contractual basis.

damages for breach of W's fencing obligation owed to B.

It has been argued by Williams[7] that to allow G to recover damages from B based, now, on a statutory action for straying livestock and then to allow B to recover an indemnity as to those damages from W, based on breach of a fencing obligation, promotes circuity of action and that a far better solution would be to deny G an action against B but to give him an action in negligence against W. Not only has this argument been considered judicially at common law and rejected,[8] but there is no warrant within the terms of the Animals Act 1971 for denying G his statutory right of action against B under s. 4.

---

[7] Williams, p. 223.
[8] *Sutcliffe* v. *Holmes,* [1947] K.B. 147, 156.

5

ANIMALS AND THE HIGHWAY

(a) Introduction

There are various bases of liability which concern harm done by animals which have strayed onto or from a highway, or have caused injuries or damage whilst lawfully on the highway. Indeed, it has been seen already that the fact that livestock was lawfully on a highway before it strayed is a defence to an action under s. 4 of the Animals Act 1971.[1] The purpose of this chapter is to gather together the examination of the various bases of liability for harm done by animals in connection with their use of the highway. Whilst liability in nuisance and in trespass does exist in such cases and will be considered in due course, the prime area for examination is that of liability in negligence, especially because of substantial changes in such liability brought about by s. 8 of the Animals Act 1971.

(b) Negligence

There are three factual situations in which discussion of liability in negligence is relevant. They are the cases of animals straying onto the highway as the result of negligence and there causing injury to users of the highway; injuries caused by an animal which has been lawfully taken onto the highway but whose keeper has acted negligently in permitting it to cause injury to persons using the highway; and the related case of such injury being caused by animals straying from the highway.

---

[1] *Supra*, pp. 112–114.

(i)   Animals straying onto the highway

The general rule at common law[2] was that an occupier of land
was under no duty to erect or maintain fences so as to fence his
land off from the highway[3] and was under no liability if his
domestic animals strayed onto the highway and there injured a
user of the highway, whether the straying was caused by his
negligent failure to build or maintain fences or by some other
factor.   This rule was confirmed in the House of Lords decision
in *Searle* v. *Wallbank*.[4] Here a cyclist collided with the
defendant's horse which was on the highway, having escaped
from an adjoining field where the defendant had put it.   The
plaintiff's claim in negligence failed, for the court held that
there was no general duty cast upon the defendant to use
reasonable care to prevent the horse from straying.

To this general rule there were a number of possible exceptions, though they were exceptions that were more often
explained than applied.   First, if the owner of a domestic
animal brought it onto the highway and it there caused damage
to persons or property on or adjoining the highway then he
would, and will,[5] be liable provided negligence can be proved.[6]
Secondly, if an animal with a known vicious propensity was
allowed to stray onto the highway or if there were other
special circumstances concerning the characteristics of the
animal which took the case out of the general rule, then the
owner might be held liable in negligence for injuries caused by
the animal,[7] as where a dog tended to act like "a missile",[8] but
not just where it was blind.[9]   There was a third probable
exception, namely where there were special circumstances
which imposed liability, other than the propensities of the

---

[2] Williams, Part 6; Winfield and Jolowicz, *Tort*, 9th ed. 400; Salmond,
Torts, 15th ed. 446–450; Bentham (1958) 3 U. Qd. L.J. 222; Toohey (1966)
7 U.W.A.L.R. 490.
[3] *Potter* v. *Perry* (1859), 23 J.P. 644.
[4] [1947] A.C. 341.
[5] *Infra*, pp. 161–162.
[6] E.g. *Deen* v. *Davies*, [1935] 2 K.B. 282; *Gomberg* v. *Smith*, [1963] 1 Q.B. 25.
[7] *Searle* v. *Wallbank*, [1947] A.C. 341, 356–357, 359–360; *Wright* v. *Callwood*,
[1950] 2 K.B. 515, 527–528, 529–530; *Brock* v. *Richards*, [1951] 1 K.B. 529,
536–538; *Gomberg* v. *Smith*, [1963] 1 Q.B. 25, 32–34, 37; *Ellis* v. *Johnstone*,
[1963] 2 Q.B. 8, 21–23, 25–26, 28–32; *Bativala* v. *West*, [1970] 1 Q.B. 716.
[8] *Ellis* v. *Johnstone*, *supra*, at pp. 25–26.
[9] *Millns* v. *Garrett* (1906), *Times*, March 6th.

animal, such as the peculiar topography[10] or the fact that the
animal was engaged in an activity which could only be carried
on under a high degree of human control,[11] but not, perhaps, the
circumstances of darkness.[12]

The general rule in *Searle* v. *Wallbank* excluding liability in
negligence has been subjected to vigorous and sustained
criticism.[13] It has been described as "an outrageous subsidy
shamelessly exacted by the farming lobby at the expense of
public safety."[14] There has long been considerable debate on
this issue in other common law jurisdictions and, although
approval of the rule has been expressed in Ireland[15] and New
Zealand,[16] it has been disapproved of in Canada,[17] Australia[18]
and Scotland.[19] Various attempts have been made in England
to abolish the rule[20] culminating in the provisions of the
Animals Act 1971, s. 8 of which states:

"(1) So much of the rules of the common law relating to liability
for negligence as excludes or restricts the duty which a person
might owe to others to take such care as is reasonable to see
that damage[1] is not caused by animals straying on to a
highway is hereby abolished.

(2) Where damage is caused by animals straying from unfenced
land to a highway a person who placed them on the land shall
not be regarded as having committed a breach of the duty to
take care by reason only of placing them there if—

(a) the land is common land, or is land situated in an area

---

[10] *Ellis* v. *Johnstone, supra,* at pp. 21, 25–26.
[11] *Bativala* v. *West,* [1970] 1 Q.B. 716.
[12] *Anderson* v. *Wilson's Trustees* 1965 S.L.T. 35, 36 (Sh. Ct. Rep.).
[13] E.g. *Gomberg* v. *Smith, supra,* at pp. 31, 39–40; *Ellis* v. *Johnstone, supra,*
at p. 27; *Bativala* v. *West, supra,* at p. 724.
[14] Fleming, *Introduction to the Law of Torts,* 170.
[15] *Gibb* v. *Comerford,* [1942] I.R. 294; *cf. Dunphy* v. *Bryan* (1962), 97 I.L.T.R.
4.
[16] *Simeon* v. *Avery,* [1959] N.Z.L.R. 1345; *Ross* v. *McCarthy,* [1970] N.Z.L.R.
449.
[17] *Fleming* v. *Atkinson* (1959), 18 D.L.R. (2d) 81.
[18] *Reyn* v. *Scott* (1968), 2 D.C.R. (N.S.W.) 13; Fleming, *Torts,* 4th ed. 309–310;
cf. Bentham (1958), 3 U.Qd. L.J. 222; *Hill* v. *Clarke* [1969] 2 N.S.W.R.
733.
[19] *Gardiner* v. *Miller* 1967 S.L.T. 29.
[20] North, (1966) 30 Conv. (N.S.) 44.
[1] Damage is defined here, as elsewhere in the Act, so as to include "the death
of, or injury to, any person (including any disease and any impairment of
physical or mental condition)": Animals Act 1971, s. 11.

where fencing is not customary, or is a town or village green; and

(b) he had a right to place the animals on that land."

This section of the Animals Act 1971 generated more Parliamentary debate than any other, indeed almost as much as all the other sections combined. The rule abolished by this section is:

"rooted in the social conditions of an earlier age when pastoral land in England was not normally fenced, and consequently straying animals on the highway were a normal hazard of the highway which any traveller on the highway had to expect and be prepared to meet. Nowadays such conditions only survive in relatively remote parts of the country; Dartmoor springs to mind as an example. Over the major part of England and Wales the relevant social conditions are vastly different."[2]

Nevertheless, it was strongly urged that to impose liability in negligence for straying animals was an intolerable burden, in terms of fencing and insurance, to place upon farmers. On the other side it was argued that the Act, in s. 8 (2), goes too far in the protection of farmers, especially in the case of animals straying from unfenced or common land. The end result is a compromise between the interest of the farmer and of the motorist which is "to some extent a judgment of Solomon."[3] In the past the scales have been weighed far too heavily against the motorist. As Lord GARDINER, L.C. said:

"Really, the farmers have been very lucky. The historical truth of the matter is that, whereas in nearly every walk of life we are all under a duty to take care to see that we do not injure our neighbours, their position has always been a complete exception. Farmers have been lucky to be in this exceptional position from the start; the dead and the injured have been unlucky."[4]

The basic effect of s. 8 (1) is to treat the case of animals straying onto a highway in no way different from other liability in negligence.[5] It does not put the owner or keeper of the

---

[2] *Bativala* v. *West*, [1970] 1 Q.B. 716, 724.
[3] 312 H.L. Deb. c. 200.
[4] 305 H.L. Deb. c. 562; *cf. Ross* v. *McCarthy*, [1970] N.Z.L.R. 449, 456.
[5] Liability under s. 8 applies to the Crown: Animals Act 1971, s. 12, discussed, *supra*, pp. 33–34.

animals in a peculiarly disadvantageous position. It merely removes a peculiar advantage. The effect of s. 8 (2) is to indicate that there is no presumption of negligence when animals stray from unfenced land. No peculiar benefit is conferred on the farmer who places animals on unfenced land. He is merely protected against an abnormal disadvantage.[6]

The effects of these two subsections will now be considered in more detail.

In abrogating the rule in *Searle* v. *Wallbank*, s. 8 (1) has rendered otiose any discussion of the scope of that rule; and, indeed, the same might be said of any discussion of the scope of s. 8 (1) itself, for when *Searle* v. *Wallbank* did not apply the common law of negligence did. Now that *Searle* v. *Wallbank* has gone, the common law of negligence applies throughout. There is no restriction on the generality of the application of negligence principles based upon either the type of animals which strayed or on the type of highway, e.g. footpath, bridle path, main road or motor-way, onto which they strayed.[7] In all cases liability will depend on general negligence principles. The law will be the same for straying dogs as for straying sheep. Indeed, it might be said that not only are the former as great an evil and danger as the latter,[8] but that s. 8 (1) will have as great an effect on the urban dog keeper as on the rural farmer.

The inherent flexibility[9] of general negligence principles applied to animals straying onto the highway means that one can but give examples of the types of factors which a court will weigh in considering whether a defendant has been negligent. If it is reasonable for him to fence and injury is attributable to a failure to fence, then, subject to s. 8 (2),[10] he may well be

---

[6] The Attorney-General would appear to have stated the position too widely when he said that s. 8 (2) "ensures that no liability shall fall on a person who grazes an animal on unfenced land in open parts of the country": 815 H.C. Deb. c. 603; *cf.* the Solicitor-General, H.C. Standing Committee A, 18th March 1971, c. 65.

[7] Law Commission Report, §§. 45–54.

[8] An average of 400–500 people are killed or seriously injured each year in road accidents caused by dogs: 810 H.L. Deb. c. 742.

[9] Twelfth Report of the Law Reform Committee for Scotland, (1963), §. 12; Report of the New South Wales Law Reform Commission (1970), L.R.C. 8, §. 21.

[10] Discussed, *infra*, pp. 157–160.

considered at fault in failing to do so.   However, his fences
need only be reasonable ones.   The fact that an animal got
through or over a normally satisfactory fence is not, as such,
conclusive of negligence.   Again, some intervening cause may
have rendered the fence inadequate; a trespasser may have
left a gate open; a motorist may have knocked part of it down;[11]
the electricity supply in an electric fence may have failed.
None of these, unless foreseeable or ignored, would indicate
fault on the part of the farmer.

Some indication of the types of conduct which may or may
not connote negligence in the case of animals straying from a
highway may be drawn from Canadian experience.   JUDSON, J.
in the Supreme Court of Canada held, in *Fleming* v. *Atkinson*,[12]
that the rule in *Searle* v. *Wallbank* did not apply in Ontario and
that—

> "there can be no difficulty in the application of the ordinary rules
> of negligence to the facts in this type of case and the matter
> should be left to the tribunal of fact to determine, with due regard
> to all the circumstances, including the nature of the highway and
> the amount and nature of the traffic that might reasonably be
> expected to be upon it, whether or not it would be negligent to
> allow a domestic animal to be at large."[13]

Although he was the only judge in that case expressly to
repudiate *Searle* v. *Wallbank*, his view has been adopted as the
law of Ontario,[14] and so, since 1959, the common law of Ontario
has achieved substantially the same result as is provided for
England and Wales by s. 8 of the Animals Act 1971.   It has
been said of JUDSON, J.'s judgment in that case that it "is a
classic example of how a judge should integrate legal and policy
considerations to justify adoption of a rule in adjudication."[15]

This judgment as to the law of Ontario has been adopted in

---

[11] He is under no obligation to report this fact: Road Traffic Act 1960, s. 79;
   Pagett v. *Mayo*, [1939] 2 K.B. 94; *Tucker* v. *Mackenzie*, 1955 S.C.(J.) 75.
[12] (1959), 18 D.L.R. (2d) 81.
[13] *Ibid.*, at p. 102.
[14] *Bonany and Bonany* v. *Gratton* (1960), 23 D.L.R. (2d) 591; *Colonial Coach
   Lines, Ltd.* v. *Bennett*, [1968] 1 O.R. 333.
[15] Weiler (1971), 21 U. Tor. L.J. 267, 273.

several other,[16] though not all,[17] Canadian Provinces with the
effect that a corpus of decisions, essentially factual, has been
built up on what constitutes negligence on the part of a farmer
whose animals stray onto the highway. This body of case law
may provide some guidance, by analogy, to the interpretation
of s. 8 (1) of the Animals Act 1971. Thus, it is not a case of
negligence if animals break through an ordinary reasonable
fence, especially if it is a new fence.[18] In many circumstances
a fence will be adequate even though insufficient to contain an
animal which is determined to escape; but it has been suggested
that if the defendant's land adjoined:

> "a heavily travelled, high speed road, he might well be required to
> use fencing, however expensive, through which his cattle could not
> possibly escape.[19] I do not think that one can require that when
> the land adjoins a gravel market road, which is lightly travelled."[20]

There is no negligence when cattle are contained by an electric
fence in good order and charged with current at all material
times and yet a cow gets onto the highway in some inexplicable
way.[1] Similarly, the use of a four foot fence to contain heifers
in heat was reasonable, even though heifers in such a condition
may become unruly and jump fences. As the judge said:

> "It would surely not be reasonable to ask farmers whose properties
> are adjacent to a public highway to erect eight-foot fences or such
> fences that no animal at any time would ever be able to break out
> of. Cows are persistent, and in spite of their apparent stupidity,
> are very resourceful when they wish to go from point A to point
> B."[2]

---

[16] E.g. Alberta: *Cooper* v. *Matteotti* (1968), 66 D.L.R. (2d) 338; British
Columbia: *Staul* v. *Crawford* (1968), 64 W.W.R. 568; Manitoba: *Gash* v.
Wood (1960), 22 D.L.R. (2d) 625; *Penner* v. *Allan* (1964), 43 W.W.R. 244;
Nova Scotia: *Crosby* v. *Curry* (1970), 7 D.L.R. (3d) 188; and in the Canadian
Exchequer Court in the case of an accident occurring in New Brunswick:
R. v. *DeWitt*, [1968] 1 Ex. C.R. 156.
[17] It has been rejected in New Brunswick: *Cormier* v. *McCarthy* (1969), 1
N.B.R. (2d) 866; and in Saskatchewan: *Lane* v. *Biel* (1971), 17 D.L.R. (3d)
632.
[18] *Cormier* v. *McCarthy, supra,* at p. 870.
[19] Whilst this may be an excessively high standard, it has been accepted that
the heavier the traffic the higher the duty of care: *R.* v. *DeWitt*, [1968]
Ex.C.R. 156.
[20] *Penner* v. *Allan* (1963), 43 W.W.R. 244, 245.
[1] *Crosby* v. *Curry* (1970), 7 D.L.R. (3d) 188.
[2] *Staul* v. *Crawford* (1968), 64 W.W.R. 568, 573.

Examples might also be given of conduct which has been considered to amount to common law negligence. The most dramatic example is provided by *Fleming* v. *Atkinson*[3] itself, where the defendant made no attempt to contain his cattle at all, the fences of his land being in a very poor state of repair and his cattle were regularly allowed to range over the highway. Again, to allow horses to roam over land adjoining a highway without any attempt to fence them in has been held to amount to negligence;[4] but even where animals are fenced in a farmer may be at fault if he does not regularly check the security of his fences, at least where they adjoin a busy road.[5] It has even been held that where A's land adjoins B's and B is under an obligation to fence, then if A knows that the fence is defective, A will be held liable in negligence if he puts animals into such an inadequately fenced field so that they stray from his land, onto B's land and thence onto a highway; though B may be liable to A for any injury to A's animals caused by a collision on the highway.[6] Finally, in the one relevant Australian decision,[7] a farmer who knew that his horse had the ability to open its paddock gate, and indeed had a propensity for so doing, was at fault in failing to take adequate steps, such as padlocking, to prevent this.

Although these common law decisions are no more than illustrative of the application of a general rule of negligence liability to the particular case of animals straying onto a highway, they give some indication of the types of issues to which the application of s. 8 (1) of the Animals Act 1971 may give rise. It does appear that in areas of heavy traffic, of fields well-stocked with animals or of high population the obligation imposed by s. 8 (1) may only be met by the provision of reasonably adequate fences. Particularly will this be true of liability for accidents in urban areas caused by dogs. Where a dog is allowed out onto the highway without a lead, or no adequate steps are taken to prevent it getting onto a highway, it will be

---

[3] (1959), 18 D.L.R. (2d) 81.
[4] *Bonany and Bonany* v. *Gratton* (1960), 23 D.L.R. (2d) 591.
[5] *Gash* v. *Wood* (1960), 22 D.L.R. (2d) 625.
[6] *Colonial Coach Lines, Ltd.* v. *Bennett*, [1968] 1 O.R. 333.
[7] *Reyn* v. *Scott* (1968), 2 D.C.R. (N.S.W.) 13.

very difficult to rebut an allegation of negligence. Animal owners put under a risk of liability by s. 8 (1) will find it prudent to insure, thereby spreading the burden over a wider sector of the community than its imposition on the victim of their negligence under the *Searle* v. *Wallbank* rule.

No definition of "animals" is provided in the Animals Act 1971. That being so, it must be furnished by the common law and it would appear that there may now be liability in negligence where not only cows, horses and sheep stray onto a highway, but also where dogs, cats and even poultry do so.[8] There is no restriction on the type of creature whose straying may involve liability in negligence,[9] and it is suggested that "animals" is apposite in this context to include poultry.[10]

Some protection for the keeper of animals is provided by s. 8 (2) of the Animals Act 1971 but only, it may be recalled, to the extent that there is to be no presumption of negligence from the fact that the animals strayed from unfenced land where such fencing is not customary and the defendant had a right to put his animals there. The detailed provisions of s. 8 (2) call for further examination. That subsection states:

"Where damage is caused by animals straying from unfenced land to a highway a person who placed them on the land shall not be regarded as having committed a breach of the duty to take care by reason only of placing them there if—

(a) the land is common land, or is land situated in an area where fencing is not customary, or is a town or village green; and

(b) he had a right to place the animals on that land."

One general comment on this subsection is that it applies to all cases of alleged liability for injury done by animals straying onto a highway and not just to such liability as is introduced by s. 8 (1) and the abrogation of the rule in *Searle* v. *Wallbank*. Section 8 (2) is drafted in terms wide enough to apply to any

[8] And, in appropriate circumstances, deer: Law Commission Report, §. 53.
[9] *Cf.* the doubts in the various Private Member's Bills on this topic; see North, (1966), 30 Conv. (N.S.) 44, 55–57.
[10] Though, undoubtedly, one factor in determining whether there was liability for allowing poultry to escape would be "the extreme difficulty of preventing poultry escaping on to the road": Twelfth Report of the Law Reform Committee for Scotland, (1963), §. 12. The same might be said of cats: see Law Commission Report, §. 54.

cases of liability which, at common law, fell outside the constricting effects of that rule, for the very scope of the rule had been "subject to qualifications of uncertain extent and authority."[11] It will now be the case that all liability in negligence for harm done by animals straying onto the highway, no matter what its provenance, will be subject to s. 8 (2).

Both that subsection and s. 8 (1) raise a number of detailed issues of definition:

(*a*) *Fencing*. The land to which s. 8 (2) applies must be "unfenced land" and, furthermore, one of the further possible conditions under s. 8 (2) (a) is that it is land where "fencing is not customary". Fencing is defined in s. 11 of the Animals Act 1971 as to include "the construction of any obstacle designed to prevent animals from straying". This includes not only fences, but also ditches whose object is not solely drainage but also the retention of animals. It would also include cattle grids. So, land which has no fences but which has some other obstacle such as a wide stock-proof ditch will not be regarded as unfenced land.

(*b*) *Types of unfenced land*. Three types of unfenced land are referred to in s. 8 (2), all of which raise issues of definition. The first is common land. This has the same meaning[12] as is given in the Commons Registration Act 1965, namely:

"(a) land[13] subject to rights of common (as defined in this Act) whether those rights are exercisable at all times or only during limited periods;

(b) waste land of a manor not subject to rights of common; but does not include a town or village green or any land which forms part of a highway."[14]

One reason for the inclusion of common land in the categories of unfenced land is that a commoner has, normally, no right to fence the land and, under the Law of Property Act 1925, s. 194, the consent of the Secretary of State for the Environment is required before common land may be fenced.[15]

---

[11] Law Commission Report, §. 30.
[12] Animals Act 1971, s. 11.
[13] Defined by s. 22 (1) of the Commons Registration Act 1965 to include "land covered with water".
[14] Commons Registration Act 1965, s. 22 (1); see Harris & Ryan, *The Law Relating to Common Land*, 8–10.
[15] See Harris & Ryan, *op. cit.*, 122.

The second type of unfenced land is a "town or village green", and, again, this is defined[16] by reference to the Commons Registration Act 1965 as:

"land which has been allotted by or under any Act for the exercise or recreation of the inhabitants of any locality or on which the inhabitants of any locality have a customary right to indulge in lawful sports and pastimes or on which the inhabitants of any locality have indulged in such sports and pastimes as of right for not less than twenty years."[17]

The third category is that of "land situated in an area where fencing is not customary". There is no definition of this provided by the Animals Act 1971 and its general vagueness may well be the source of considerable difficulty. The custom is that of the area and not that of the particular land in question. If it is customary to fence in the area, then the fact that the defendant's land has never been fenced may not bring the protection of s. 8 (2) into play; though it is difficult to assess the ambit of "area" for it can mean "anything from a couple of farms to Cumberland or South-East England".[18] Underlying this provision is the fact that some account must be taken of the circumstance that, in some areas of the country, highways run through unenclosed land, especially moorland, and it would be unreasonable to consider that a farmer who exercised his rights to graze sheep on such moorland should be held to be negligent merely because they strayed onto a road running across the moor. Whether fencing is "customary" will have to be decided according to the general usages of the area in question, but it may be that this provision could act as a deterrent against the very fencing that s. 8 is designed, in part, to encourage. No farmer will wish to upset a local custom of leaving land unfenced if no liability necessarily accrues from the failure to fence. If a farmer then does fence, he will have to maintain his fences and may be held liable if his animals stray as a result of the disrepair of his fences. An area of decaying walls and rotting fences is, probably, an area where fencing is

---

[16] Animals Act 1971, s. 11.
[17] Commons Registration Act 1965, s. 22 (1); Harris & Ryan, *op. cit.*, 27-29.
[18] 313 H.L. Deb. c. 460.

customary.   There is no provision for those areas, often on the
edge of moorland, where "bad or inadequate fencing is
customary".   Furthermore, no provision is made for the fact
that it may be customary not to fence although it is widely
agreed that the custom, in that area, is bad.

(c) *Right to place animals on unfenced land.*   In order for
there to be no presumption of negligence when animals stray
from unfenced land, the defendant must have had a right to
put his animals on that land.   A variety of persons will have
rights to pasture animals on unfenced land.   They will include
the owner or occupier of the land, a person with a contractual
right as under a contract of agistment, a non-contractual
licensee and, as with much unfenced land, a person with rights
of common over the land.

It might be asked what the effect on liability is, under s. 8,
of animals straying from unfenced land where they had no
right to be or where the right has been exceeded.[19]   What
s. 8 (2) suggests is that there is no presumption of negligence "by
reason only" of animals being placed on unfenced land if there
was a right to do so.   It does not also say that there is a
presumption of negligence if there was no right to place them
there.   Indeed it is difficult to see how the mere fact that
animals are kept on unfenced land for one day longer than they
are contractually permitted to be there makes it any more
foreseeable that they will stray onto a highway and cause
injury.   Perhaps the most that can be said for s. 8 (2) is that it
excludes the operation of the maxim *res ipsa loquitur* in determining the negligence of someone who has a right to pasture
his animals on unfenced land.

(d) *Highway.*   No definition is provided in the Animals Act
1971 of a "highway".   The rule in *Searle* v. *Wallbank* had been
applied not only to highways where there was a right of passage
for vehicular traffic, but also to public footpaths.[20]   It is
suggested that the meaning of "highway" for the purposes of
s. 8 is the general common law meaning of "all portions of land

---

[19] It could be exceeded, for example, by the animals being kept on the land for
    too long a period or by too many being pastured on the land.
[20] *Fitzgerald* v. *E.D. & A.D. Cooke Bourne (Farms), Ltd.,* [1964] 1 Q.B. 249.

over which every subject of the Crown may lawfully pass."[1]
This is an unlimited definition which would include footpaths
and bridleways as well as all public roads. This has the result
that not only will a farmer be under a duty of care in relation to
his animals straying onto roads, but he will also owe a duty of
care to those persons who use a highway, such as a footpath,
across his land. If that footpath crosses a field wherein animals
are pastured and those animals injure users of the highway, then
the farmer will be held liable if such injuries are the result of
his negligence. He will, however, only be liable if he has
been negligent and it has been suggested that:

> "it would be too much to expect that an 'ordinarily careful' owner
> of fillies should refrain from keeping them in a field where there is
> a public highway merely because there is a chance that one of the
> fillies in a playful mood might . . . come in contact with and
> injure someone lawfully walking along the highway."[2]

(*ii*) *Animals lawfully on the highway causing injury there*

It has been settled since the seventeenth century that an
obligation of care is imposed on anyone who takes a horse out
onto a highway.[3] This is a general obligation which is, in fact,
applicable to all who take any animals onto the highway. For
example, if a horse bolts and knocks a cyclist over;[4] if a pony is
insecurely tethered so that it escapes and injures a pedestrian;[5]
if a pony is left unattended for so long that it becomes restive
and causes injury;[6] if a large St. Bernard dog escapes and
collides with a car,[7] then in all these cases there will be liability
for such damage or injury if negligence is proved.

It is undoubtedly true, as in all negligence cases, "that what
constitutes 'reasonable care' is a question of fact in each case".[8]
All that one can do is to point to a variety of factors which may
be relevant in deciding whether adequate care has been taken.

---

[1] Pratt & Mackenzie, *Law of Highways*, 21st ed. 3.
[2] *Fitzgerald* v. *E.D. & A.D. Cooke Bourne (Farms), Ltd.*, *supra*, at p. 265.
[3] *Mitchil* v. *Alestree* (1676), 1 Vent. 295.
[4] *Turner* v. *Coates*, [1917] 1 K.B. 670.
[5] *Deen* v. *Davies*, [1935] 2 K.B. 282.
[6] *Aldham* v. *United Dairies (London), Ltd.*, [1940] 1 K.B. 507.
[7] *Gomberg* v. *Smith*, [1963] 1 Q.B. 25
[8] *Ibid.*, at p. 30.

The standard of care may vary as between town and country,[9] and as between day and night.[10]   Other factors would be the number[11] and age[12] of the animals involved, the extent to which they were used to traffic conditions,[13] the number of people available to control them,[14] the measures taken to secure unattended animals,[15] whether the animals were adequately lit at night,[16] the weather conditions[17] or even the width of the road.[18]

Not only may there be liability in negligence for harm done by animals which are lawfully being taken or driven along a highway, but, for example, there may also be liability in negligence for injuries caused by animals which are kept in a parked car on the highway.[19]   Again, however, liability depends on the facts of the particular case.[20]

(*iii*)   *Animals straying from the highway*

There was no liability in cattle trespass where animals lawfully on the highway strayed from the highway onto the plaintiff's land.[1]   Similarly, there is no liability for damage done by straying livestock under s. 4 of the Animals Act 1971 if such animals stray from the highway.   This is because of the special defence provided by s. 5 (5) of that Act to protect the owner of livestock lawfully on the highway from such liability.[2]

---

[9] *Gomberg* v. *Smith*, [1963] 1 Q.B. 25; and see *Deen* v. *Davies, supra,* at pp. 286, 299.
[10] *Turner* v. *Coates, supra; Griffith* v. *Turner,* [1955] N.Z.L.R. 1035.
[11] *Paul* v. *Rowe* (1904), 24 N.Z.L.R. 641.
[12] *Turner* v. *Coates, supra.*
[13] *Ibid.;* and see *Purdon* v. *Scott,* [1968] N.Z.L.R. 83.
[14] *Hill* v. *Clark,* [1969] 2 N.S.W.R. 733.
[15] *Gayler and Pope, Ltd.* v. *B. Davies & Son, Ltd.,* [1924] 2 K.B. 75.
[16] *Turnbull* v. *Wieland* (1916), 33 T.L.R. 143; *Gardner* v. *Della Santa,* [1968] S.A.S.R. 345; *cf. Catchpole* v. *Minster* (1913), 30 T.L.R. 111.
[17] *E. J. Lett & Co.* v. *Air Contracts, Ltd.* (1968), 12 M.C.D. 360.
[18] *Nickells* v. *Melbourne Corpn.* (1938), 56 C.L.R. 219.
[19] *Sycamore* v. *Ley* (1932), 147 L.T. 342, 345.
[20] *Fardon* v. *Harcourt-Rivington* (1932), 146 L.T. 391; *Sycamore* v. *Ley, supra.*
[1] *Tillett* v. *Ward* (1882), 10 Q.B.D. 17; *Goldston* v. *Bradshaw,* [1934] L.J.N. C.C.R. 355; *Esso Petroleum Co., Ltd.* v. *Southport Corpn.,* [1956] A.C. 218, 244.
[2] *Supra,* pp. 112–114.

Thus, "a bull may stray from the highway into a china shop without imposing liability on its owner".[3]   In the leading case of *Tillett* v. *Ward*[4] an ox strayed into an ironmonger's shop from the highway.   No negligence was proved.   There was no liability.

Although occupiers of land adjoining a highway are deemed to assume the risks of livestock straying from the highway where there is no fault on the part of the defendant,[5] the position is quite different where that straying is caused by negligence.   The leading authority is *Gayler and Pope, Ltd.* v. *B. Davies & Son, Ltd.*[6]   The defendants' pony and milk van had been left unattended in the street.   The pony bolted and crashed through the plaintiffs' shop window causing a good deal of damage to the goods inside the plaintiffs' drapers shop. Although a claim in trespass failed, McCARDIE, J. held that "when a pony and van, wholly unattended, dash into a plaintiff's shop window adjoining a highway there is a prima facie case of negligence."[7]   The defendants were held liable in negligence.

Although there is no liability under s. 4 of the Animals Act 1971 when livestock stray from the highway onto the plaintiff's land,[8] a problem may arise when such animals do stray and are not removed by their owner.   Under the Animals Act 1971 this failure to remove them does not affect their owner's non-liability under s. 4.   It is possible, however, that an action might lie against him in negligence.   The problem arose, at common law, in *Goodwyn* v. *Cheveley*.[9]   The plaintiff's drover was driving cattle along the highway when some strayed onto the defendant's land.   The drover left them where they were and took the remaining cattle to their destination for the night and returned an hour later for the errant ones.   By that time

---

[3] *Manton* v. *Brocklebank*, [1923] 2 K.B. 212, 231.
[4] (1882), 10 Q.B.D. 17.
[5] *Fletcher* v. *Rylands* (1866), L.R. 1 Exch. 265, 286; *Tillett* v. *Ward* (1882), 10 Q.B.D. 17, 20; *Gayler and Pope, Ltd.* v. *B. Davies & Son, Ltd.*, [1924] 2 K.B. 75, 82–84; Animals Act 1971, s. 5 (5).
[6] [1924] 2 K.B. 75.
[7] *Ibid.*, at p. 87.
[8] Section 5 (5), *supra*, pp. 112–114.
[9] (1859), 4 H. & N. 631; see also *Butcher* v. *Smith* (1868), 5 W.W. & a'B 223; *Bourchier* v. *Mitchell* (1891), 17 V.L.R. 27.

the defendant had impounded them. The plaintiff sued in
trespass and, in defence, it was argued that as the plaintiff had
not removed his cattle within a reasonable time the defendant
was justified in impounding them. The court held that it was
for the jury to decide what constituted a reasonable time in all
the circumstances of the case which included not only time to
remove the straying cattle but also time to make the others
safe. Nevertheless, it is clear that where cattle strayed from a
highway onto the defendant's land, although this gave rise to no
action in cattle trespass, the defendant could impound them if
there were left on his land for an unreasonable length of time.
Presumably the basis for this right is dependent upon the fact
that once the reasonable period had elapsed, a right of action in
cattle trespass arose.

When one turns to the statutory position under the Animals
Act, it will be recalled[10] that the defence to an action under s. 4
of the Animals Act 1971 provided by s. 5 (5) of that Act, i.e.
animals lawfully on the highway straying onto the plaintiff's
land, has no requirement or qualification that the animals be
removed within a reasonable time. Nevertheless, there could
be great inconvenience caused to an occupier of land adjoining
the highway if livestock straying there from the highway were
left to graze on his land for any great length of time. The right
to detain straying livestock, under s. 7 of the Animals Act
1971,[11] is of little real assistance; for, if the person onto whose
land they have strayed had no claim under s. 4, the right to
detain until the livestock is claimed by the plaintiff[12] is worth-
less in terms of recompense for the damage resulting from the
inordinate delay in the plaintiff's collecting them. If he has no
claim under s. 4, he cannot keep the proceeds of any sale in
exercise of his rights under s. 7 to offset his expenses and loss.[13]
One possible solution to this dilemma is to adapt the principle
of *Goodwyn* v. *Cheveley*[14] to present circumstances and hold that
he who unreasonably leaves his animals on another's land after

---

[10] *Supra*, pp. 112–114.
[11] *Supra*, pp. 115–123.
[12] Animals Act 1971, s. 7 (3) (c).
[13] Animals Act 1971, s. 7 (5), *supra*, p. 120.
[14] (1859), 4 H. & N. 631.

they have strayed from the highway will be liable in negligence for any harm that they do as a result of the unreasonable delay. In other words, although there is no liability under s. 4 of the Animals Act 1971 for allowing them to stray from the highway, this should not preclude liability, at common law, in negligence for unreasonable delay in removing them.

(c) Nuisance

If animals stray onto the highway in such numbers that their presence causes an obstruction, then it is probable that that constitutes an actionable public nuisance if it interferes with the right of free passage.[15] The presence, however, of a single animal[15] or even of a few animals[17] is much less likely to be considered to constitute a nuisance. For, as Lord DU PARCQ has said:

"The stray horse on the road does not seriously interfere with the exercise of a common right, and is no more a nuisance in law, merely by reason of its presence there, than the fallen carthorse or its modern analogue, the lorry which has temporarily broken down."[18]

If a dog or some other animal escapes whilst on the highway or, perhaps, escapes onto the highway, this may well constitute a nuisance if the animal poses some hazard additional to that of its mere presence. In *Pitcher* v. *Martin*,[19] it was held that a dog running on the highway with a long lead trailing from its collar constituted an actionable nuisance.[20] The dog had escaped whilst being taken for a walk on the highway and its lead had become entangled with the plaintiff's legs causing her to fall and injure herself.

---

[15] *Ellis* v. *Banyard* (1911), 106 L.T. 51, 52, 53; *Cunningham* v. *Whelan* (1917), 52 I.L.T.R. 67; *Hall* v. *Wightman*, [1926] N.I. 92, esp. at pp. 102–103; and see *Price* v. *Godfrey* (1884), 2 N.Z.L.R. 300, 302.
[16] *Higgins* v. *Searle* (1909), 100 L.T. 280, 281; *cf.* Williams, 384–385; *Howarth* v. *Straver* (1953), Bingham, *Motor Claims Cases*, 6th ed., 207–208.
[17] *Maddy* v. *Rutter*, [1934] L.J.C.C.R. 259.
[18] *Searle* v. *Wallbank*, [1947] A.C. 341, 361; *cf.* *Cox* v. *Burbidge* (1863), 32 L.J.C.P. 89, 92 (the report in 13 C.B.N.S. 430, 441 is slightly different); *Wood* v. *Madders*, [1935] L.J.C.C.R. 253, 254 (this last case would probably be regarded as wrongly decided in the light of *Searle* v. *Wallbank*).
[19] [1937] 3 All E.R. 918.
[20] It was decided by ATKINSON, J. that there was also liability in negligence.

It is a nuisance to leave a dead animal on the street for an unreasonable length of time[1] and, therefore, it is possible that an owner who allows his animals to stray onto the highway where they are later killed may be liable in nuisance for failure to remove their corpses.

(d)   Trespass and liability for straying livestock

As with negligence, there are three different situations to examine here in relation to liability in trespass for animals straying onto or from a highway.

(i)   *Straying onto the highway*

If an animal falling within the definition of "livestock"[2] strays onto a highway, then the owner or occupier of the highway would appear to be able to maintain an action under the Animals Act 1971, s. 4, for any damage done to the land or property thereon in the ownership or possession of the plaintiff.[3] It appears clear that, at common law, an action of cattle trespass[4] would lie in such circumstances.[5]   Certainly an action lay at the suit of the occupier of the highway[6] against a person who had put his animal out to graze on the highway.[7]   It may well be that this latter right of action is more properly classified as ordinary trespass to land, rather than as cattle trespass.[8]   If that is so, it remains unaffected by the fact that the Animals Act 1971 has abolished the tort of cattle trespass[9] and replaced

---

[1] *Percy Bros.* v. *Fly and Young,* [1917] N.Z.L.R. 451.
[2] Animals Act 1971, s. 11.
[3] Liability for straying livestock is discussed in Chapter 3, *supra.*
[4] *Durand* v. *Child* (1611), 1 Bulst. 157, *per* CROKE, J.; *Cox* v. *Burbidge* (1863), 13 C.B.N.S. 430, 435, 441; *Hadwell* v. *Righton,* [1907] 2 K.B. 345, 349; *Higgins* v. *Searle* (1909), 100 L.T. 280, 280–281; *Heath's Garage, Ltd.* v. *Hodges,* [1916] 2 K.B. 370, 377; Williams, 367–369; and see *Hayes* v. *Shire of Fitzroy* (1913), 7 Q.J.P.R. 42.
[5] It was also possible to distrain such animals damage feasant: *Dovaston* v. *Payne* (1795), 2 Hy. Bl. 527.   See now Animals Act 1971, s. 7, *supra,* pp. 115–123.
[6] *Cf. Haigh* v. *West,* [1893] 2 Q.B. 19; and see *Lade* v. *Shepherd* (1734), 2 Stra. 1004.
[7] *Stevens* v. *Whistler* (1809), 11 East 51.
[8] *R.* v. *Pratt* (1855), 4 E. & B. 860; *Hunt* v. *Shanks,* [1918] S.A.L.R. 254, 261–262; and see *Buckle* v. *Holmes* (1925), 42 T.L.R. 147, 148.
[9] Animals Act 1971, s. 1 (1) (c).

it with liability, under s. 4, for harm done by straying livestock. Moreover, such action for trespass to land applies to all animals whether "cattle", "livestock" or anything else. It will be a trespass to take an animal onto the highway for a purpose other than normal use of the highway and, for example, this might apply to the use of a highway by fox-hounds other than for normal passage and repassage.[10]

No action of cattle trespass lay, nor will an action lie under s. 4 of the Animals Act 1971, at the suit of a *user* of the highway against the person to whom an animal which has strayed onto the highway belongs. This is because the highway user's rights are limited to rights of passage and he has no necessary interest, unless he is the owner or occupier,[11] in the highway.[12]

(ii) *Straying from the highway onto the plaintiff's land*

It may be recalled[13] that, provided the use of the highway by the defendant is lawful, no action will lie under s. 4 of the Animals Act 1971 at the suit of an owner or occupier of land onto whose property livestock stray from the highway.[14] If, however, the defendant's use of the highway is unlawful[15] then not only is he liable to an action under s. 4, at the suit of the occupier of the highway, but also at the suit of the occupier or owner of land onto which the livestock stray from the highway.

If a lawful user of the highway, without authority, sends or takes his animals, including those other than "livestock", such as dogs, from the highway onto the plaintiff's land, then an action will lie against the defendant for trespass to land.[16] There is also liability for damage done by animals straying from the highway on proof of negligence.[17]

---

[10] *Cf. Paul* v. *Summerhayes* (1878), 4 Q.B.D. 9. As to what constitutes unlawful use of the highway, see *supra*, pp. 112–113.

[11] Animals Act 1971, s. 4 (1).

[12] *Cox* v. *Burbidge* (1863), 13 C.B.N.S. 430; *Hadwell* v. *Righton*, [1907] 2 K.B. 345; *Higgins* v. *Searle* (1909), 100 L.T. 280; and see *Heath's Garage, Ltd.* v. *Hodges*, [1916] 2 K.B. 370.

[13] *Supra*, Chapter 3, pp. 112–114.

[14] Animals Act 1971, s. 5 (5).

[15] Unlawful use of the highway is discussed, *supra*, pp. 112–113.

[16] *R.* v. *Pratt* (1855), 4 E. & B. 860, 864, 868.

[17] E.g. *Tillett* v. *Ward* (1882), 10 Q.B.D. 17, *supra*, p. 163.

(iii)   Straying onto the highway and thence onto the plaintiff's land

In these circumstances there would seem to be no reason why an action should not lie under s. 4 of the Animals Act 1971 in the case of straying "livestock", just as an action lay at common law for cattle trespass[18] in this type of case.   No defence is available to a claim under s. 4 of the Animals Act 1971 based on user of the highway, under s. 5 (5),[19] for the use of the highway would not appear to be lawful in this type of case.

It does seem anomalous that:

> "a person who puts his stock on a highway is not liable for their trespasses in the absence of negligence though, if they stray out to the highway without negligence on his part, [and thence stray onto other land] he is."[20]

The justification that adjoining landowners take the risk of accidental straying from the highway provided the animals are lawfully thereon is rather hollow in the light of the fact that they do not assume the risk of animals straying from neighbouring fields even though lawfully there. As Fleming has said: "None of this makes a great deal of sense."[1]

(e) Breach of statutory duty

Although it may constitute a criminal offence[2] for an owner to allow his animals, of various kinds, to stray onto the highway, such criminal liability is most unlikely to give rise to any civil liability for breach of statutory duty.[3]   NEVILLE, J. has

---

[18] *D'Agruima* v. *Seymour* (1951), 69 W.N. (N.S.W.) 15; and see *Poupart* v. *Brazil*, [1941] L.J.C.C.R. 223; *Creasy* v. *Abell*, [1945] L.J.C.C.R. 148; *Morris* v. *Curtis*, [1947] L.J.C.C.R. 284; *Cooke* v. *Skinner* (1948), 98 L. Jo. 38.

[19] Discussed, *supra*, pp. 112–114.

[20] *D'Agruima* v. *Seymour* (1951), 69 W.N. (N.S.W.) 15, 17.

[1] Fleming, *Torts*, 4th ed. 299.

[2] E.g. under the Highways Act 1959, s. 135 (1), as amended by the Criminal Justice Act 1967, Sched. 3, and the Highways Act 1971, s. 33; or under the Road Traffic Act 1960, s. 220.   See North (1966), 30 Conv. (N.S.) 44, 46; Law Commission Report, §§. 42, 49.

[3] *Cox* v. *Burbidge* (1863), 13 C.B.N.S. 430, 435–436; *Heath's Garage, Ltd.* v. *Hodges*, [1916] 2 K.B. 370, 376, 383–384; *Searle* v. *Wallbank*, [1947] A.C. 341, 362; and see *Maddy* v. *Rutter*, [1934] L.J.N.C.C.R. 259; *Creasy* v. *Abell*, [1945] L.J.C.C.R. 148, 154–155.   A similar view has been taken in New Zealand: *Simeon* v. *Avery*, [1959] N.Z.L.R. 1345, 1346; *Ross* v. *McCarthy*, [1969] N.Z.L.R. 691, affirmed, [1970] N.Z.L.R. 449; *cf. Turner* v. *August* (1909), 11 G.L.R. 715.

said, of the forerunners of the Highways Act 1959, that they:

> "do not, in my opinion, impose any civil liability in respect of animals trespassing upon the highway. So far as I know they have never been held so to do, and from their form I do not think they could have been intended to do so".[4]

It has been held, furthermore, that breach of bye-laws relating to London parks and open spaces does not give rise to a cause of action for injury caused by a dog.[5]

[4] *Heath's Garage, Ltd.* v. *Hodges*, [1916] 2 K.B. 370, 383–384.
[5] *Newman* v. *Francis*, [1953] 1 W.L.R. 402; and see *Rowan* v. *Mann* (1959), 19 D.L.R. (2d) 163; *Thordarson* v. *Zastre* (1968), 65 W.W.R. 555.

6

LIABILITY AT COMMON LAW

There is no doubt that there can be liability for harm done by animals outside the ambit of the Animals Act 1971. That Act deals primarily with the instances of strict liability for harm done by animals; but liability may also arise in the context of other heads of tortious liability, such as nuisance or negligence. So far as the problems of liability for harm done by animals on or by straying off the highway are concerned, these other heads of liability have been considered already,[1] but it is proposed in this chapter to consider, generally, such common law liabilities as remain unaffected by the Animals Act 1971.

It is quite clear that the torts of negligence, nuisance, trespass, liability under the Rule in *Rylands* v. *Fletcher*[2] and under the rules of occupiers' liability may arise through the use or agency of animals. This fact poses no particular problems for the application of the principles of these heads of tortious liability, but it may be helpful to consider instances where there may be such liability.

(a) Trespass[3]

It is undoubtedly an actionable trespass to the person to set a dog onto the plaintiff or to cause his horse to throw him off,[4] provided it is done intentionally. Equally it is a trespass to goods to set a dog onto the plaintiff's animals.[5]

---

[1] Chapter 5, *supra*.
[2] (1866), L.R. 1 Exch. 265, affirmed (1868), L.R. 3 H.L. 330.
[3] Williams, 340.
[4] *Scott* v. *Shepherd* (1773), 3 Wils. K.B. 403, 408.
[5] *Baker* v. *Webberley* (1631), Het. 171.

The action of trespass to land will lie when committed through the agency of an animal. It is actionable as trespass to land intentionally to take[6] or send an animal onto the plaintiff's land[7] or to drive the animal onto the land,[8] without the plaintiff's permission. Again, to leave cattle which have strayed onto the plaintiff's land on that land for an unreasonable length of time is a common law trespass.[9] It may even be a trespass although the cattle originally strayed as a result of the plaintiff's failure to fence.[10]

There is an obvious affinity between the action of trespass to land through the medium of an animal, on the one hand, and the action of cattle trespass or, as it now is, the statutory action for straying livestock under s. 4 of the Animals Act 1971, on the other hand. The basic distinction between the two forms of liability has been explained thus:

"If one's cattle stray, of their own volition, onto the land of another, without his consent, one thereby commits the tort of cattle-trespass; on the other hand if one's cattle get onto the land, not by straying, but because one deliberately drives them onto the land, one commits the ordinary tort of trespass to land. In the case of the ordinary tort of trespass to land, the cattle are merely the means whereby one commits the trespass. It would be equally ordinary trespass to land if one drove onto the land not cattle but a motor car."[11]

Important reasons for distinguishing between the statutory liability for straying livestock, under s. 4 of the Animals Act 1971, and liability at common law for trespass are that the former is restricted to "livestock", is a tort of strict liability and is subject to only the limited statutory defences, whereas the latter can apply to all animals, its defences exist at common law and it is unclear whether liability is based upon proof of

[6] *Beckwith* v. *Shordyke* (1767), 4 Burr. 2092.
[7] *R.* v. *Pratt* (1855), 4 E. & B. 860, 864–865; *Buckle* v. *Holmes* (1925), 42 T.L.R. 147, 148; and see *Dimmock* v. *Allenby* (1810), cited 2 Marsh, at p. 582.
[8] *Cf. Paul* v. *Summerhayes* (1878), 4 Q.B.D. 9.
[9] *Hunt* v. *Shanks*, [1918] S.A.L.R. 254.
[10] Williams, 223–224.
[11] Report of the New South Wales Law Reform Commission on Civil Liability for Animals, (1970), L.R.C. 8, §. 23.

fault.[12]   The nature of the distinction is put most cogently by
MURRAY, C.J. in *Hunt* v. *Shanks*:[13]

> "A man is answerable for the trespass of his cattle, if they stray
> without his knowledge and against his will into another person's
> land; but he is also answerable for his own acts of trespass, and
> if he unlawfully drives his cattle into another's land or permits
> them to remain there for an unreasonable time after he has become
> aware that they are trespassing, or breaks a fence, or opens a gate,
> with a view to inducing them to pass through, and they do pass
> through, the resulting trespass, in my opinion, is his trespass, and
> not merely the trespass of his cattle."

(b) Nuisance[14]

It is possible that an action for public nuisance will lie for
the obstruction of the highway by animals.[15] Further, an
action for private nuisance may lie where animals escape from
the defendant's land onto that of the plaintiff.   This can be
very relevant where, for example, a statutory action under s. 4
of the Animals Act 1971 is inapplicable because the animals do
not fall into the category of "livestock", as where they are
cats, dogs, or wild animals.   Thus, the owner of a dog which
escapes onto his neighbour's property, constantly fouling it,
may be liable in nuisance.[16]

If wild animals escape from the defendant's land they may
constitute a nuisance to the plaintiff's use and enjoyment of his
land, provided the animals in question have been brought or
attracted onto the defendant's land in the first place.   If they
are naturally there, then the defendant is unlikely to be held
liable in nuisance if they multiply and escape onto adjoining
land.   The basis of the liability should be that the defendant

---

[12] Street, *Torts,* 4th ed. 67; Fleming, *Torts,* 4th ed. 39; *National Coal Board* v.
J. E. Evans & Co. Cardiff, Ltd., [1951] 2 K.B. 861; *Fowler* v. *Lanning,*
[1959] 1 Q.B. 426; *Letang* v. *Cooper,* [1965] 1 Q.B. 232; *cf.* Treitel (1952),
15 M.L.R. 84.

[13] [1918] S.A.L.R. 254, 261.

[14] Williams, Chapter 14.   For a discussion of statutory nuisances by animals,
see Pearce & Meston, *Law of Nuisances,* Chapter 8; and also Garrett, *Law
of Nuisances,* 3rd ed. Chapter 6.

[15] See Chapter 5, *supra*; and see Report of the New South Wales Law Reform
Commission on Civil Laibility for Animals, (1970), L.R.C. 8, §. 32.

[16] *Cf. Curtis* v. *Thomson* (1956), 106 L.Jo. 61.

is "liable for damage caused . . . by extraordinary, non-natural, or unreasonable action".[17]

Thus, to bring an abnormal number of pheasants onto one's land can lead to liability in nuisance if they escape;[18] but there will be no such liability if the increase in the number of pheasants is due to unusually favourable weather rather than to any unreasonable action by the defendant.[19] If rabbits are naturally on the land, then their escape to the plaintiff's land should give rise to no liability in nuisance;[20] but if they are allured onto the defendant's land and then escape onto the plaintiff's land, then there may well be liability in nuisance.[1] The presence on the defendant's land of heaps of bones which attracted rats which later went onto the plaintiff's land and ate his crops has been considered not to be unreasonable, and not an actionable nuisance.[2] Yet an unusual and excessive collection of manure which attracted flies which bred in the manure and then went onto the plaintiff's land has been considered to be a nuisance,[3] as has a rubbish dump which attracted seagulls which damaged the plaintiff's plants.[4] So far as bees are concerned, it would seem clear that their escape can constitute a nuisance.[5] However, it is only in the keeping of an excessive number of bees, or keeping them in such a place as to cause discomfort to neighbours through their escape, that there will be liability.[6]

All the cases of nuisance considered so far have been ones where animals have interfered with the use and enjoyment of the plaintiff's land by escaping from the defendant's land.

---

[17] *Peech* v. *Best.* [1931] 1 K.B. 1, 14; and see *Farrer* v. *Nelson* (1885), 15 Q.B.D. 258, 260.
[18] *Farrer* v. *Nelson, supra.*
[19] *Seligman* v. *Docker,* [1949] 1 Ch. 53; and see *Robson* v. *Marquis of Londonderry* (1900), 34 I.L.T.R. 88; *Foley* v. *Berthoud* (1903), 37 I.L.T.R. 123.
[20] *Brady* v. *Warren,* [1900] 2 I.R. 632; *cf. Boulston's Case* (1597), 5 Co. Rep. 104b.
[1] *Pratt* v. *Young* (1952), 69 W.N. (N.S.W.) 214.
[2] *Stearn* v. *Prentice Bros., Ltd.,* [1919] 1 K.B. 394.
[3] *Bland* v. *Yates* (1914), 58 Sol. Jo. 612.
[4] *Plater* v. *Town of Collingwood* (1968), 65 D.L.R. (2d) 492.
[5] *O'Gorman* v. *O'Gorman,* [1903] 2 I.R. 573; *Parker* v. *Reynolds* (1906), *Times,* December 17th; and see Frimston, *Bee Keeping and the Law,* 7–8; Swan, *A Receiver of Stolen Property,* 8–9.
[6] *O'Gorman* v. *O'Gorman, supra,* at pp. 581–582; *Lucas* v. *Pettit* (1906), 12 O.L.R. 448, 451–452; *Johnson* v. *Martin* (1950), 100 L.Jo. 541; and see the county court cases cited by Frimston, *op. cit.,* 8.

Just as such escapes may constitute a nuisance, so also may the conduct of animals remaining on the defendant's land. If pigs are kept on the defendant's land so that the smell from them unreasonably interferes with the plaintiff's enjoyment of his land, this is a nuisance;[7] and the same may be said for other smells, such as those from horses.[8] Liability in nuisance extends also to unreasonable noise made by animals on the defendant's land, as with the crowing of cockerels,[9] the barking of dogs[10] or the noises of horses in a stable.[11] Also the noise of pigeons, both on the defendant's land and in flight over the plaintiff's land, may constitute a nuisance.[12] It is probable also that it is an actionable nuisance to keep diseased animals on one's own land in circumstances such that their disease infects one's neighbour's animals, and thereby interferes with his use of his land.[13]

(c) Rylands v. Fletcher Liability[14]

The basis of liability under this head is that an occupier of land who brings onto and keeps on his land, as a non-natural user of the land, anything likely to do mischief if it escapes, is liable for all the direct consequences of such an escape.[15]

---

[7] *Aldred's Case* (1610), 9 Co. Rep. 57b; *A.-G.* v. *Squire* (1906), 5 L.G.R. 99.

[8] *Rapier* v. *London Tramways Co.*, [1893] 2 Ch. 588; *Drysdale* v. *Dugas* (1896), 26 S.C.R. 20; *Munro* v. *Southern Dairies, Ltd.*, [1955] V.L.R. 332; and see *Treadwell* v. *Wellington Dairy Co.* (1910), 29 N.Z.L.R. 906.

[9] *Leeman* v. *Montagu*, [1936] 2 All E.R. 1677; *cf. Hunt* v. *W. H. Cook, Ltd.* (1922), 66 Sol. Jo. 557; *Ruthning* v. *Ferguson*, [1930] Qd. S.R. 325; *Randall* v. *Harper*, [1955] C.L.Y. 1940.

[10] *Mallock* v. *Mason and Mason*, [1938] L.J.C.C.R. 387; and see Williams, 236–237.

[11] *Ball* v. *Ray* (1873), 8 Ch. App. 467; *Broder* v. *Saillard* (1876), 2 Ch.D. 692; *Rapier* v. *London Tramways Co.*, [1893] 2 Ch. 588; *Drysdale* v. *Dugas* (1896), 26 S.C.R. 20; *Painter* v. *Reed*, [1930] S.A.S.R. 295; *Munro* v. *Southern Dairies, Ltd.*, [1955] V.L.R. 332.

[12] *Fraser* v. *Booth* (1949), 50 S.R.N.S.W. 113; *cf. Mobbs* v. *Shephardson*, [1937] L.J.C.C.R. 277.

[13] *Cf. R.* v. *Henson* (1852), Dears. C.C. 24; *Ruhan* v. *Water Conservation and Irrigation Commission* (1920), 20 S.R.N.S.W. 439; Williams, 342–343. Similarly, it may be an actionable nuisance to contaminate your neighbour's water supply with droppings from animals on your land: Report of the New South Wales Law Reform Commission on Civil Liability for Animals, (1970) L.R.C.8, §. 32.

[14] Williams, 197–199, 261–262, 352–353. The Report of the New South Wales Law Reform Commission, *supra*, §. 15, recommends that the Rule in *Rylands* v. *Fletcher* should not be applied to damage done by animals.

[15] *Rylands* v. *Fletcher* (1866), L.R. 1 Exch. 265, affirmed (1868) L.R. 3 H.L. 330.

He keeps it at his peril and his liability does not depend on his being negligent.

There would seem, in principle, to be no reason why there should not be liability under the Rule in *Rylands* v. *Fletcher* for harm done to the plaintiff by animals escaping from the defendant's land. Indeed, in *Rylands* v. *Fletcher* itself, BLACKBURN, J.[16] regarded the law of cattle trespass as but an instance of the wider and more generalised head of liability there being laid down. Nevertheless, it remains true that authorities, both academic[17] and judicial,[18] have regarded cattle trespass and liability under *Rylands* v. *Fletcher* as quite separate heads of liability. Furthermore, one could have said the same for the relationship between the *scienter* action and the Rule in *Rylands* v. *Fletcher.*[19]

Whilst accepting that liability under *Rylands* v. *Fletcher* was separate from liability in cattle trespass or the *scienter* action and is now separate from the strict liability imposed by sections 2 to 4 of the Animals Act 1971, this does not mean that liability for harm done by escaping animals cannot fall within the Rule in *Rylands* v. *Fletcher.* On the other hand, it is unlikely that many cases of harm done by animals will fall within that rule. The reason for such a conclusion is that for liability to exist under the Rule, not only must there be an escape of the animal from the defendant's land,[20] but the keeping and accumulating there of the animal must constitute a non-natural user of the land. The pasturing of domestic livestock, as with the keeping of domestic pets, is, one assumes, a natural user of the land.[1] Furthermore, the animals which

---

[16] (1866), L.R. 1 Exch. 265, 280 *et seq.*
[17] Williams, 197–199; Salmond, *Torts*, 15th ed. 453; Winfield, *Tort*, 8th ed. 455; and see Report of the New South Wales Law Reform Commission, *supra*, §. 15.
[18] E.g. *Manton* v. *Brocklebank,* [1923] 2 K.B. 212, 222, 230; *cf.,* e.g. *Holgate* v. *Bleazard,* [1917] 1 K.B. 443; *Miles* v. *Forest Rock Granite Co. (Leicestershire), Ltd.* (1918), 34 T.L.R. 500.
[19] Salmond, *op. cit.,* 453; Winfield, *op. cit.,* 464–465; Williams, 353–354; *Fardon* v. *Harcourt-Rivington* (1932), 146 L.T. 391, 392; *Read* v. *J. Lyons & Co. Ltd.,* [1947] A.C. 156, 166–167; *Behrens* v. *Bertram Mills Circus, Ltd.,* [1957] 2 Q.B. 1, 21–22; *cf.,* e.g. *Baker* v. *Snell,* [1908] 2 K.B. 825, 835–836; *Lowery* v. *Walker,* [1910] 1 K.B. 173, 182; *Knott* v. *L.C.C.,* [1934] 1 K.B. 126, 139.
[20] *Read* v. *J. Lyons & Co., Ltd.,* [1947] A.C. 156.
[1] *Cf. Stearn* v. *Prentice Bros., Ltd.,* [1919] 1 K.B. 394. *Holgate* v. *Bleazard,* [1917] 1 K.B. 433, must surely be wrongly decided in so far as it is based on *Rylands* v. *Fletcher.*

escape must fall within the class of "dangerous things" and, again, domestic animals such as horses,[2] or dogs[3] cannot normally be classified as dangerous things.   To keep a wild animal such as a tiger on your land would appear to be a non-natural user of the land and, if the tiger, being a dangerous thing, escaped, then there could well be liability under *Rylands* v. *Fletcher*.[4]   It is possible that there might be such liability for harm caused by an escaping fox[5] or even, in appropriately unusual circumstances, for a dangerous dog.[6]

(d) Negligence

There has never been any doubt since the seventeenth century[7] that an action will lie for the negligent keeping of animals which causes harm to the plaintiff.   There is, therefore, a common law duty to take reasonable care to prevent your animals from causing injury, whether or not they escape from your land or control.   This liability was quite independent of the common law heads of liability peculiar to animals and is quite independent of any statutory liability imposed in their place by the Animals Act 1971.[8]   As Lord ATKIN has said:

"It is also true that, quite apart from the liability imposed upon the owner of animals or the person having control of them by reason of knowledge of their propensities, there is the ordinary duty of a person to take care either that his animal or his chattel is not put to such a use as is likely to injure his neighbour—the ordinary duty to take care in the cases put upon negligence."[9]

It is necessary for all the elements of the tort of negligence to

---

[2] *Manton* v. *Brocklebank,* [1923] 2 K.B. 212.
[3] *Cf. Hines* v. *Tousley* (1926), 95 L.J.K.B. 773.
[4] See *Behrens* v. *Bertram Mills Circus, Ltd.,* [1957] 2 Q.B. 1, 22.
[5] *Brady* v. *Warren,* [1900] 2 I.R. 632, 651.   As to the situation with regard to bees, see *Rolins* v. *Kennedy and Columb,* [1931] N.Z.L.R. 1134, 1142.
[6] *Hines* v. *Tousley, supra,* at p. 774.
[7] *Mitchil* v. *Alestree* (1676), 1 Vent. 295.
[8] See Chapters 2, 3, 7.
[9] *Fardon* v. *Harcourt-Rivington* (1932), 48 T.L.R. 215, 217.   See also *Hinckes* v. *Harris* (1921), 65 Sol. Jo. 781, 782; *Lathall* v. *Joyce & Son,* [1939] 3 All E.R. 854; *Brackenborough* v. *Spalding U.D.C.,* [1942] A.C. 310, 321–322; *Ellis* v. *Johnstone,* [1963] 2 Q.B. 8, 29–30; *Fitzgerald* v. *E.D. & A.D. Cooke (Bourne) Farms, Ltd.,* [1964] 1 Q.B. 249.

be satisfied. There must be a duty of care owed to the plaintiff by the defendant, breach of that duty by the defendant
and reasonably foreseeable damage suffered by the plaintiff
as a consequence of that breach of duty. Liability is based
upon foresight and not upon the defendant's knowledge of the
dangerous characteristics of the animal which caused the
injury.[10] Thus, where a pony was left unattended in the
street which, when it became restive, attacked the plaintiff,
the defendants were held liable in negligence for such injuries
despite a finding that they did not know of the animal's propensity to injure.[11] They ought to have foreseen the likelihood
of such injury from leaving the pony unattended.

A further significance of determining whether the action for
injury done by an animal is one in negligence or one of strict
liability under the Animals Act 1971 is that for the latter no
fault on the part of the defendant needs to be proved. Liability is strict with the one qualification of proof of knowledge
under s. 2 (2), though this may often be equivalent to proof of
fault. A corollary of this general distinction between liability in negligence and under the Animals Act 1971 is that the
rules of remoteness of damage appear to be different. It has
been suggested already[12] that, just as with the *scienter* action
and cattle trespass at common law, the statutory liability
under s. 2 and s. 4 of the Animals Act 1971 attracts a test of
remoteness based upon direct consequences. However, the
test of remoteness in negligence is now[13] that of reasonable
foresight of consequences.[14] Thus the statutory actions based
on strict liability could give rise to a greater extent of liability
than in negligence.

---

[10] *Fardon* v. *Harcourt-Rivington, supra;* and see *Matheson* v. *G. Stuckey & Co.
Pty., Ltd.,* [1921] V.L.R. 637; *Sycamore* v. *Ley* (1932), 147 L.T. 342.
[11] *Aldham* v. *United Dairies, Ltd.,* [1940] 1 K.B. 507; and see *Hinckes* v.
Harris, supra, at p. 782; *cf. Cooke* v. *Waring* (1863), 2 H. & C. 332, which is
probably to be considered as wrongly decided in that it required proof of
knowledge of the diseased nature of the defendant's cattle for liability in
negligence to arise; see Williams, 341–342; and see *Earp* v. *Faulkner*
(1875), 34 L.T. 384, affirmed (1876), 24 W.R. 774.
[12] *Supra,* pp. 47–48, 58, 107–108.
[13] *Cf. Aldham* v. *United Dairies, Ltd.,* [1940] 1 K.B. 507, 513.
[14] *The Wagon Mound,* [1961] A.C. 388; *The Wagon Mound (No. 2),* [1967]
1 A.C. 617; and see *Whycherley* v. *Grave,* [1967] C.L.Y. 91.

Another basic difference between liability in negligence and under the Animals Act 1971 for harm caused by animals is that the only defendant in the latter case is the keeper of the animal. Although there may be more than one keeper,[15] liability is confined to that particular class of defendant. There are no such limitations on liability in negligence. Anyone who is negligent in the keeping or care of an animal may be liable for harm that it does. Furthermore, under the statutory actions the keeper will be liable even though he has taken all possible care, whereas, at common law, negligence liability will depend on fault.

It is a basic requirement of liability in negligence that the plaintiff's injury is caused by and is a reasonable consequence of the defendant's negligence. Without this link the plaintiff must fail, as is illustrated by *Bradley* v. *Wallaces, Ltd.*[16] Here the deceased was killed when passing behind a horse which kicked him. The horse had been left unattended by the defendants in the deceased's employers' yard. As the deceased's injury was considered not to have been a natural or probable consequence of the negligence of the defendants in leaving the horse unattended, the action by his dependants failed.

Just as negligence is a very flexible basis of liability, so also are the instances where there has been such liability for harm done by animals very varied. Where animals are taken out onto the highway and there cause injury as a result of the negligent conduct or lack of care on the part of the person who took them out onto the highway there will be liability for such injury.[17] Such a duty of care on the part of the person who takes animals onto a highway has been applied to the case of leaving a dog in a parked car[18] and has been suggested on the part of the owner of animals who takes them to market.[19] All

---

[15] Animals Act 1971, s. 6 (3).

[16] [1913] 3 K.B. 629; and see *Abbott* v. *Freeman* (1876), 35 L.T. 783; *Lathall* v. *Joyce*, [1939] 3 All E.R. 854, 856.

[17] E.g. *Deen* v. *Davies*, [1935] 2 K.B. 282; *Brackenborough* v. *Spalding U.D.C.*, [1942] A.C. 310; Williams, 377–378. The whole problem of liability for harm done by animals on the highway is examined in Chapter 5.

[18] *Fardon* v. *Harcourt-Rivington* (1932), 48 T.L.R. 215; *Sycamore* v. *Ley* (1932), 147 L.T. 342, esp. at p. 345.

[19] *Brackenborough* v. *Spalding U.D.C.*, [1942] A.C. 310, 331.

the more will there be liability where the defendant does a positive act which causes the animal to injure the plaintiff, as with the negligent whipping of a horse causing it to lash out.[20]

Another situation where a duty of care might arise is where an animal has escaped from one building or part of a building to another where it has caused the injury. Thus in *Hines* v. *Tousley*[1] the plaintiff was injured when the defendant's dog collided with her on the staircase of a building in which she was employed. The defendant lived on the top floor of the building and the dog was coming downstairs when the incident occurred. The action failed because:

> "there was no evidence at all that the dog on this occasion was rushing or doing anything other than proceeding in a way in which a well-behaved dog would go downstairs."[2]

However, the Court of Appeal was prepared to accept that there could well be circumstances where the owner of a dog would be liable for causing such injury.[3] It would not appear to be a breach of the duty of care to allow a large dog, playing in a small garden, to jump over a garden wall and land on the neck of the plaintiff who was digging in the adjoining garden.[4]

If the defendant's dog strays onto the plaintiff's land and fouls his garden, then it has been held[5] that, as there is no liability for the straying or the trespass[6] in such a case there is no liability in negligence for failing to prevent the trespass. It might be argued, nevertheless, that although there may be no strict liability for straying livestock, yet if the animal escapes through the neglect of the defendant there should be liability in negligence. The exclusion of dogs from the statutory definition of "livestock" should not operate as an exclusion, also, of liability in negligence.

---

[20] *Abbott* v. *Freeman* (1876), 34 L.T. 544; reversed on a different view of the facts, 35 L.T. 783.
[1] (1926), 95 L.J.K.B. 733.
[2] *Ibid.*, at p. 774.
[3] *Ibid.*, at pp. 774, 775.
[4] *Sanders* v. *Teape and Swan* (1884), 51 L.T. 263; though it was such a breach to allow a large collie dog to knock the plaintiff over in *Morris* v. *Baily* (1970), 13 D.L.R. (3d) 150.
[5] *Curtis* v. *Thompson* (1956), 106 L.Jo. 61.
[6] Neither in cattle trespass at common law, for a dog is not "cattle", nor under s. 4 of the Animals Act 1971 for neither is it "livestock".

Where a defendant whose land adjoined the plaintiff's mink farm allowed his dog to run at large during the whelping season, the defendant was held liable in negligence for damage done to the plaintiff's mink when the dog jumped into the mink pen. The defendant was at fault in that he should have known of the dangers to mink from strange dogs at that time, and he failed to take steps to control his dog.[7]

There may also be liability in negligence for allowing a diseased animal to escape onto neighbouring land and there infect the plaintiff's cattle,[8] or even the plaintiff. In *Earp* v. *Faulkner*[9] the defendant's diseased cattle escaped into the plaintiff's field and infected the latter's cattle with foot and mouth disease. There was evidence that the defendant's servants knew that the cattle were diseased when they were placed in a field adjoining the plaintiff's. It was held that such conduct amounted to negligence on the part of the defendant.[10]

Two final examples might be given to illustrate the scope of liability in negligence for harm done by animals. Where a riding school is negligent in the selection of the horse which it supplies to a rider, it will be held liable in negligence for the rider's injuries.[11] Secondly, it is actionable negligence to keep bees in excessive numbers without taking due care, if such conduct causes injury to the plaintiff.[12]

(e) Occupiers' Liability[13]

If the plaintiff is injured by the defendant's animal when visiting the defendant's premises this poses the question whether

---

[7] *Caine Fur Farms* v. *Kokolsky* (1963), 39 D.L.R. (2d) 134; and see (1962), 31 D.L.R. (2d) 556.

[8] Equally there would be liability under s. 4 of the Animals Act 1971, *supra,* pp. 102–103.

[9] (1875), 34 L.T. 284, affirmed (1876), 24 W.R. 774; and see *Cooke* v. *Waring* (1863), 3 H. & C. 332.

[10] There is no reason to doubt that such an action will lie if only the disease and not the animals escapes: *Earp* v. *Faulkner, supra,* at p. 286, provided the plaintiff's cattle are infected; *cf. Weller & Co.* v. *Foot and Mouth Disease Research Institute,* [1966] 1 Q.B. 569.

[11] *Collins* v. *Richmond Rodeo Riding, Ltd.* (1966), 56 D.L.R. (2d) 428; and see *Saari* v. *Sunshine Riding Academy, Ltd.* (1968), 65 D.L.R. (2d) 92.

[12] *O'Gorman* v. *O'Gorman,* [1903] 2 I.R. 573; *Robins* v. *Kennedy and Columb,* [1931] N.Z.L.R. 1134.

[13] See North, *Occupiers' Liability,* 91–92.

the special rules relating to the liability of an occupier for harm done to visitors are applicable. This issue must be examined on the alternative hypotheses that the plaintiff is a lawful visitor or a trespasser.

(i)　*Lawful visitor*

The obligations of an occupier to lawful visitors are governed by the Occupiers' Liability Act 1957, and there are no fully reported decisions thereunder concerned with injuries to visitors caused by the occupier's animals.[14]　The basic liability under the 1957 Act is that the occupier shall take reasonable care to make the premises reasonably safe for the purpose for which the lawful visitor visits them.[15]　It is suggested that an occupier fails in that duty if he exposes a lawful visitor to risk of injury from an animal on the premises.　Certainly, so far as the pre-1958 common law position was concerned, there seems little doubt not only that the *scienter* action would lie when the injury occurred on the defendant's premises, but also that the specialised common law rules relating to an occupier's liability could be applied to cases of harm caused by animals on premises visited by the plaintiff.　Thus in *Kavanagh* v. *Stokes*[16] the plaintiff recovered on the basis of the duty owed to her as an invitee of the defendant when she was bitten by the defendant's dog whilst she was walking up the drive of the defendant's guest house.

The likely situation for the plaintiff to base his case on the rules of occupiers' liability rather than upon strict liability under the Animals Act 1971 is the case of an injury caused by an animal of a non-dangerous species where the defendant occupier has no actual knowledge of the animal's dangerous nature but ought to have used reasonable care for the safety of his lawful visitors.[17]　The likeliest animals to fall into this category will be bulls and dogs and, so far as the latter are

---

[14] *Cf. Carroll* v. *Garford* (1968), 112 Sol. Jo. 948.
[15] Occupiers' Liability Act 1957, s. 2.
[16] [1942] I.R. 596; and see *Gould* v. *McAuliffe*, [1941] 1 All E.R. 515, affirmed, [1941] 2 All E.R. 527.
[17] Such was the opinion of the Divisional Court in *Clinton* v. *J. Lyons & Co., Ltd.*, [1912] 3 K.B. 198, so far as the common law obligations of an occupier to invitees were concerned; and see *McNeill* v. *Frankenfeld* (1964), 44 D.L.R. (2d) 132, 139–140; *Andrews* v. *Patullo*, [1955] C.L.Y. 1835.

concerned, it should be remembered that if a dog bites the plaintiff there will be no liability under s. 3 of the Animals Act 1971, for the strict liability there laid down relates only to damage by killing or injuring livestock.[18]   The basic principle of liability in such a case is still that expressed by TINDAL, C.J. in *Sarch* v. *Blackburn*:[19]

> "Undoubtedly, a man has a right to keep a fierce dog for the protection of his property, but he has no right to put the dog in such a situation, in the way of access to his house, that a person innocently coming for a lawful purpose may be injured by it.   I think he has no right to place a dog so near to the door of his house, that any person coming to ask for money, or on other business, might be bitten."

(ii)   Trespassers[20]

There is very little direct authority on the question of the liability of an occupier to a trespasser injured by animals on the land trespassed upon.[1]   The general common law rule, unaffected in the case of trespassers by the Occupiers' Liability Act 1957, is that the occupier must not wilfully injure a trespasser nor act with reckless disregard of his presence on the land; but there is no liability merely for the negligent infliction of injury upon a trespasser.[2]

If an occupier keeps on his land an animal of whose dangerous characteristics he has actual or presumed knowledge, then the occupier should not be liable at common law for injuries to a trespasser unless the keeping of the animals was aimed at causing injury to trespassers.   No liability should normally

---

[18] See Chapter 7.

[19] (1830), 4 C. & P. 297, 300.

[20] North, *op. cit.*, Chapter 11.   Liability to trespassers under s. 2 of the Animals Act 1971 is discussed *supra*, pp. 77–83.

[1] See *Murphy* v. *Zoological Society of London*, [1962] C.L.Y. 68.   A number of cases dealing with an occupier's liability for harm done by animals are concerned, primarily, with the issue of whether or not the plaintiff was a trespasser: *Lowery* v. *Walker*, [1910] 1 K.B. 173, reversed, [1911] A.C. 10; *Gould* v. *McAuliffe*, [1941] 1 All E.R. 515, affirmed, [1941] 2 All E.R. 527; and see *Pearson* v. *Coleman Bros.*, [1948] 2 K.B. 359.

[2] *Robert Addie & Sons (Collieries), Ltd.* v. *Dumbreck*, [1929] A.C. 358; *Commissioner for Railways* v. *Quinlan*, [1964] A.C. 1054; *Herrington* v. *British Railways Board*, [1971] 2 Q.B. 107.

ensue from a trespasser being gored by a bull,[3] or kicked by a horse[4] which is kept in the field into which the plaintiff trespassed. Neither will liability attach if the animal was put there to protect the property and deter trespassers.[5] Similarly, if the plaintiff trespasses by climbing into a lion's enclosure[6] or by walking into a zebra's cage,[7] he cannot complain if he is injured.

The Animals Act 1971 considers the effect on liability under s. 2 of the fact that the plaintiff was trespassing on the land where he was injured and provides that the keeper of a dangerous animal shall not be liable for injuries to a trespassing plaintiff if the animal was not kept on the premises for the protection of persons or property or, if it was kept there for those purposes, such keeping was not unreasonable.[8] No provision is made in the Animals Act 1971 for liability to trespassers generally. The common law rules are unaffected by that Act. The reason for this partial treatment of the position of trespassers is that the Law Commission did not:

"consider that it would be appropriate within the terms of reference set by the topic of civil liability for damage or injury done by animals to make recommendations which would affect the common law covering occupiers and trespassers generally."[9]

---

[3] *Cf. Brook v. Copeland* (1701), 1 Esp. 203, 201; *Blackman v. Simmons* (1827), 3 C. & P. 138, 140.

[4] *Lowery v. Walker*, [1910] 1 K.B. 173, reversed on the basis that the plaintiff was not a trespasser, [1911] A.C. 10.

[5] *Sarch v. Blackburn* (1830), 4 C. & P. 297, 300.

[6] *Murphy v. Zoological Society of London*, [1962] C.L.Y. 68; *cf. Pearson v. Coleman Bros.*, [1948] 2 K.B. 359.

[7] *Cf. Marlor v. Ball* (1900), 16 T.L.R. 239.

[8] Animals Act 1971, s. 5 (3), discussed *supra*, pp. 77–83.

[9] Law Commission Report, §. 58. The Law Commission did suggest, however, that if it were decided to impose a general duty on occupiers to trespassers, the relevant considerations in the case of injuries or damage caused by animals might include the following: "(i) The purpose (if any) for which the animal is on the premises at the time in question and how far it is a reasonable use of the premises to keep or bring the animal thereon for that purpose; in particular, if the purpose or one of the purposes for which the animal is on the premises is that of deterring trespassers, how far it is reasonable to use the animal in question for that purpose. (ii) Whether the precautions (including warning notices, if any) taken to keep trespassers off the premises or to provide for the safety of persons thereon were in the circumstances reasonably adequate, having in particular regard to the nature of potential trespassers and the likelihood of their entry." Law Commission Report, §. 58, n. 90.

7

SPECIAL PROVISIONS RELATING TO DOGS

Dogs are singled out for special treatment by the Animals Act 1971 in two different, though related, respects. Strict liability for damage caused by a dog killing or injuring livestock is imposed on its keeper by s. 3. However, the owner of the livestock does not have to wait until they have been killed or maimed before taking action. Section 9 defines the circumstances in which a person may kill or injure another's dog for the protection of livestock. These two separate provisions must now be examined.

(a) Liability for harm done by dogs

Dogs, it may be recalled, fall outside the statutory definition of "livestock"[1] for the purposes of liability under s. 4 of the Animals Act 1971 for damage caused by trespassing livestock;[2] just as they fell outside the definition of "cattle" for the purposes of the common law action of cattle trespass.[3] On the other hand, there may be strict liability for damage caused by dogs under s. 2 (2) of the Animals Act 1971,[4] if they cause damage of a kind which they were likely to cause as a result of abnormal characteristics known to their keeper. Similarly, there was, at common law, liability for injuries caused by dogs under the

---

[1] Animals Act 1971, s. 11.
[2] *Supra,* Chapter 3.
[3] E.g. *Buckle* v. *Holmes,* [1926] 2 K.B. 125, 128–129, 130; *Tallents* v. *Bell and Goddard,* [1944] 2 All E.R. 474.
[4] *Supra,* Chapter 2.

scienter action,[5] dogs being classed as animals *mansuetae naturae*. Furthermore, there will also be liability for harm caused by dogs under the common law of negligence[6] and nuisance.[7]

Apart from these forms of liability, it has long been thought necessary to provide some special form of strict liability in the case of certain types of injuries by dogs, such liability being imposed irrespective of proof of negligence or *scienter*. The Dogs Act 1865 imposed such general liability. This was replaced by the Dogs Act 1906,[8] as amended by the Dogs (Amendment) Act 1928[9] which have themselves been replaced insofar as they relate to civil liability by the provisions of the Animals Act 1971.[10]

Section 3 of the Animals Act 1971 provides that:

> "Where a dog causes damage by killing or injuring livestock, any person who is a keeper of the dog is liable for the damage, except as otherwise provided by this Act."

A number of elements in this head of liability merit separate discussion.

(i) *Kinds of damage*

Liability is imposed for "damage by killing or injuring livestock". Livestock is defined in terms similar to but not identical with its meaning for the purposes of liability under

---

[5] E.g. *M'Kone* v. *Wood* (1831), 5 C. & P. 1; *Card* v. *Case* (1848), 5 C.B. 622; *Barnes* v. *Lucille, Ltd.* (1907), 96 L.T. 680.
[6] E.g. *Fardon* v. *Harcourt-Rivington* (1932), 146 L.T. 391; *Gomberg* v. *Smith*, [1963] 1 Q.B. 25.
[7] E.g. *Mallock* v. *Mason and Mason*, [1938] L.J.C.C.R. 387; and see *Curtis* v. *Thompson* (1956), 106 L.Jo. 61. Common law obligations which are unaffected by the Animals Act 1971 are considered in Chapter 6.
[8] Section 1 (1)–(3).
[9] Section 1 (1).
[10] Section 1 (1) (b). The relevant provisions of the Dogs Acts 1906–1928 are repealed by s. 13 (2) of the Animals Act 1971. One effect of this is to repeal s. 1 (3) of the Dogs Act 1906 which empowered a court of summary jurisdiction to award damages of up to £5 for injury caused by a dog to livestock as a civil debt. A suggestion that a similar jurisdiction, up to £25 damages, should be conferred on magistrates' courts by the Animals Act 1971 was not accepted: 306 H.L. Deb. cc. 72–74; H.C. Standing Committee A, March 16th 1971, cc. 9–19, 815 H.C. Deb. cc. 590–600.

s. 4 for damage caused by straying livestock.[11]   Section 11
of the Animals Act 1971 states:

> " 'livestock' means cattle, horses, asses, mules, hinnies, sheep,
> pigs, goats and poultry, and also deer not in the wild state and, in
> sections 3 and 9, also, while in captivity, pheasants, partridges
> and grouse."

Poultry is further defined in the same section as "the domestic
varieties of the following, that is to say, fowls, turkeys, geese,
ducks, guinea-fowls, pigeons, peacocks and quails." If the
creature injured falls outside these varieties, there will be no
liability under s. 3.[12]   It will, therefore, still be the case, as
under the Dogs Acts 1906–1928, that there will be no such liability where a dog kills or injures rabbits, whether domestic
or wild.[13]

The damage covered by s. 3 must involve the killing or
injuring of livestock by dogs.   Damage caused directly to
people or to other property is not actionable hereunder; it
falls to be dealt with under either s. 2 or s. 4 of the Animals
Act 1971, or at common law.   Section 3 of the Animals Act
1971, as with the Dogs Acts, "placed cattle and sheep in a
better position than human beings".[14]

Undoubtedly, there is liability under s. 3 if a dog attacks and
thereby kills or injures livestock.   Thus, the keeper would be
liable if his dog attacked a horse[15] or worried and killed sheep[16]
or if the dog chased and killed chickens.[17]

There was also liability under the Dogs Acts 1906–1928 if a
dog caused an appropriate animal to be injured even though it
was not attacked.   For example, it was held that it would
suffice for liability if the dog merely frightened a horse so that

---

[11] Discussed, *supra*, pp. 92–94.
[12] No protection would be given to a game park where a dog attacked wild
swans, geese or duck.
[13] *Tallents* v. *Bell and Goddard*, [1944] 2 All E.R. 474.
[14] *Grange* v. *Silcock* (1897), 77 L.T. 340, 341.
[15] *Wright* v. *Pearson* (1868), L.R. 4 Q.B. 582; *McKinnon* v. *Dwyer*, [1906]
V.L.R. 28; *cf. Raisbeck* v. *Desabrais* (1971), 16 D.L.R. (3d) 447.
[16] *Grange* v. *Silcock, supra;* and see, e.g. *Strachan* v. *M'Leod* (1884), 5 N.S.W.
L.R. 191; *Priest* v. *Davidson* (1922), 17 M.C.R. 105; *Nicol* v. *Humphreys*
(1922), 18 M.C.R. 22; *Burchmore* v. *Rawson,* [1932] G.L.R. 283.
[17] *Ives* v. *Brewer* (1951), 95 Sol. Jo. 286.

it bolted and was thereby injured;[18] though the injury had to
be to the animal in question and there could be no recovery for
consequential injury to, for example, a horse's harness or the
trap that the horse was pulling.[19]   The question arises whether
there will be liability under s. 3 of the Animals Act 1971 for
injuries caused in similar circumstances.   The Dogs Acts
speak of "injury done to any cattle by that dog".[20]   The
equivalent phrase in s. 3 is "Where a dog causes damage by
killing or injuring livestock".   It would seem that a dog has as
much "caused injury to livestock" as "done injury to cattle"
by causing a horse to bolt so that it is injured.   Therefore, it
is suggested that there will still be strict liability, now under
s. 3 of the Animals Act 1971, for injuries to a horse by its being
caused by a dog to bolt.

Will there, in such a case, be liability for damage to the horse's
harness or trap?   It has already been suggested that s. 3
relates to injuries to livestock rather than to people or other
property.   Although the marginal note to s. 3 talks of "Liability for injury done by dogs to livestock", the actual section
talks of a dog which "causes damage by killing or injuring
livestock".   Undoubtedly there must be death of or injury to
livestock for liability to arise under s. 3; but what if there is
further damage caused by the injury?   If a horse is bitten in
the leg by a dog and so bolts and wrecks its trap, is the latter
damage caused by the injury to the horse?   To take another
example: if a dog kills a man's prize pig, will the owner of the
pig who has a heart attack on discovering the slaughter be able
to recover for such personal injuries?   There has been death
or injury to livestock.   There has been damage caused, for
s. 11 defines damage so as to include "the death of, or injury
to, any person (including any disease and any impairment of
physical or mental condition)".   The one debateable issue is
whether that damage is caused by the dog killing the pig.
It is hard to see why it is not.

---

[18] *Elliott* v. *Longden* (1901), 17 T.L.R. 648; and see *Cowell* v. *Mumford* (1886),
3 T.L.R.1.   It would appear that an actual attack is required in Ireland:
Campbell v. *Wilkinson* (1909), 43 I.L.T.R. 237, and New Zealand: *Chittenden*
v. *Hale*, [1933] N.Z.L.R. 836; and see Williams, 354–355.
[19] *Cowell* v. *Mumford, supra.*
[20] Dogs Act 1906, s. 1 (1).

A final series of examples of the problems raised as to the scope of s. 3 might be given which relate in part to the issue of who can properly complain of the damage. A variety of situations may be posed:

1. A dog bites a cow, thereby injuring it. The owner of the cow may recover under s. 2.

2. A dog runs at a cow, causing it to bolt and injure itself. It is suggested that the owner can recover under s. 3.

3. A dog bites a cow causing it to run into a car. The cow has been injured and it is, at the least, arguable that that injury has caused the damage to the car.[1] If so, then both the owner of the cow and of the car might recover under s. 3. Similarly:

4. A dog bites a cow causing it to bolt and knock a man off his bicycle. Both this case and Case 3 raise the issue whether the plaintiff under s. 3 must be the person whose livestock is injured. There is nothing in the Animals Act 1971 to indicate that that must be the case. There is an arguable case that the injured plaintiff could recover under s. 3 on the basis that his damage is caused by the injury to the cow.

5. A dog barks at a cow causing it to bolt. In running away it collides with a car, or knocks a man off his bicycle. As a result of that collision it is injured. No doubt the owner of the cow can succeed under s. 3 (as in Case 2). Can the owner of the car or the man knocked off his bicycle recover for their damage under s. 3? Was the damage caused by the injury to the livestock? The dog injured the cow by causing it to be involved in the collision. That which actually injured the cow is the same incident as caused the plaintiff's damage. Here again, however, it is arguable that the dog caused the cow to bolt and to collide with car, or the plaintiff, thereby injuring the cow and causing damage to the plaintiff.

6. A dog bites, or barks at and causes to bolt, another dog which is injured and causes damage to the plaintiff in any of the ways envisaged in Cases 1–5. There will be

---

[1] *Cf. Knowlson* v. *Solomon,* [1969] N.Z.L.R. 686, 690.

no liability under s. 3, for the animal injured is not "livestock". It does seem a little strange that to cause a cow to knock the plaintiff off his bicycle might involve strict liability whilst to cause a dog to do so will not. One can but recall that the purpose of s. 3 is, in the words of the Law Commission, "that the opportunity should be taken to provide a clearer statement of the law".[2]

(ii) *Who is liable?*

Although liability under the Dogs Acts 1906–1928 was placed on the owner of the dog or the occupier of the premises where the dog was kept, unless he could prove that he was not the owner,[3] this was generally regarded as unsatisfactory.[4] Liability under s. 3 of the Animals Act 1971 is imposed on the keeper of the dog.   The keeper is defined, by s. 6 (3) and s. 6 (4), in exactly the same way for the purposes of liability under s. 3 as for liability under s. 2 and this definition has already been examined in detail in that latter context.[5]

Briefly, liability as a keeper will be imposed on the owner of the dog or the person who has it in his possession.[6]   Also, the head of a household wherein there is a keeper under the age of sixteen will be a keeper.[7]   If the dog has been taken into possession to prevent it causing damage or to return it to its keeper, that possession, as such, will not create the obligations of a keeper.[8]

Thus, the owner of a dog will be liable for the damage it has caused even though he was not in possession of it.[9]   Conversely, the possessor will also be liable even though he is not the owner.[10] If there is neither ownership nor possession, actual or constructive, then there will be no liability.   Therefore, an employer

---

[2] Law Commission Report, §. 73.
[3] Dogs Act 1906, s. 1.
[4] Law Commission Report, §. 74.
[5] *Supra*, pp. 23–34.
[6] Animals Act 1971, s. 6 (3) (a).   Liability may be imposed on the Crown: Animals Act 1971, s. 12, discussed, *supra*, pp. 33–34.
[7] Animals Act 1971, s. 6 (3) (b).
[8] *Ibid*, s. 6 (4);   *cf. Roberts* v. *McCready* (1921), 14 M.C.R. 4.
[9] *Cf. Grigg* v. *Murname,* [1934] V.L.R. 295.
[10] *Cf. Jackson* v. *Croft* (1879), 2 S.C.R. (N.S.W.) (N.S.) 295; and see *Tobin* v. *Dorman,* [1937] N.Z.L.R. 937.

is not liable for damage done by his employee's dog;[11] nor would the organisers of a drag hunt be held liable if the dogs, a pack of beagles, attacked the plaintiff's sheep after the end of the hunt; for, in both cases the defendants would be neither owners nor possessors of the dogs.[12]

(*iii*)   *Strict liability*

Liability under s. 3 of the Animals Act 1971 is strict, though not absolute.[13]   The keeper of the dog will be liable for damage done without proof of fault on his part.   No proof of knowledge of the dog's vicious or abnormal characteristics is required; nor will proof by the defendant of lack of knowledge[14] or absence of fault[15] afford a defence.   The existence of strict liability under s. 3 will not affect other heads of liability either at common law or under other provisions of the Animals Act 1971.[16]

(*iv*)   *Defences*

As liability under the Dogs Acts 1906–1928 has been abolished by the Animals Act 1971,[17] to be replaced by the new head of liability under s. 3, the only defences to the new statutory liability will be those provided by the Animals Act 1971.   Two of these are general in that they apply not only to liability under s. 3, but also to liability for dangerous animals[18] and to liability for straying livestock,[19] but the third is peculiar to liability under s. 3.   The first two are that a person will not be liable for any damage which is due wholly to the fault of the person suffering it,[20] and the defence of contributory negligence.[1] It might well be said that, if a dog is provoked by the owner of livestock, the ensuing damage to such livestock is due wholly

---

[11] *Cf. Knott* v. *L.C.C.*, [1934] 1 K.B. 126.
[12] *Cf. Crean* v. *Nolan* (1963), 97 I.L.T.R. 125.
[13] Defences are discussed *infra*.
[14] *Cf. R.* v. *Hare* (1888), 14 V.L.R. 89; *Stremple* v. *Wilson* (1904), 7 W.A.R. 101.
[15] *Cf. Knowlson* v. *Solomon*, [1969] N.Z.L.R. 686, 690.
[16] *Cf. Ex parte Finneran* (1897), 18 N.S.W.R. 353; *Torpy* v. *Hart* (1915), 11 Tas. L.R. 6.
[17] Animals Act 1971, s. 1 (1) (b), s. 13 (2).
[18] Animals Act 1971, s. 2.
[19] *Ibid.*, s. 4.
[20] *Ibid.*, s. 5 (1), discussed, *supra*, Chapter 2, pp. 83–86.
[1] *Ibid.*, s. 10, discussed, *supra*, Chapter 2, pp. 86–89.

to the fault of the provoker.[2]   Again, if livestock is being
driven negligently so that it bolts and is injured when barked
at by a dog, this might well constitute contributory negligence
and justify the apportionment of damages under the Law
Reform (Contributory Negligence) Act 1945.[3]

The third defence provided by the Animals Act 1971, and the
only one which relates solely to liability under s. 3, concerns
liability for injury to livestock which has strayed onto the
defendant's land.   It was no defence to an action under the
Dogs Acts that the animals injured by the defendant's dog were
trespassing on the defendant's land.[4]   This situation has been
criticised[5] and so it is provided by s. 5 (4) of the Animals Act
that:

> "A person is not liable under section 3 of this Act if the livestock
> was killed or injured on land to which it had strayed and either
> the dog belonged to the occupier or its presence on the land was
> authorised by the occupier."[6]

There are three main elements in this defence.   First, the
livestock must have strayed onto the land where they were
injured or killed.   There will be no problem where the livestock are trespassing, i.e. where there is no doubt that their
straying is wrongful.   There is, however, no suggestion in the
Animals Act that this defence is inapplicable where the
livestock have strayed as a result of the fault of the defendant.
Such a case might be where the defendant was under an obliga
tion to fence the livestock out.   If he is in breach of that
obligation then he will be unable to maintain an action, under
s. 4, for damage done by straying livestock;[7] but it appears
that he will have a good defence, under s. 5 (4), to any claim

---

[2] *Cf. Elliott* v. *Longden* (1901), 17 T.L.R. 648, 649; and see *R.* v. *Hare* (1888)
14 V.L.R. 89, 94.
[3] *Cf. Campbell* v. *Wilkinson* (1909), 43 I.L.T.R. 237.
[4] *Grange* v. *Silcock* (1897), 77 L.T. 340.   It may have been a defence that the
animals were injured in the course of use by the occupier and his dog of
reasonable force to expel such trespassing animals: *Grange* v. *Silcock, supra,*
at p. 341.
[5] Law Commission Report, §. 73; Williams, 356–357; and see *Trethowan* v.
Capron, [1961] V.R. 460.
[6] This subsection is modelled on the existing defence to a criminal charge
under the Dogs (Protection of Livestock) Act 1953, s. 1 (3).
[7] Animals Act 1971, s. 5 (6).

under s. 3 for damage to the livestock done by his dog. This may be of little real help to him, for there is no reason why he should not be liable, independently of s. 3, for harm caused to the livestock as a result of his breach of his fencing obligation and it is suggested that exposure to injury from his dog could lead to such liability.[8]

The other two elements are really alternatives. The first is that the dog belonged to the occupier of the land on which the livestock were injured. The obvious case is that where the owner of the dog is also the occupier of the land strayed upon. More difficult is it to determine the meaning of "belonged to", especially in the light of the fact that a keeper of a dog for the purpose of s. 3 may be either the owner or the possessor.[9] This has the effect that any keeper may rely on the defence provided by s. 5 (4) even though he is not the occupier of the land where the livestock were injured. If one may borrow, by analogy, the definition of "belonged" from s. 4 (2),[10] a dog would belong to the person in whose possession it is. Such a person would always be a keeper, but not necessarily the only keeper, of the dog. For example, if a dog is owned by A and is in the possession of B, then both are keepers of it and both may rely on the protection of s. 5 (4), provided that the dog "belongs" to whichever of them is the occupier of the land strayed upon. It would be sensible to regard the dog as belonging to both, so that whichever occupies the land both are protected. If, however, the analogy is drawn with s. 4 (2), the dog would only belong to its possessor. This would have the curious effect, in the above example, that if B occupied the land where the livestock strayed, both he and A would be protected by s. 5 (4); but if A occupied the land, then it would appear that neither would be protected. The dog belonged to B who was not the occupier, whilst the land was occupied by A to whom the dog did not "belong", even though he was its owner. This is, it must be admitted, a most unlikely factual situation.

---

[8] See Chapter 4, *supra,* pp. 131–133; *cf. Dobbie* v. *Henderson* 1970 S.L.T. (Sh. Ct. Rep.) 27.

[9] Animals Act 1971, s. 6 (3).

[10] Where it relates to liability for straying livestock. The definition in s. 4 (2) is expressed to be for the purpose of s. 4.

What is the result if "belong to" is defined as meaning "owned by"?[11] If, in the earlier example, A occupies the land, then both he and B are protected because the dog belongs to the occupier and this brings s. 5 (4) into operation whichever keeper is the defendant. This is an unlikely circumstance for it would mean that the dog caused injury whilst on the owner's land though not in the owner's possession. The more likely case is the converse where B occupies the land and possesses the dog. Here neither B nor A appears, on this hypothesis, to be protected by s. 5 (4) for the dog does not "belong" to the occupier.

The alternative element, and one which ought to resolve most of the problems posed by the varied possible definitions of "belong", is that the defence provided by s. 5 (4) is satisfied if the presence of the dog on the land was authorised by the occupier, even though the dog does not belong to him. This will deal with the difficult case provided by a definition of "belong to" as "owned by", i.e. the situation where the dog is possessed by the occupier but owned by someone out of occupation. There is no doubt here that the occupier would authorise the presence of the dog on his land. This alternative provision also accommodates the situation where there is only one keeper, and so no problem as to whom the dog belongs, but that keeper is not the occupier of the land. So long as the occupier has authorised the dog's presence, then the keeper is protected from liability. If, for example, a shepherd is working with his dog on land occupied by someone else, then if the dog injures sheep that have strayed onto the land the shepherd will be protected from liability under s. 3 if the presence of his dog on the land is authorised by the occupier.

If might be mentioned, finally, that the three defences which have been considered are the only defences provided by the Animals Act 1971 to liability for dogs under s. 3.[12] It is no

---

[11] The Dogs (Protection of Livestock) Act 1953, s. 1 (3) speaks of a dog "owned by, or in the charge of, the occupier".

[12] It has been argued with regard to similar legislation in other jurisdictions that all common law defences apart from the need to prove *scienter* applied : *Wilkins* v. *Manning* (1897), 13 W.N. (N.S.W.) 220; *Simpson* v. *Bannerman* (1932), 47 C.L.R. 378; *Trethowan* v. *Capron*, [1961] V.R. 460; *Chittenden* v. *Hale*, [1933] N.Z.L.R. 836; and see *Christian* v. *Johannesson*, [1956] N.Z.L.R. 664.

defence, for example, that the dog has not escaped from control, or that the injury has been caused by the act of a third party. Furthermore, although it is a defence to liability under s. 2 of the Animals Act 1971 that the damage is suffered by a person who has voluntarily accepted the risk thereof,[13] there is no such defence of "consent" to liability under s. 3.[14]

(v) *Joint Liability*[15]

There are two main problems to consider here. The first is where damage is done by more than one dog. If two dogs act together in causing damage to livestock, then it is suggested that the keepers of both dogs will be liable. They are to be treated as either concurrent[16] or joint[17] tortfeasors, so that each will be liable for the whole of the damage caused,[18] subject to apportionment between them under the Law Reform (Married Women and Tortfeasors) Act 1935, s. 6. If the two dogs do not act together, but each separately causes injury to the plaintiff's livestock, then each keeper is liable only for the damage done by his own dog.[19]

The second problem arises from the fact that there may be more than one keeper of the same dog. Both the owner and possessor of the dog may be liable, as keepers, for damage caused by the dog under s. 3 of the Animals Act 1971. It is suggested that they will be classed as joint tortfeasors[20] and each will be liable for the whole damage, though this may, again, be apportioned between them in accordance with the Law Reform (Married Women and Tortfeasors) Act 1935, s. 6. Such apportionment will be on the basis of what is "just and equitable having regard to the extent of that person's responsibility for

---

[13] Animals Act 1971, s. 5 (2).

[14] *Cf. Chittenden* v. *Hale*, [1933] N.Z.L.R. 836, 848.

[15] See further Williams, 321–323; Williams, *Joint Torts and Contributory Negligence*, 20–21.

[16] Williams, *Joint Torts and Contributory Negligence*, 20–21.

[17] *Bank View Mills, Ltd.* v. *Nelson Corpn.*, [1942] 2 All E.R. 477, 483; Winfield and Jolowicz, *Tort*, 9th ed. 556.

[18] *Arneil* v. *Paterson*, [1931] A.C. 560; and see *Piper* v. *Winnifrith* (1917), 34 T.L.R. 108, 109.

[19] *Piper* v. *Winnifrith, supra;* and see *Popp* v. *Hoffman* (1953), 10 W.W.R. 337; cf. *Lankshear* v. *Farr,* [1930] N.Z.L.R. 347.

[20] Williams, *Joint Torts and Contributory Negligence*, 9.

the damage".[1] It may well be that in cases of strict liability where neither of the keepers of the dog is to blame the apportionment can only be an equal division; though the courts should look both to the relative blameworthiness of the defendants and to the extent to which each contributed to the cause of the damage.[2]

(b) Protection of livestock against dogs

(i) *Introduction*

Although there was no liability at common law in cattle trespass for the incursions of dogs, there were circumstances where such trespassing dogs might be shot.[3] Such action could be justified as reasonable defence of property. The best statement of the common law rules applicable to this type of case is that of SCOTT, L.J. in *Cresswell v. Sirl*[4]:

"The relevant rules of law may be thus stated: (1) The onus of proof is on the defendant to justify the preventive measure of shooting the attacking dogs. (2) He has, by proof, to establish two propositions, but each proposition may be established in either of two ways: *Proposition No.* 1: That at the time of shooting, the dog was either (a) actually . . . attacking the animals in question, or (b) if left at large would renew the attack so that the animals would be left presently subject to real and imminent danger unless renewal was prevented. *Proposition No.* 2: That either (a) there was in fact no practicable means, other than shooting, of stopping the present attack or preventing such renewal, or (b) that the defendant, having regard to all the circumstances in which he found himself, acted reasonably in regarding the shooting as necessary for the protection of the animals against attack or renewed attack."

It would appear that such action against the dog had to be taken by the owner of the animals in question or, presumably, by someone acting on his behalf.

---

[1] Law Reform (Married Women and Tortfeasors) Act 1935, s. 6 (2).
[2] Clerk & Lindsell, *Torts*, 13th ed., §. 184.
[3] This was, of course, apart from any civil liability under the Dogs Acts 1906–1928 or criminal liability under the Dogs (Protection of Livestock) Act 1953.
[4] [1948] 1 K.B. 241, 249; approved in *Ramage v. Evans*, [1948] V.L.R. 391.

Applying these rules, the owner of animals has been considered to have acted lawfully when he shot a dog attacking chickens[5] or worrying sheep.[6] It must be emphasised that there was no right to shoot the dog unless there was a real or imminent danger to the animals in question.[7] There would appear to have been no right to shoot a trespassing dog attacking wild animals, such as pheasants, even though the person shooting the dog had sporting rights over the land in question.[8]

The Law Commission considered that the rules laid down in *Cresswell* v. *Sirl* to govern the circumstances in which measures might be taken against trespassing dogs were inadequate in two respects.[9] They required the measures to be taken against the dog during an attack or when there was a likelihood of an imminent renewal of an attack; they did not apply to the imminence of the first attack.   Secondly, they gave no right to take the measures against the dog after the attack and when it was escaping.[10] The Law Commission, therefore, reformulated the rules governing the right to take action against marauding dogs.   These rules are now to be found in the Animals Act 1971, s. 9 of which provides:

"(1) In any civil proceedings against a person (in this section referred to as the defendant) for killing or causing injury to a dog it shall be a defence to prove—

---

[5] *Cf. Goodway* v. *Becher*, [1951] 2 All E.R. 349.   The rules have also been considered applicable to the case of the right to shoot homing pigeons eating one's crops: *Hamps* v. *Darby*, [1948] 2 K.B. 311; and see *Taylor* v. *Newman* (1863), 4 B. & S. 89.   In Queensland it has been doubted whether there is a right to shoot turkeys which are injuring crops: *Kelly* v. *Nufer*, [1918] Qd. W.N. 13; or whether there is a right to shoot a trespassing bull to protect property: *R.* v. *Rogers*, [1916] Qd. S.R. 38.   The suggestion in the former case that "the more valuable the class of animal trespassing, the more difficult such a defence would be" might be compared with the comment of BLACKBURN, J. in *Taylor* v. *Newman, supra,* at p. 91, that "a person might shoot even a valuable greyhound which is chasing a hare, if the hare was in peril."

[6] *Cresswell* v. *Sirl*, [1948] 1 K.B. 241; and see *Stephenson* v. *Auton*, [1934] L.J.C.C.R. 423; *Raine* v. *Temple*, [1943], L.J.C.C.R. 99; *Thayer* v. *Newman* (1953), 51 L.G.R. 618.

[7] *Workman* v. *Cowper*, [1961] 2 Q.B. 143.

[8] *Gott* v. *Measures*, [1948] 1 K.B. 234.

[9] Law Commission Report, §. 85.

[10] As is provided, in part, by the Dogs Act (Northern Ireland) 1960, s. 1; abrogating *Eccles* v. *McBurney*, [1959] N.I. 15.

(a) that the defendant acted for the protection of any livestock and was a person entitled to act for the protection of that livestock; and

(b) that within forty-eight hours of the killing or injury notice thereof was given by the defendant to the officer in charge of a police station.

(2) For the purposes of this section a person is entitled to act for the protection of any livestock if, and only if—

(a) the livestock or the land on which it is belongs to him or to any person under whose express or implied authority he is acting; and

(b) the circumstances are not such that liability for killing or causing injury to livestock would be excluded by section 5 (4) of this Act.

(3) Subject to subsection (4) of this section, a person killing or causing injury to a dog shall be deemed for the purposes of this section to act for the protection of any livestock if, and only if, either—

(a) the dog is worrying or is about to worry the livestock and there are no other reasonable means of ending or preventing the worrying; or

(b) the dog has been worrying livestock, has not left the vicinity and is not under the control of any person and there are no practicable means of ascertaining to whom it belongs.

(4) For the purposes of this section the condition stated in either of the paragraphs of the preceding subsection shall be deemed to have been satisfied if the defendant believed that it was satisfied and had reasonable ground for that belief.

(5) For the purposes of this section—

(a) an animal belongs to any person if he owns it or has it in his possession; and

(b) land belongs to any person if he is the occupier thereof."

The basic effect of this section is that anyone who kills or injures a dog in protection of livestock which belongs to him or is on his land will not be liable in civil proceedings for the death of or injury to the dog. Before considering the elements of this defence in further detail, three general points might be made. First, the defence applies only to civil proceedings brought

against the person who killed or injured the dog.[11]   Any defence
to criminal proceedings for so acting, for example, a prosecution
for criminal damage,[12] must rest either on specific statutory
defences thereto,[13] or on the common law rules as laid down in
Cresswell v. *Sirl*.[14] Secondly, s. 9 of the Animals Act 1971 applies
to all cases of killing or injuring dogs and not just to the shooting of them.   As the Law Commission said,

> "What are being discussed are the circumstances in which measures
> taken against a dog, which would normally give cause for a civil
> action, may be excused."[15]

The defence provided by s. 9 will apply, therefore, whether the
dog is shot or hit with a stick or any other weapon, such as
stones thrown at it.   Thirdly, s. 9 applies only to action taken
against dogs.   The common law rules will continue to apply to
causing the death of, or injury to, other animals in protection
of one's property, as in the case of the depredations of pigeons.[16]

(ii)   Scope of the defence

The various elements of the defence provided by s. 9 must
now be examined:

(1) Livestock.   The purpose of s. 9 is to protect "livestock".
It must be proved that the defendant acted for the protection
of livestock.   This means that it is only when animals within
the definition of livestock are threatened by a dog that it may,
under s. 9, be killed or injured.   "Livestock" is defined by
s. 11 as:

> "cattle, horses, asses, mules, hinnies, sheep, pigs, goats and
> poultry, and also deer not in the wild state and, in sections 3 and
> 9, also, while in captivity, pheasants, partridges and grouse."

---

[11] These are most likely to be proceedings for trespass to goods.
[12] Criminal Damage Act 1971.   This repeals and replaces most of the Malicious
Damage Act 1861.   The leading decisions under the latter Act which concerned dogs, i.e. *Gott* v. *Measures,* [1948] 1 K.B. 234; *Goodway* v. *Becher,*
[1951] 2 All E.R. 349; *Workman* v. *Cowper,* [1961] 2 Q.B. 143, are criticised
in Smith & Hogan *Criminal Law,* 2nd. ed., 463–466.
[13] Criminal Damage Act 1971, s. 5.   There is power, under s. 8 of that Act, for
the court on conviction to award compensation to the person to whom the
property belonged.
[14] [1948] 1 K.B. 241.
[15] Law Commission Report, §. 85, n. 144.
[16] As in *Hamps* v. *Darby,* [1948] 2 K.B. 311.

Poultry is itself defined as "the domestic varieties of the following, that is to say, fowls, turkeys, geese, ducks, guinea-fowls, pigeons, peacocks and quails". Therefore, if a dog has been injured by the owner of livestock he may resist an action for trespass to goods where the dog was attacking sheep,[17] a horse,[18] domestic fowls[19] or deer in a deer-park.[20]

There are, however, two particular comments to be made on the definition of livestock. The first is that, for the purposes of the defence provided by s. 9, a dog may be killed or injured when threatening pheasants, partridges or grouse, but only when they are in captivity.[1] There will be no such right in the case of such birds when wild, even though they attacked on the defendant's land or on land over which he has shooting rights.[2] Secondly, if the animal threatened by the dog falls outside the definition of livestock, no defence will be provided by s. 9. It will not apply, for example, to injuries inflicted on a dog in protection of a cat, another dog,[3] or rabbits kept either as pets or for commercial purposes. In all such cases reliance will have to be placed on the common law rules as to defence of property.[4] It will not be sufficient, at common law, to justify shooting a dog that it was merely trespassing. It is wrongful to shoot another's dog when it has just come onto your land to play with your dog;[5] but it is lawful to shoot a trespassing dog which is killing your rabbits. If there is no property in the rabbits[6] or in hares[7] then there is no right to shoot the dog which is attacking them even if it is doing so on your land. There is no property in the animals in whose defence you are acting.[8]

---

[17] *Cf. Cresswell* v. *Sirl*, [1948] 1 K.B. 241.
[18] *Cf. Quigley* v. *Pudsey* (1894), 26 N.S.R. 240.
[19] *Cf. Janson* v. *Brown* (1807), 1 Camp. 41.
[20] *Cf. Barrington* v. *Turner* (1681), 3 Lev. 28; *Protheroe* v. *Matthews* (1833), 5 C. & P. 581.
[1] As in *Miles* v. *Hutchings*, [1903] 2 K.B. 714.
[2] *Cf. Gott* v. *Measures*, [1948] 1 K.B. 234.
[3] *Cf. Wright* v. *Ramscot* (1667), 1 Saund. 84.
[4] E.g. *Cresswell* v. *Sirl*, [1948] 1 K.B. 241; and see Clerk & Lindsell, *Torts*, 13th ed. §. 562.
[5] *Cf. Barnard* v. *Evans*, [1925] 2 K.B. 794.
[6] *Cf. Wadhurst* v. *Damme* (1604), Cro. Jac. 45, in the light of *Sutton* v. *Moody*, (1697), 1 Ld. Raym. 250.
[7] Contrast *Vere* v. *Lord Cawdor* (1809), 11 East 568.
[8] *Gott* v. *Measures*, [1948] 1 K.B. 234, 239.

(2) *Notice to the police.* The defendant in the civil proceedings who has killed or injured the dog must, in order to avail himself of the protection of s. 9, have notified the police of the killing or injury within forty-eight hours thereof.[9] There is no need to give notice to the owner of the dog. Failure to give notice will only deprive the defendant of the protection of s. 9. There is no reason to believe that he would be unable to rely on his, admittedly less extensive, common law rights.

(3) *Defendant entitled to act for the protection of livestock.* The person who injured or killed the dog must have been someone who, within the terms of s. 9, was entitled to act for the protection of livestock.[10] Two requirements must be satisfied. First, the livestock or the land on which it is must belong to the defendant or to a person under whose authority he is acting.[11] Livestock belongs to its owner or possessor.[12] Therefore, a man may shoot a dog which is injuring his livestock even though the livestock are not on his own land. He may also so act even though he has merely possession of them without ownership. Furthermore, the occupier of the land where the livestock are has the same rights against threatening dogs, even though he is neither possessor nor owner of the livestock, for land is taken to belong to its occupier.[13] Anyone authorised by the owner or possessor of the livestock, or the occupier of the land where the livestock are, may act against a dog within s. 9. This authorisation may be either express or implied. It will mean, therefore, that no action will lie against an employee of such a person for killing or injuring a dog which is threatening his employer's livestock, for there can be little doubt that such employees will be impliedly authorised to protect their employer's livestock.

A corollary of the definition of the person entitled to rely on the defence provided by s. 9 is that there is no requirement that

---

[9] Animals Act 1971, s. 9 (1) (b). A suggestion that the period should be 6 hours was not accepted in the House of Lords: 312 H.L. Deb. cc. 905–909.
[10] Animals Act 1971, s. 9 (1) (a).
[11] *Ibid.*, s. 9 (2) (a).
[12] *Ibid.*, s. 9 (5) (a). The subsection actually talks of "an animal" belonging to its owner or possessor, but the relevant animals are those which constitute livestock. It is assumed that poultry may be classed as animals for this purpose.
[13] *Ibid*, s. 9 (5) (b).

the dog be trespassing on the defendant's land when it is killed or injured. It does not matter whether the dog is on or off the defendant's land or whether the livestock are or not, subject to qualification where they are trespassing on the dog keeper's land.[14] If livestock are worried by a dog whilst on the highway, the defendant who kills or injures the dog will fall within the protection of s. 9 if he owns or possesses the livestock or acts under the authority of such a person. Equally it may be a defence to a civil action for killing or injuring a dog that it was worrying livestock, even though the dog was lawfully brought onto the land where the livestock are.[15]

The second requirement is that "the circumstances are not such that liability for killing or causing injury to the livestock would be excluded by section 5 (4)".[16] The object of this provision is to deal with the case where livestock have strayed onto another's land and they are threatened by a dog which belongs to the occupier of that land or whose presence on the land has been authorised by the occupier. If, therefore, livestock owned or possessed by A stray onto B's land and are worried there by B's dog, there will be no statutory right in A to kill or injure B's dog in order to protect his livestock. This is because had B's dog killed or injured A's livestock, s. 5 (4) would have prevented A from successfully claiming damages under s. 3 for harm done by the dog, as the livestock had strayed onto B's land.

One problem, which has already been encountered,[17] is that s. 5 (4) merely talks of livestock which have "strayed" and it may be that they have strayed as a result of the failure of the person onto whose land they have strayed to fence them out. If they are then attacked by that person's dog, there

---

[14] *Ibid.*, s. 9 (2) (b), *infra.*
[15] Subject to the requirement, discussed *infra*, p. 204, that there were no other reasonable means (such as the owner calling it off) of ending the worrying.
[16] Animals Act 1971, s. 9 (2) (b). Section 5 (4), which has been discussed *supra*, pp. 191–193, provides that "A person is not liable under section 3 of this Act if the livestock was killed or injured on land on to which it had strayed and either the dog belonged to the occupier or its presence on the land was authorised by the occupier."
[17] *Supra*, pp. 191–192.

would not appear to be any right, under s. 9, for their owner to kill or injure the dog in protection of his own livestock.

(4) Defendant acted for the protection of livestock.   The person who injured or killed the dog must not only have been someone who is entitled to act for the protection of livestock, but he must also have actually acted for the protection of that livestock.[18]   He must act in protection of the livestock that he is entitled to protect.   If he is the owner or possessor of sheep then he may only kill or injure a dog which is worrying his sheep.   He may not take action against the dog, under s. 9, if it is worrying someone else's sheep, unless they are on his land, or unless, perhaps, the fact that it has worried other sheep causes him to believe that it is about to worry his sheep.[19]

Section 9 lays down the only two circumstances where a person who kills or injures a dog is deemed to act for the protection of livestock.   The first is where "the dog is worrying or is about to worry the livestock and there are no other reasonable means of ending or preventing the worrying.[20]"   The first element of this requirement to be considered is the meaning of "worry".   No definition is provided in the Animals Act 1971, though it is defined in the Dogs (Protection of Livestock) Act 1953 as:

"(a) attacking livestock, or (b) chasing livestock in such a way as may reasonably be expected to cause injury or suffering to the livestock or, in the case of females, abortion, or loss of or diminution in their produce."[1]

Whilst this definition cannot be regarded as necessarily authoritative for the purposes of different legislation, it does indicate the type of conduct which might be thought to fall within the term "worry" for the purposes of the Animals Act 1971.   If livestock are stampeded by a dog without their being attacked then, if there is no reasonable danger of injury to them, there will be no "worrying".   The passage of a pack of hounds down

---

[18] Animals Act 1971, s. 9 (1) (a).
[19] Animals Act 1971, s. 9 (3) (a), *infra,* pp. 202–205.
[20] *Ibid.,* s. 9 (3) (a).
[1] Dogs (Protection of Livestock) Act 1953, s. 1 (2).

a road might frighten livestock nearby, but this should not justify the killing of the hounds.[2]

The meaning of "worry" has fallen for consideration in other jurisdictions with legislation similar to that of s. 9 of the Animals Act 1971. In *Hanlin* v. *O'Sullivan*[3] it was pleaded in defence to a prosecution for unlawfully killing a dog that the dog had been worrying sheep and that this was a defence both at common law[4] and by statute.[5] There was no evidence that the dog had attacked the sheep, bitten them or caused them any external injury. It had chased them into a corner of the paddock where they were kept. The court was prepared to interpret "worry" as being substantially wider than its etymological meaning of "seize by the throat". It was not to be confined to "mangled or lacerated by the teeth". It was considered that "worrying" is a "comprehensive term, which connotes or includes an attack, which the common law would accept as a justification for preventive measures".[6] Furthermore, the court held that:

"chasing by dogs, which causes any real and present danger of serious harm to the animals chased—as it must when the animals are 'ewes heavily in lamb'—constitutes an attack which, at common law, entitles the owner to take effective measures of prevention."[7]

On this definition, the dog in question was held to have been worrying sheep. It is suggested that this interpretation accords with the definition in the Dogs (Protection of Livestock) Act 1953 and provides a reliable guide to the meaning of "worry" in s. 9 of the Animals Act 1971.

A difficult type of case is that where a dog runs out at a horse, frightening it and causing it to run off in fear. If this is likely to cause injury to the horse, then it is suggested that the horse is being "worried" and the dog may be shot with

---

[2] *Cf. Bond* v. *Belville,* [1963] Crim. L.R. 103.
[3] [1954] S.A.S.R. 286.
[4] Relying on *Cresswell* v. *Sirl,* [1948] 1 K.B. 241.
[5] Registration of Dogs Act, 1924–1948, s. 21 (South Australia).
[6] [1954] S.A.S.R. 286, 295.
[7] *Ibid.*

impunity.[8] It might be thought strange if there was not such a right to kill the dog, for if the horse is in fact injured then there would appear to be liability imposed on the keeper of the dog by reason of s. 3 of the Animals Act 1971.[9] It should be the case that all conduct which would involve liability under s. 3 ought to justify the killing or injuring of the dog under s. 9. If the conduct of a dog puts the rider of a horse in jeopardy then he has a common law right to act in self-defence,[10] though such conduct falls outside the scope of s. 9. He cannot be said to be acting for the protection of livestock, unless he acts both to protect himself and his horse.

Under s. 9 (3) (a) the dog need not be actually worrying livestock. It is sufficient that it "is about to worry the livestock". This will enable a farmer to take precautionary measures to protect his livestock. If he thinks that they will be attacked or otherwise worried, he can prevent the dog from doing this. This is wider than the common law rule for that dealt only with an actual attack or the threat of a renewed attack. Section 9 permits action against the dog to prevent the first attack.

Before a dog which is worrying or about to worry livestock may be killed or injured, there must be no other reasonable means of ending or preventing the worrying. If it is reasonable to call the dog off before shooting it then this must be tried first.[11] This requirement would also suggest that it might be reasonable to act in a way likely to injure, rather than likely to kill. It might be reasonable to throw stones at a dog, thereby injuring it, rather than shoot it dead outright.[12] On the other hand, where a dog is actually worrying sheep, it is probable that shooting is the only practicable remedy.

---

[8] See *Quigley* v. *Pudsey* (1894), 26 N.S.R. 240.

[9] *Supra,* pp. 186–189; and see *Cowell* v. *Mumford* (1886), 3 T.L.R. 1.

[10] *Morris* v. *Nugent* (1836), 7 C. & P. 572; *Quigley* v. *Pudsey, supra.*

[11] Nevertheless, a dog may be killed or injured, under s. 9 (3) (a), even though it is under the control of another person, as where it is set on the livestock by its keeper.

[12] This requirement of reasonableness ought to be adequate to deal with cases of brutal killing or maiming of dogs. Such conduct would not be reasonable means of ending or preventing the worrying; *cf. Wilgress* v. *Ritchie,* [1920] 2 W.W.R. 421. Would castration be reasonable to prevent future worrying? See *Robinson* v. *Wagner* (1910), 30 N.Z.L.R. 367.

It will not matter that the defendant in killing or injuring a dog has been mistaken as to the dog's behaviour. The requirements of s. 9 (3) are regarded as satisfied if the defendant believed that they were satisfied and had reasonable ground for that belief.[13] If he reasonably thinks that the dog is worrying or is about to worry livestock, or if he reasonably believes that there is no other way to prevent it so doing or of ending the worrying, then he will be justified in killing or injuring it.

Finally, there is no requirement under s. 9 (3) (a) that the defendant should be unaware of to whom the dog belongs.[14] He can kill or injure a dog even though he is well aware of whose it is.

The second circumstance where a person who kills or injures a dog is deemed to act for the protection of livestock is where

"the dog has been worrying livestock, has not left the vicinity and is not under the control of any person and there are no practicable means of ascertaining to whom it belongs."[15]

This is an extension of the common law which was limited to the type of circumstance covered by s. 9 (3) (a).[16] This second case is, in part, an act of vengeance against a dog for what it has already done. It is only preventative in the long term. If the dog is about to worry livestock then action is justified on that basis, rather than on the ground that it has already worried. The justification for killing the dog which has already worried is that it might do it again, even though it is not just about to do so, and that the defendant does not know to whom it belongs so that he is unable to take steps against the owner to prevent any future worrying. This second circumstance is narrower than that where the dog is actually worrying or about to worry and a number of conditions have to be satisfied.

The first is that the dog has been worrying livestock,[17] or that the defendant reasonably believes that it has.[18] The one

---

[13] Animals Act 1971, s. 9 (4).
[14] *Cf.* Animals Act 1971, s. 9 (3) (b).
[15] Animals Act 1971, s. 9 (3) (b).
[16] See *Cresswell* v. *Sirl*, [1948] 1 K.B. 241; *Ramage* v. *Evans*, [1948] V.L.R. 391; and see *Wells* v. *Head* (1831), 4 C. & P. 568; *Crow* v. *Palmer* (1888), 6 N.Z.L.R. 408; *Sommers* v. *Sandilands* (1910), 13 W.A.L.R. 53; *O'Leary* v. *Therrien* (1915), 27 D.L.R. 701; *Austin* v. *Laking*, [1933] G.L.R. 543 *cf. Deep* v. *Cook* (1938), 55 W.N. (N.S.W.) 115.
[17] "Worrying" will have the same meaning as in s. 9 (3) (a), *supra*.
[18] Animals Act 1971, s. 9 (4).

difficulty raised here is as to whether the livestock which has been worried must have belonged to the defendant who shot the dog. There seems to be a difference in this respect between the wording of s. 9 (3) (a) and s. 9 (3) (b). In the first case the defendant is deemed to act for the protection of *any* livestock if the dog is worrying or about to worry *the* livestock. The words italicised would indicate that the livestock to be protected is, naturally, that which is being or is about to be worried. On the other hand, s. 9 (3) (b) provides that a person is deemed to act for the protection of *any* livestock if the dog has been worrying livestock. There is no indication that, in this case, the dog must have been worrying the same livestock as its killing or injuring is meant to protect. This becomes of some importance when one looks also at the question of who may act in protection of livestock.[19] If the dog is about to worry, or is actually worrying, livestock then the only people who are entitled to injure it are the owner or possessor of that livestock, the occupier of the land where it is, or any person acting with their authority.[20] If the dog has actually worried livestock and the other requirements of s. 9 (3) (b) are satisfied, then anyone who owns or possesses livestock or occupies land whereon there is livestock may kill or injure the dog in protection of their livestock, even though the livestock which has been worried or the land where the worried livestock was kept does not belong to them.[1]

The second requirement under s. 9 (3) (b) is that the dog has not left the vicinity. There would seem, from this, little doubt that the dog need not still be on the land where it worried the livestock. It must still be in the neighbourhood, and it is not sufficient that it has been away and has later returned, unless the defendant reasonably believes that it has not been away. The problem here is to know how large an area "the vicinity" is. The narrower the courts choose to define it, the greater will be the defendant's difficulty in escaping liability

---

[19] Discussed *supra,* pp. 200–202.
[20] Animals Act 1971, s. 9 (2) (a), s. 9 (5).
[1] It would clearly seem to have been the intention of the Law Commission that the person who could rely on s. 9 (3) (b) was to be only the person to whom the livestock which had been worried belonged, or the occupier of the land where it was kept: Law Commission Report, §. 88.

for shooting a dog which has undoubtedly worried the defendant's sheep, but which he has had to track down in order to kill it and thereby protect his flocks in future.

The third requirement is that the dog is not under the control of any person.[2] The defendant may not shoot a dog which has worried livestock and is still in the vicinity if it is under the control of its keeper. Furthermore, he may not do so if *any* person has it in his control. This would seem to include himself. If he catches the dog he is then prevented from killing it. He is only allowed to kill or injure it whilst it is at large. The defendant will be protected if he kills a dog which is under the control of some person if he reasonably believed that it was not under control. No definition of "control" is given in the Animals Act 1971. No doubt a dog which is on a lead or under some form of physical control may not be killed or injured. It is suggested that also included is the situation where the dog, if trained, is "subject to disciplinary control".[3] If a dog is responding to its keeper's commands, it is under his control and may not be shot or injured.

Finally, the defendant may only kill or injure a dog which has been worrying livestock if there are no practicable means of ascertaining to whom the dog belongs, or if the defendant reasonably believed that there were no such means. The object of this condition is to allow action to be taken against an apparently ownerless dog which has already worried livestock, but not against one where it is known to whom it belongs. A dog is held, for these purposes, to belong to any person who owns it or has it in his possession.[4] There must also be no practicable means of discovering to whom it belongs. In many cases it will be impossible to discover to whom it belongs without catching it, which is likely to be almost impossible; and, once it has been caught, then it cannot be killed or injured within s. 9. Just as the scope of phrases such as "the vicinity" or "under the control of any person" are essentially factual questions for the court in each case, so also is the determination of whether there were, or the defendant reasonably believed

---

[2] *Cf. R. (Mino)* v. *Corliss* (1957), 120 Can. Crim. Cas. 341.
[3] *Jolliffe* v. *Dean* (1954), 54 S.R. (N.S.W.) 157, 159
[4] Animals Act 1971, s. 9 (5) (a).

that there were, no practicable means of ascertaining to whom the dog belonged.

There is one problem which is concerned with the inter-relation of s. 9 (3) (a) and s. 9 (3) (b). It will be apparent that the right to kill or injure a dog is wider when it is actually worrying livestock than when it has been worrying them. In the former case, it does not matter that the defendant knows to whom the dog belongs, nor does it have to be out of anyone's control. These differences mean that it is important to know when the scope of one subsection ends and the other takes over. When can it be said that a dog ceases to worry and must be regarded as "having been worrying"? If the dog has made off and is several fields away when shot,[5] then it is suggested that the dog must be treated as one which "has been worrying". This type of problem has arisen in other jurisdictions which have had statutory provisions relating to the shooting of dogs for some years. In New Zealand, where a dog which is "biting or attacking" any person or livestock, may be destroyed,[6] it has been held that a dog which has been worrying and attacking sheep has ceased to do so when chased into another field and shot ten minutes later whilst lying down.[7] In New South Wales, it is lawful to destroy a dog which is "attacking any person or animal".[8] Where a dog which was attacking sheep was shot as it ran away from the sheep at the approach of the defendant, it was held to be lawful to kill it.[9] JORDAN, C.J. was:

> "disposed to think that, even if a dog when detected in the act of killing sheep attempted to escape when it saw that it was detected, it could, nevertheless, be killed so long as it was killed at once and incidentally to the actual detection."[10]

It is suggested that this dictum might provide a guide line for an English court in order to determine when a dog has ceased to worry livestock for the purposes of the inter-relation of s. 9 (3) (a) and s. 9 (3) (b).

---

[5] E.g. *Wells* v. *Head* (1831), 4 C. & P. 568.
[6] Dogs Registration Act 1955, s. 25 (New Zealand).
[7] *Crow* v. *Palmer* (1888), 6 N.Z.L.R. 408, decided under the Dog Registration Act 1880, the fore-runner of the 1955 Act.
[8] Dog and Goat Act 1898, s. 20 (N.S.W.).
[9] *Deeps* v. *Cook* (1938), 55 W.N. (N.S.W.) 115.
[10] *Ibid.*, at p. 117. See also *Hanlin* v. *O'Sullivan*, [1954] S.A.S.R. 286.

APPENDIX

The marginal notes to the sections are printed in bold type after each section number.

ANIMALS ACT 1971

(1971 c. 22)

An Act to make provision with respect to civil liability for damage done by animals and with respect to the protection of livestock from dogs; and for purposes connected with those matters.

[12th May 1971]

Strict liability for damage done by animals

1. New provisions as to strict liability for damage done by animals

(1) The provisions of sections 2 to 5 of this Act replace—

(a) the rules of the common law imposing a strict liability in tort for damage done by an animal on the ground that the animal is regarded as ferae naturae or that its vicious or mischievous propensities are known or presumed to be known;

(b) subsections (1) and (2) of section 1 of the Dogs Act 1906 as amended by the Dogs (Amendment) Act 1928 (injury to cattle or poultry); and

(c) the rules of the common law imposing a liability for cattle trespass.

(2) Expressions used in those sections shall be interpreted in accordance with the provisions of section 6 (as well as those of section 11) of this Act.

2. Liability for damage done by dangerous animals

(1) Where any damage is caused by an animal which belongs to a dangerous species, any person who is a keeper of the animal is liable for the damage, except as otherwise provided by this Act.

(2) Where damage is caused by an animal which does not belong to a dangerous species, a keeper of the animal is liable for the damage, except as otherwise provided by this Act, if—

(a) the damage is of a kind which the animal, unless restrained, was likely to cause or which, if caused by the animal, was likely to be severe; and

(b) the likelihood of the damage or of its being severe was due to characteristics of the animal which are not normally found in animals of the same species or are not normally so found except at particular times or in particular circumstances; and

(c) those characteristics were known to that keeper or were at any time known to a person who at that time had charge of the animal as that keeper's servant or, where that keeper is the head of a household, were known to another keeper of the animal who is a member of that household and under the age of sixteen.

3. Liability for injury done by dogs to livestock

Where a dog causes damage by killing or injuring livestock, any person who is a keeper of the dog is liable for the damage, except as otherwise provided by this Act.

4. Liability for damage and expenses due to trespassing livestock

(1) Where livestock belonging to any person strays on to land in the ownership or occupation of another and—

(a) damage is done by the livestock to the land or to any property on it which is in the ownership or possession of the other person; or

(b) any expenses are reasonably incurred by that other person in keeping the livestock while it cannot be restored to the person to whom it belongs or while it is detained in pursuance of section 7 of this Act, or in ascertaining to whom it belongs;

the person to whom the livestock belongs is liable for the damage or expenses, except as otherwise provided by this Act.

(2) For the purposes of this section any livestock belongs to the person in whose possession it is.

5. Exceptions from liability under sections 2 to 4

(1) A person is not liable under sections 2 to 4 of this Act for any damage which is due wholly to the fault of the person suffering it.

(2) A person is not liable under section 2 of this Act for any damage suffered by a person who has voluntarily accepted the risk thereof.

(3) A person is not liable under section 2 of this Act for any damage caused by an animal kept on any premises or structure to a person trespassing there, if it is proved either—

(a) that the animal was not kept there for the protection of persons or property; or

(b) (if the animal was kept there for the protection of persons or property) that keeping it there for that purpose was not unreasonable.

(4) A person is not liable under section 3 of this Act if the livestock was killed or injured on land on which it had strayed and either the dog belonged to the occupier or its presence on the land was authorised by the occupier.

(5) A person is not liable under section 4 of this Act where the livestock strayed from a highway and its presence there was a lawful use of the highway.

(6) In determining whether any liability for damage under section 4 of this Act is excluded by subsection (1) of this section the damage shall not be treated as due to the fault of the person suffering it by reason only that he could have prevented it by fencing; but a person is not liable under that section where it is proved that the straying of the livestock on to the land would not have occurred but for a breach by any other person, being a person having an interest in the land, of a duty to fence.

6. Interpretation of certain expressions used in sections 2 to 5

(1) The following provisions apply to the interpretation of sections 2 to 5 of this Act.

(2) A dangerous species is a species—

(a) which is not commonly domesticated in the British Islands; and

(b) whose fully grown animals normally have such characteristics that they are likely, unless restrained, to cause severe damage or that any damage they may cause is likely to be severe.

(3) Subject to subsection (4) of this section, a person is a keeper of an animal if—

(a) he owns the animal or has it in his possession; or

(b) he is the head of a household of which a member under the age of sixteen owns the animal or has it in his possession; and if at any time an animal ceases to be owned by or to be in the possession of a person, any person who immediately before that time was a keeper thereof by virtue of the preceding provisions of this subsection continues to be a keeper of the animal until another person becomes a keeper thereof by virtue of those provisions.

(4) Where an animal is taken into and kept in possession for the purpose of preventing it from causing damage or of restoring it to its owner, a person is not a keeper of it by virtue only of that possession.

(5) Where a person employed as a servant by a keeper of an animal incurs a risk incidental to his employment he shall not be treated as accepting it voluntarily.

Detention and sale of trespassing livestock

7. Detention and sale of trespassing livestock

(1) The right to seize and detain any animal by way of distress damage feasant is hereby abolished.

(2) Where any livestock strays on to any land and is not then under the control of any person the occupier of the land may detain it, subject to subsection (3) of this section, unless ordered to return it by a court.

(3) Where any livestock is detained in pursuance of this section the right to detain it ceases—

(a) at the end of a period of forty-eight hours, unless within that period notice of the detention has been given to the officer in charge of a police station and also, if the person detaining the livestock knows to whom it belongs, to that person; or—

(b) when such amount is tendered to the person detaining the livestock as is sufficient to satisfy any claim he may have under section 4 of this Act in respect of the livestock; or

(c) if he has no such claim, when the livestock is claimed by a person entitled to its possession.

(4) Where livestock has been detained in pursuance of this section for a period of not less than fourteen days the person detaining it may sell it at a market or by public auction, unless proceedings are then pending for the return of the livestock or for any claim under section 4 of this Act in respect of it.

(5) Where any livestock is sold in the exercise of the right conferred by this section and the proceeds of the sale, less the

costs thereof and any costs incurred in connection with it, exceed the amount of any claim under section 4 of this Act which the vendor had in respect of the livestock, the excess shall be recoverable from him by the person who would be entitled to the possession of the livestock but for the sale.

(6) A person detaining any livestock in pursuance of this section is liable for any damage caused to it by a failure to treat it with reasonable care and supply it with adequate food and water while it is so detained.

(7) References in this section to a claim under section 4 of this Act in respect of any livestock do not include any claim under that section for damage done by or expenses incurred in respect of the livestock before the straying in connection with which it is detained under this section.

Animals straying on to highway

8. Duty to take care to prevent damage from animals straying on to the highway

(1) So much of the rules of the common law relating to liability for negligence as excludes or restricts the duty which a person might owe to others to take such care as is reasonable to see that damage is not caused by animals straying on to a highway is hereby abolished.

(2) Where damage is caused by animals straying from unfenced land to a highway a person who placed them on the land shall not be regarded as having committed a breach of the duty to take care by reason only of placing them there if—

(a) the land is common land, or is land situated in an area where fencing is not customary, or is a town or village green; and

(b) he had a right to place the animals on that land.

Protection of livestock against dogs

9. Killing of or injury to dogs worrying livestock

(1) In any civil proceedings against a person (in this section referred to as the defendant) for killing or causing injury to a dog it shall be a defence to prove—

(a) that the defendant acted for the protection of any livestock and was a person entitled to act for the protection of that livestock; and

(b) that within forty-eight hours of the killing or injury notice thereof was given by the defendant to the officer in charge of a police station.

(2) For the purposes of this section a person is entitled to act for the protection of any livestock if, and only if—

(a) the livestock or the land on which it is belongs to him or to any person under whose express or implied authority he is acting; and

(b) the circumstances are not such that liability for killing or causing injury to the livestock would be excluded by section 5 (4) of this Act.

(3) Subject to subsection (4) of this section, a person killing or causing injury to a dog shall be deemed for the purposes of this section to act for the protection of any livestock if, and only if, either—

(a) the dog is worrying or is about to worry the livestock and there are no other reasonable means of ending or preventing the worrying; or

(b) the dog has been worrying livestock, has not left the vicinity and is not under the control of any person and there are no practicable means of ascertaining to whom it belongs.

(4) For the purposes of this section the condition stated in either of the paragraphs of the preceding subsection shall be deemed to have been satisfied if the defendant believed that it was satisfied and had reasonable ground for that belief.

(5) For the purposes of this section—

(a) an animal belongs to any person if he owns it or has it in his possession; and

(b) land belongs to any person if he is the occupier thereof.

Supplemental

10. Application of certain enactments to liability under sections 2 to 4

For the purposes of the Fatal Accidents Acts 1846 to 1959,

the Law Reform (Contributory Negligence) Act 1945 and the Limitation Acts 1939 to 1963 any damage for which a person is liable under sections 2 to 4 of this Act shall be treated as due to his fault.

11. General interpretation

In this Act—

"common land", and "town or village green" have the same meanings as in the Commons Registration Act 1965;

"damage" includes the death of, or injury to, any person (including any disease and any impairment of physical or mental condition);

"fault" has the same meaning as in the Law Reform (Contributory Negligence) Act 1945;

"fencing" includes the construction of any obstacle designed to prevent animals from straying;

"livestock" means cattle, horses, asses, mules, hinnies, sheep, pigs, goats and poultry, and also deer not in the wild state and, in sections 3 and 9, also, while in captivity, pheasants, partridges and grouse;

"poultry" means the domestic varieties of the following, that is to say, fowls, turkeys, geese, ducks, guinea-fowls, pigeons, peacocks and quails; and

"species" includes sub-species and variety.

12. Application to Crown

(1) This Act binds the Crown, but nothing in this section shall authorise proceedings to be brought against Her Majesty in her private capacity.

(2) Section 38 (3) of the Crown Proceedings Act 1947 (interpretation of references to Her Majesty in her private capacity) shall apply as if this section were contained in that Act.

13. Short title, repeal, commencement and extent

(1) This Act may be cited as the Animals Act 1971.

(2) The following are hereby repealed, that is to say—

(a) in the Dogs Act 1906, subsections (1) to (3) of section 1;
    and
(b) in section 1 (1) of the Dogs (Amendment) Act 1928 the
    words "in both places where that word occurs".

(3) This Act shall come into operation on 1st October 1971.

(4) This Act does not extend to Scotland or to Northern
Ireland.

INDEX

centered:*Index* 223

EMPLOYER,
liability of, for risks incidental to employment, 73–76
safe working conditions, provision of, 73, 74

ESCAPE,
dangerous animals, of,
captor, liability of, 23, 32
common law, at, 68–71
escape from control not required, 69–71
keeper, liability of, 23, 28–32
non-dangerous species, of, 30, 68
wild animals, of,
dangerous animals, where, 28, 29
nuisance, as, 172
Rylands v. *Fletcher*, liability under, for, 176

EXPENSES,
detention of straying livestock, of, 92, 103, 211

F

FATAL ACCIDENTS ACT 1946 1959,
application of, to liability under Act, 46*n*., 57, 215–216

FAULT,
definition of, 85, 110, 216
plaintiff, of, damage due to,
Act, provisions of, as to, 83, 211
dangerous animals, where, 82, 83 86
dogs, where damage to livestock by, 190
straying livestock, where, 110–111
trespasser, where, 82–83
what amounts to, 84–86

FENCE,
breach of obligation to,
Act, provisions of, as to, 111, 135, 212
common law defence, as, 136–139, 140, 143
dominant tenant, owed to, and relied on by third party, 139–142
injury by dog where, 191–192
lawfully on dominant tenement, where livestock, 140
person other than defendant, owed by plaintiff to, 136–139

FENCE—*cont.*
breach of obligation to—*cont.*
person other than plaintiff, owed by, 142–145
unlawfully on dominant tenement, where livestock, 140–142
effects of failure to,
damage to land, 133–134
defence to action under Act, as, 135–148
injury to livestock, 131–133
recapture of straying livestock, 134
repair of fence, 130–131
failure to,
negligence, amounting to, 153–156
straying livestock, as defence to damage by, 106, 111, 135–148
obligation to,
common law, at, 127
common or unenclosed land, against, 99–100, 138–139, 142
fencing, definition of, 158, 216
highway, where animals straying on to, 153–156
livestock in ordinary circumstances, against, 128–130, 145
multiple obligations, 146–148
quasi-easement, as, 125–127
reasonable fence, provision of, 129, 145, 154–156
standard of, 128–130
statute, by, 106, 127–128
tenant, by, 136–139

FENCING,
customary in area, whether, **157**, 159
definition of, 158, 216

FOOT AND MOUTH DISEASE,
straying animal suffering from, 102

FOOTPATH,
highway includes, 160–161

G

GAME BIRDS,
livestock, whether, [93–94, 199, 216
protection of, injury to dog in, 199